D1230821

Universal Design for Learning

Theory and Practice

by
ANNE MEYER,
DAVID H. ROSE, *and*
DAVID GORDON

Copyright © 2014 by CAST, Inc.

All rights reserved. No part of this publication may be reproduced or transmitted in any form or by any means, electronic or mechanical, including photocopy, recording, or any information storage and retrieval systems, without permission in writing from the publisher.

ISBN 978-0-9898674-0-5
E-book ISBN: 978-0-9898674-1-2

Full text published online at http://udltheorypractice.cast.org

Published by:
CAST Professional Publishing
an imprint of CAST, Inc.

40 Harvard Mills Square
Suite 3
Wakefield, MA 01880
www.cast.org
Tel: (781) 245-2212
TDD/TTY: (781) 245-9320

Cover and Interior Design by:
Happenstance Type-O-Rama

Contents

Re-Envisioning Education through UDL

In 1984—the year we founded CAST—
education, technology, and society were
about to undergo enormous changes. Apple
had just introduced the Macintosh, the first
mass-market, user-friendly personal computer
that offered a graphical user interface, display
options, multimedia, and networking.[1]

Microsoft took up the challenge, vowing to provide the software
that would make it possible to put personal computers in every home
in the world.[2] The nascent Internet was just beginning to serve as a
means of communication and document exchange, primarily in university and government communities.

At the same time, the landmark report *A Nation at Risk*,
commissioned by the Reagan administration, decried the state
of education in the United States and urged massive reforms
to guarantee greater educational opportunities for all.[3] This,
in turn, coincided with a burgeoning civil rights movement to
grant individuals with disabilities access to all areas of society,
including education. The aspiration to provide all individuals with full and equal educational opportunities had been
thwarted by the limitations of existing technologies, prejudice
and low expectations—and other barriers that impede societal change.
Now, as new technologies promised to be powerful agents for change,
and society had become more open to diversity, it began to seem possible to turn the aspiration of free and appropriate education for all
into reality.[4]

> " New technologies and a
> more widespread appreciation for diversity promised
> to turn the aspiration of free
> and appropriate education
> for all into reality.

When we were forming CAST in the 1980s, we envisioned the new technologies as learning tools that could be radically different from the medium of print. Because digital tools offered flexibility in how content was displayed and acted on, we believed that they could be powerful levers for students who most needed better leverage—students with disabilities. We had met each other at a children's hospital clinic where we were members of a multidisciplinary team of diagnosticians evaluating children with learning difficulties. Coming from this medical model, our early work focused on the problems of diverse learners, those "in the margins" who struggled with learning. We didn't question the diagnostic findings, but we were dissatisfied with our recommendations which seemed to have limited effectiveness.

Sensing the promise of technology, we sought to find, adapt, and even invent technologies that would help students with disabilities overcome the barriers they faced in their environments, especially in schools. The idea was to provide tools that would amplify areas of strength and support areas of weakness, specifically chosen and set up for each learner. A simple example of such a tool was the word processor and spell checker, which, for a learner who had great ideas but had difficulty with handwriting and spelling, could enable the writing of a coherent paper even as the learner worked to shore up those areas of weakness. Our work let us see first-hand the barriers these students faced and helped us to design solutions that helped them overcome the barriers. But much of our work took place outside of classrooms, in our offices and our Learning Lab. Integrating these tools into students' and teachers' lives at schools was a big challenge.

Over time we became restless with our initial approach. The more we followed our "patients" into their classrooms, the more we became convinced that our future lay not in helping students overcome the barriers they found there but in helping schools and educators to lower or eliminate those barriers. In the future that we imagined, more students would thrive in their schools and fewer students would have to be referred to clinics like ours and labeled "patients." The new technologies could go beyond changing students. They could change schools.

VIDEO 1.1
Anne Meyer and David Rose explain what motivated the founding of CAST in 1984.

▸ http://udlvideo.org/ch1/1

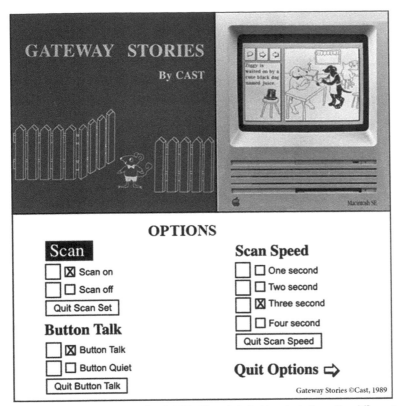

FIG. 1.1. Gateway Stories by CAST offered digital books tailored to different learners' needs. © *1989 CAST, INC.*

VIDEO 1.2 Over time our focus shifted from helping individuals overcome barriers to eliminating barriers in the print-based curriculum altogether.

▶ http://udlvideo.org/ch1/2

VIDEO 1.3 UDL was born as researchers shifted from creating individual electronic books tailored to the needs of specific individuals to designing flexible digital materials with customizable options to suit all learners.

▶ http://udlvideo.org/ch1/3

VIDEO 1.4 Matthew, a young boy "locked in" by physical disabilities, made stunning progress when given appropriate tools to communicate.

▶ http://udlvideo.org/ch1/4

We began creating individual versions of digital books tailored to each learner's needs. Those with reading challenges needed to have text read aloud to them; those with limited vocabulary needed linked definitions; those with physical challenges needed to be able to turn pages with a single-switch interface; those with low vision needed large buttons that voiced their functions. Soon we realized that we could make a single digital book with all of these options embedded and with a customizable interface so that each learner could find the supports they needed. This led to a major breakthrough in our overall approach: the realization that the curriculum, rather than the learners, was the problem. By "curriculum" we meant the learning goals, the means of assessment, the teaching methods, and the materials.

Of course, the learner and the curriculum are just two definable parts of what is really a process or interaction. Strictly speaking, considering either part by itself—learner or curriculum—sets up a false dichotomy, as if we could assess either on its own rather than in relation

VIDEO 1.5
Samantha Daley explains why designing for the "average learner" is ineffective for most students.

▶ http://udlvideo.org/ch1/5

VIDEO 1.6
Students who struggle and students who are under-challenged have all been marginalized by curriculum built for the "average learner."

▶ http://udlvideo.org/ch1/6

VIDEO 1.7
Illustrating her point by describing two students with differing emotional/motivational profiles, Anne Meyer emphasizes the importance of affect in learning and curriculum design.

▶ http://udlvideo.org/ch1/7

to each other. Success, we realized, can only occur when the learner and the curriculum interact in ways that help them both improve at the same time.[5] We knew that most curricula are designed and developed as if students were homogeneous, and the most common approach to curriculum design is to address the needs of the so-called "average student." Of course this average student is a myth, a statistical artifact not corresponding to any actual individual. But because so much of the curriculum and teaching methods employed in most schools are based on the needs of this mythical average student, they are also laden with inadvertent and unnecessary barriers to learning.

The traditional approach to learning—as we now understand it—was dictated by the predominant learning medium of the time: printed text. After all, standardization, uniformity, and affordable reproduction were among the chief advantages of the print revolution brought about by Johannes Gutenberg's invention in 1440.[6] Printed text made mass education possible. But along the way, as proficiency with printed materials became synonymous with schooling and with literacy, education became narrowly defined by the print medium, and the typical variability of students was seen as a huge problem.[7]

Furthermore, the fact that curriculum was designed for the mythical average learner, adept at navigating the print environment, created significant barriers for students in the margins, for whom the print-based environment simply did not work as the single means to access and express knowledge.[8] These students showed up in clinics, where they were diagnosed and usually referred to special education. If they were fortunate, they were able to find alternatives to print in the form of adapted, retrofitted materials. This retrofitting process was arduous, expensive, and largely ineffective: solutions were created on a case-by-case basis, hardly an efficient way to address learner diversity.

The unnecessary barriers in traditional education extended beyond those that impeded students from accessing content and expressing knowledge. Even more important in motivating our work were the *affective* barriers. Students coming to school with curiosity and a strong desire to learn found that fire quenched when they were stigmatized—not because of anything that was in their control but because of inaccessible learning environments.

These environments blocked learning progress and, more significantly, blocked students from falling in love with learning, engaging with their creativity, and seeing themselves as experts in the making. Many of our early clients were students whose enthusiasm for learning had been overwhelmed by feelings of incompetence and discouragement that had generalized from a few areas of challenge to a sense of being altogether inadequate. This disengagement from the enterprise of school and damage to self-esteem was a pernicious result of a rigid system, one we felt could in fact be made flexible now that digital technologies had emerged.

A NEW APPROACH TO EDUCATION: UNIVERSAL DESIGN FOR LEARNING

In the early 1990s, we shifted our approach to address the disabilities of schools rather than students. We later coined a name for this new approach: universal design for learning (UDL). UDL drew upon neuroscience and education research, and leveraged the flexibility of digital technology to design learning environments that from the outset offered options for diverse learner needs. This approach caught on as others also recognized the need to make education more responsive to learner differences, and wanted to ensure that the benefits of education were more equitably and effectively distributed. Our early work culminated in the 2002 publication of *Teaching Every Student in the Digital Age: Universal Design for Learning*, the first major explication of the concepts of UDL.[9]

The education community began to recognize that many students—not just students with disabilities—faced barriers and impediments that interfered with their ability to make optimal progress and to develop as educated and productive citizens. Advances in neuroscience that gave us a much better understanding of the nature of learning differences between individuals and within individuals over time, as well as the increased power and flexibility of networked media, provided a foundation for our ongoing work. Today, the public mindset is beginning to shift away from a medical model of disability towards a recognition that context and self-awareness as a learner both play a huge role in whether any given condition is disabling or not.[10]

VIDEO 1.8
We coined the term "universal design for learning" after learning about the UD movement in architecture.

▶ http://udlvideo.org/ch1/8

> 66 We shifted our emphasis to address the disabilities of schools rather than students and coined a name for this approach: universal design for learning, or UDL.

VIDEO 1.9–1.11 (SERIES)
Dr. Paul Yellin says that evaluating and understanding a child's learning requires collaboration and input from parents, teachers, and the child.

▸ http://udlvideo.org/ch1/9

Education has come a long way in the past two decades—but there is a long way to go. First, most learners are still being educated in standardized and uniform ways. Too many individuals continue to be under-challenged, stressed, or simply disaffected because of the narrow and rigid kinds of teaching and learning that schools continue to promulgate. Second, systematic application of UDL in our schools is just beginning. We have much to learn about effective, large-scale implementation. Third, the growing field of UDL needs a stronger research base to sustain it, and a broader set of innovative tools and methods to implement it at scale.

We are convinced that UDL has enormous promise. We have seen countless discouraged, unmotivated learners catch fire when given ways to learn that are optimized for their particular strengths and weaknesses. We have seen classrooms become exciting, collaborative hotbeds of learning for all students. We have seen students with dyslexia

FIG. 1.2. UDL aims to fix the curriculum, not the learner.
ILLUSTRATION BY CHRIS VALLO © 2013 CAST, INC.

or other "print disabilities" read and write complex material in digital learning environments. We've witnessed students with significant intellectual disabilities learn to read and improve their comprehension skills when few thought it was possible. We have seen gifted students, all too accustomed to boredom, become stimulated by challenges that stretch their minds. We have seen teachers who have recovered a sense of how important and satisfying teaching all of their students can be. And we have seen school systems become communities of expert learning.[11]

We offer this new publication in the hope that it will stimulate genuine change and make optimal learning a promise fulfilled—not just for some, but for all. Many signs suggest that the time is ripe. In the following pages, we highlight some of those signs—key developments that suggest that UDL will become a significant catalyst for far-reaching change.

Much has changed in the theory and practice of UDL, but it is worth highlighting an important piece that has not changed: the three core principles of the UDL framework. These principles articulate the basic UDL premise that to provide equitable opportunities to reach high standards across variable students in our schools, we must:

- Provide Multiple Means of Engagement

- Provide Multiple Means of Representation

- Provide Multiple Means of Action & Expression

Over the past decade CAST has expanded and developed these three principles. The changes reflect recent research on the learning brain, significant developments in technology, and experiences in classrooms. With input from the field, we have also expanded the three principles by developing nine guidelines, each with multiple checkpoints offering specific approaches to implementation. These checkpoints are researched and applied in classrooms around the world, and this information is helping us refine and enhance the framework.

Provide Multiple Means of Engagement	Provide Multiple Means of Representation	Provide Multiple Means of Action & Expression

FIG. 1.3. The UDL principles © 2011 CAST, INC.

UDL itself is ever-changing, a living concept evolving as a result of ongoing interaction among researchers, educators, and learners. With the help of UDL partners and practitioners around the world, we aim in this publication to capture the state of what we have learned, enriching the ideas with multiple exemplars and models of the principles in practice. Several kinds of changes are introduced and highlighted:

- Changes in the theory and practice of UDL,

- Changes in the environment of UDL, and

- Changes in the media used to convey UDL.

Changes in the Theory and Practice of UDL

An Updated View of Goals

In our early work on UDL, we focused on learning goals for individuals. We identified inherent barriers in the way some standards and goals were worded, especially when means were unnecessarily tied to goals. For example, the goal to "write a story" constrains the medium to text, while the goal "create a narrative" leaves the door open for any number of media. In both cases, the learner needs to understand and create the key elements of a narrative, but more diverse pathways enable more learners to succeed. To be clear, we know that sometimes a text-based outcome *is* required, in which case "write a story" is an appropriate goal. In that case, learners can still be given much flexibility and leeway as to their paths. Options to begin with images or sounds, to scaffold writing mechanics with digital tools, and to embed other media into text provide the flexibility needed to meet learner differences.

Of course, individual progress and specific learning goals are critically important for teaching and learning. In our current view, however, we see these competency-based goals in a larger context: they are components to serve the overall aim of education—to develop learning expertise in students, teachers, and systems as a whole. This broadened scope is necessary if we are to bring about true change. Essentially, the goal of education has shifted from knowledge acquisition to learner expertise. As we discuss below, becoming an expert learner is a process, not a fixed goal. We elaborate our latest thinking about UDL goals in Chapter 2, "Expert Learning."

VIDEO 1.12
The goal of education should be to develop a love of learning and the ability to learn.

▶ http://udlvideo.org/ch1/12

From Individual Differences to Variability

Our early articulation of UDL focused on individual differences. We recommended looking at each learner's patterns of strength and weakness in each of the three kinds of neural networks in the brain as they pertained to a particular learning goal. While it is true that each learner is unique, this approach was limited in two ways. First, extensive analysis of each learner in multiple classes with large numbers of students was probably not feasible. Second, the focus on the individual points in subtle ways back to the old medical model of disability or difference, and inadvertently reinforces the concept of a dichotomy between "typical" and "atypical." And third, this approach suggests that students have the same "profile" regardless of context.

Recent advances in neuroscience have provided a different understanding of individual differences, characterizing them instead as predictable, normal variability that exists across the population. Brain

VIDEO 1.13
CAST's thinking has shifted from the disability of any individual student to focusing on the variability of all learners.

▸ http://udlvideo.org/ch1/13

FIG. 1.4. Flexible options for meeting goals enable more learners to succeed.
ILLUSTRATION BY CHRIS VALLO © 2013 CAST, INC.

functions and characteristics fall along a continuum of systematic variability. Thus differences are incremental, distributed, and dynamic rather than stable and categorical within an individual. This contradicts the idea of bright lines between an idea of normalcy and deviation from normalcy, and challenges the practice of diagnosing and labeling individuals.

From a practical viewpoint, it means that a UDL curriculum designer or teacher can plan for expected variability across learners and provide curriculum that has corresponding flexibility. The lesson or curriculum should then have the flexibility and affordances to amplify natural abilities and reduce unnecessary barriers for most students, and enable teachers to customize easily for each learner. Of course there will be outliers who may require on-the-fly individualization or innovative single solutions. But with most of the variability addressed in the curriculum itself, teachers will have the time and attention to devote to this. Further, instead of seeing variability as problem, we now understand it to be an actively positive force in learning for the group as a whole. We elaborate these concepts in Chapter 3, "The Variability of Learners."

From Individual Interactions to Individual-Context Interactions

Much of our early work in UDL focused on learners' strengths and weaknesses as if these resided within the individual, regardless of environmental circumstances. Perhaps because of our roots in neuropsychological diagnostics, we tended to see students' abilities as inherent, stable, and consistent over time and across different contexts. But advances in almost all of the hard sciences—from physics to biology—increasingly emphasize a highly dynamic and interactional view of almost any facet of nature. Where genetics, for example, was formerly seen as something quintessentially individual and innate, the emphasis in the field is now on epigenetics—the study of the very strong effects of the environment on gene expression.

Similarly, the learning context exerts very strong effects on whether a particular individual characteristic becomes an impediment to learning or not. Taking a simple example, a bright student who has trouble reading text may be viewed as having a "disability" in an

VIDEO 1.14
Whatever a person's biology may be, whether that biology has a positive or a negative impact on learning is completely dependent upon the context.

▸ http://udlvideo.org/ch1/14

environment where printed text is the only avenue to content, but might function at a high level if alternative ways to gain information are provided.

FIG. 1.5. A student may be bored in one context ...

FIG. 1.6. ...and engaged and motivated in another.

ILLUSTRATIONS BY CHRIS VALLO, © *2013 CAST, INC.*

In our current work we emphasize that learning occurs in a dynamic interaction between student and learning environment, and that the learning environment—or context—is itself complex and dynamic. Think of a seed. You might first consider any seed as having a fixed or standard potential to grow. However, if you move that seed to Antarctica, does it still retain the same potential to grow? This is an example of the impact of context on growth and learning. Consider another example—the group dynamics of engagement. Engagement with the learning task depends on the provision of a sufficiently flexible curriculum so that each learner can find the right balance of challenge and support. Without support for sustained effort, persistence, and emotion regulation, even students who are momentarily excited about learning can become disengaged, losing out on deep learning. And when some students lose out on deep learning, everyone is affected. Active engagement with learning is gained through social processes. All students need alternative models of how to achieve a goal, and a sense that the steps to get there are achievable. Engaged students can model these different pathways for one another, but they need UDL to be able to do so.[13]

> **The learning context exerts very strong effects on whether a particular individual characteristic becomes an impediment to learning.**

It's not only the individual student that benefits from UDL, but the totality of learners that make up the learning environment, which, in turn, can be an environment of expert learners only when all students are actively involved in creating knowledge and establishing its value. In other words, the learning environment itself is impacted by the engagement and progress of each learner.

Research confirms that environmental changes can lead to physiological and psychological changes, including improved learning, and this bolsters the case for designing flexible learning environments to meet learner variability. The core UDL principles, based on the three kinds of networks of the learning brain, remain in their original form. However, with a stronger awareness of the importance of context, we have enhanced the original principles to reflect a more nuanced and refined understanding of learner/context interactions. These are explained in Chapter 4, "Universal Design for Learning."

From Cognition or Affect to the Interdependency of Cognition and Emotion

Traditionally, society as a whole has treated cognition and emotion as separate functions. Emotion has predominantly been viewed as something that needs to be contained, filtered, or otherwise overcome to allow for logical, rational thought. Until recently, research in the learning sciences has also maintained this false distinction. Most of the 20th century saw the role of emotion neglected in education and psychological research in favor of behaviorism and cognitivism. Now cognitive scientists are addressing feelings and emotion, motivation and behavior, and they are now coming to realize that emotion organizes, drives, amplifies, and attenuates students' thinking and reasoning.[14]

In his book *Descartes' Error*, neuroscientist Antonio Damasio debunked Descartes' view of the rational ideal, i.e., that it is necessary to curb and control emotion in order to make rational decisions.[15] While it might be useful to look at a phenomenon from the viewpoint of either cognition or emotion for research purposes, in reality the two never function separately. More recently, Richard Davidson has studied the neuroplasticity of the brain, obtaining evidence that

VIDEO 1.15
Sam Johnston explains research that shows that supporting multiple pathways to success is essential for the development of a sense of self-efficacy for all learners.

▸ http://udlvideo.org/ch1/15

VIDEO 1.16
Dr. Yellin describes the inextricable interactions, both positive and negative, of affect and cognition.

▸ http://udlvideo.org/ch1/16

shows that brain function and structure actually change, particularly in response to positive social-emotional experiences.[16]

At CAST, we have always recognized the importance of emotion and affect in learning, yet in the past we have treated affect as somewhat separable from cognition. And our nation's education system has mostly been built around this assumption. A curriculum centered on content and skills implies that affect is secondary—it can enhance or interfere with the "real" business of learning. But it is now clear that affect is core.

Many of us will recall the proverb "a chain is only as strong as its weakest link" to make the case for a business developing each of its units to the maximum. The marketing department will have only short-term success if the quality control department is ineffective. Yet we rarely think about how this proverb applies to education. We don't realize that under-developing even one student's potential will negatively impact the development of all other students.

Research suggests that core beliefs and behaviors that enable a learner to persist when faced with challenge—those that we often think develop intrinsically—in fact develop through social interactions. In other words, both positive and negative thinking are "catchy" in social situations—they can spread from person to person. In developing the theory of self-efficacy—that is, a person's belief in his or her own abilities and competence—psychologist Albert Bandura found that efficacy expectations develop socially through performance accomplishments, vicarious experience, verbal persuasion, and emotional arousal. He suggests that diverse models are better at improving self-efficacy: "If people of widely differing characteristics can succeed, then observers have a reasonable basis for increasing their own sense of self-efficacy."[17] Much like strong links in a chain, well-supported students can reinforce one another's efficacy expectations, providing a wide variety of models of how to reach learning goals.

The UDL Guidelines

Since our previous explications of UDL, we have moved towards the close linkage of affect with recognition and with strategy. We have developed the UDL Guidelines to help educators design, choose, and implement effective teaching strategies and tools. Built upon the three UDL principles, the Guidelines offer insight into specific kinds of systematic learner variability and specific ways to build curricular flexibility around this variability. They explicitly call for the integration of emotion and cognition. We know that students continuously appraise their environment as good for them or bad for them—beneficial or threatening. When they find the environment threatening on an emotional level, they will not be able to leverage instruction in the service of learning, even if the instruction is well designed. If they appraise the learning environment as positive and engaging, students will be able to make better use of instructional resources. The UDL Guidelines help educators manage resources and challenges in the learning environment to move students' perception of the environment in a positive direction.

Thus, under the UDL Guidelines, engagement—which is needed for successful learning—is achieved by employing a curriculum with options built in such that each learner will appraise the environment positively in part because each student can find the right level of challenge and support. UDL informs the design of the environment so that it is flexible enough to address variability; with this flexibility, meeting specific needs is more feasible. UDL "happens" both in the design, and in the use of the design to facilitate the appropriate, dynamic interaction between learner and context.

The Guidelines offer a way for teachers and school systems to correctly represent how cognition and emotion are interrelated when they design learning and interact with students. Every checkpoint under the Guidelines can be seen to deal explicitly with both cognition and emotion. If we are trying to manage demands and resources flexibly, the checkpoints are levers or means by which to do this. This balance is essential to the development of self-regulation, where appropriate goals and feedback play a key role. We introduce the concept and overview of the UDL Guidelines in Chapter 5, "A Framework for UDL Implementation."

Bringing Assessment to the Fore

In our previous writings, we defined curriculum as having four instructional components: goals, methods, materials, and assessment. This definition—broader than traditional definitions of curriculum as a sequence of content conveyed by a fixed set of instructional materials—aimed to emphasize how essential it is to be clear about instructional goals, and to stay flexible about the methods and materials used to accomplish those goals. "Tight on goals, loose on means" is how U.S. Secretary of Education Arne Duncan has described his expectations of accountability systems, and that phrase aptly describes our aim for curriculum. When the means of learning are restrictive, the goals of learning get warped.[18]

We used to talk about goals, methods, materials, and assessment in precisely that order, with assessment at the end. However, this suggested that assessment should somehow be a summative act. That idea was never our intention, and in recent years we have moved assessment up the line—so we now discuss goals, assessment, methods, and materials.

The distinction is an important one. The most important kind of assessment, from a UDL perspective, is formative assessment. Formative assessment is defined by the Council of Chief State School Officers (CCSSO) as "a process used by teachers and students during instruction that provides feedback to adjust ongoing teaching and learning to improve students' achievement of intended instructional outcomes."[19]

As CCSSO notes, this "process" is not separate and apart from curriculum but is an essential, embedded feature of the learning process. Teachers collect evidence of student progress through observations and conversations with learners; learners collect data about their own performance, or that of their peers. All of this knowledge is used during the instructional episode—before students succeed or fail—to inform and adjust instruction so that each individual has optimal opportunities to learn. CCSSO also emphasizes how essential it is to include both teachers and learners in formative assessment. Students learn to become proactive in monitoring their own progress, and to take responsibility for their own learning. In doing so, they (and their teachers) develop a better grasp of learning goals and what methods and materials work best for them. In contrast, summative assessments—tests at the end of a unit, state-mandated exams at the end of a year—provide general data for teachers and administrators on how a student or groups of students have done, but that data cannot improve instruction for those learners. It's too late. In Chapter 6, we address the four parts of the curriculum, including assessment, in more detail.

Changes in the Environment of UDL

The Societal Changes and the Context of UDL

UDL itself has evolved over the past two decades and will continue to evolve as we learn more. And the context in which UDL is maturing has also changed significantly—in public policy, in technology, and in the ways educators practice. Advances in society, education, and science will inform and guide how we articulate and practice UDL in the coming decades.

The context of public policy has changed in the past ten years. UDL has spread beyond the boundaries of special education as advocates, educators, funders, and policy makers have realized its potential for transforming education for all. In 2008, for the first time, a definition of the term *universal design for learning* was included under

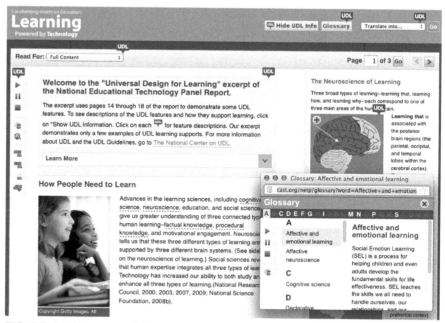

FIG. 1.7. A UDL version of the National Education Technology Plan
© CAST, INC. (PRESENTATION ONLY). PLAN IN PUBLIC DOMAIN.

federal law in the Higher Education Opportunity Act.[20] In 2010, the U.S. Department of Education's National Education Technology Plan emphasized UDL as a framework that can benefit all learners, in particular those who have been underserved.[21] (To demonstrate UDL in action, CAST created a UDL version of an excerpt of that Plan: http://cast.org/netp/page/NETP/I28/)

Trends in federal education funding also indicate a growing awareness and acceptance of the promise of UDL. For example, the National Science Foundation (NSF) allocated both regular and special education funds to develop science curricula for middle and high school students that are designed, right from the start, with UDL principles and options to ensure that science education will reach and engage all learners. Meanwhile, numerous states, school districts, and colleges and universities across the United States and Canada are launching UDL initiatives. Interest in UDL has spread well beyond North America, with growing activity in countries such as Australia, South Korea, and Spain.

VIDEO 1.17
Ricki Sabia describes the beginnings of the UDL Task Force, an alliance of more than 45 organizations to promote UDL in federal and state policy.

▶ http://udlvideo.org/ch1/17

VIDEO 1.18
Yvonne Domings describes an international UDL initiative involving the University of the Azores, the Azorean government, CAST, and Lesley University.

▶ http://udlvideo.org/ch1/18

State Level UDL Initiatives

Map Key
- ■ = Statewide Initiative
- ■ = ≤ 2 State Activities
- □ = 1 State Activity
- ▨ = 0 State Activities

FIG. 1.8. Numerous states have adopted UDL and related initiatives. *© 2012 CAST, INC.*

VIDEO 1.19
TED-Ed Director Logan Smalley highlights ways the network effect of interactive media can shape and sharpen online learning environments.

▶ http://udlvideo.org/ch1/19

VIDEO 1.20
After lagging behind by ten years in technology, schools should benefit from the latest developments in networked tools.

▶ http://udlvideo.org/ch1/20

VIDEO 1.21
According to Logan Smalley, the printed book has huge untapped potential; when the content is made digital, we can "split it like an atom" and release it, providing opportunities for far greater engagement.

▶ http://udlvideo.org/ch1/21

(To explore these and other recent policy developments surrounding UDL, please visit the National Center on UDL: www.udlcenter.org).[22]

UDL and the Internet

Not surprisingly, the Internet is fueling this dissemination. In 2013 alone, people from more than 200 countries visited CAST's websites, including the UDL Center. As of this writing, the UDL Guidelines have been translated into eight languages. CAST's web-based UDL Book Builder—which enables individuals to create and publish online their own multimedia books and instructional materials based on UDL principles—includes publicly shared books written in 10 different languages, including English, Spanish, Mandarin Chinese, and Russian.[23]

Indeed, digital technology has always been a cornerstone in the theory and practice of UDL. Without the development of digital media, it would have been impossible to conceive of flexible learning environments that could be tuned and adjusted to varied learners. As new technologies come along, they will enable new visions and innovations for learning designs.

The initial technological cornerstone for our thinking in UDL was the malleability of digital media, its quality of being able to remain forever flexible (if so designed) and therefore adaptable for individual learners and for different educational purposes. This enabled alternate representations, including multiple media to represent concepts, on-the-fly transformation from one medium to another (as in text to speech) and adjustability of display (size, color saturation and contrast, etc.). The malleability of digital media also opened the door to true interactivity—embedded prompts, linked glossaries, and background information and, most importantly, the opportunity for students to act on texts while learning. This interactivity enables students to construct meaning actively by changing the text itself. Release from print as the main instructional medium enabled customization and interactivity. But this was only the beginning.

All of these qualities were present in the early digital media we worked with in the 1980s, before the widespread use of the Internet or even email. The Internet changed the landscape, especially in terms of how we access information. Now, the Internet has transformed how we share information, too, and much of that sharing is very personal and instantaneous via social networking. The growing capacity for two-way and multiparty exchange online is transforming education through online courses, communities of practice, and so forth. The sharable, manipulable Web—where individuals are not just receiving content but are creating, co-authoring, and remixing—opens vast new possibilities for education, and especially for creating UDL environments with multiple levers for growth. This so-called "network effect" has important implications for education.

It is important to remember that UDL is not primarily about technology: it is about *pedagogy*. The most radical aspect of UDL is that it raises our expectations about education. Instead of seeing students as limited, we see traditional curricula as limited and too uniform to enable all learners to reach goals that really matter. UDL provides an approach for designing learning environments that support high expectations and results for *all* students.

Changes in the Media Used to Convey UDL

From Printed Book to Digital River

When we published our first book about UDL, *Teaching Every Student*, printed books were still the dominant medium of expression and information. We wanted to walk the talk of UDL. So, simultaneous to the print release, we launched an interactive web site where UDL principles were applied to support varied readers and to provide interactive learning experiences. Nonetheless, we saw the printed book as the primary version and the digital version as an enhancement or adaptation. The positions are reversed in this current publication. Today, it seems obvious that the digital version must be the definitive edition, with the print edition a derivative, for several key reasons.

First, the digital version (go to http://udltheorypractice.cast.org) offers a dynamic, interactive environment with options for different readers and learning contexts. Many voices—of learners, teachers, administrators, and policy makers—are presented via video, audio, and text, offering the perspective of thinkers and practitioners in the field. We offer multiple means of engagement, representation, and action and expression via display options, tools, supports, and links.

Second, the digital version is embedded in a rich knowledge network—more like a hub than a stand-alone source. Those who are researching, advocating, and implementing UDL concepts share their

VIDEO 1.22
This publication reflects our current understanding, a glimpse into UDL. Based on developing research, feedback, and submissions of others' work via our online edition, its content will change with time, making it more like a "digital river" than a book.

▶ http://udlvideo.org/ch1/22

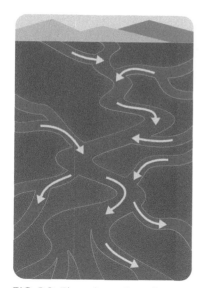

FIG. 1.9. The online edition (go to http://udltheorypractice.cast.org) is a "digital river," where the flow of ideas from research and practice will continually refine and expand UDL concepts. *ILLUSTRATION BY CHRIS VALLO © 2013 CAST, INC.*

insights and ideas through various media and through links to their own work. Links to related research also enrich and extend the core content, inviting deeper exploration of related ideas.

Third, the digital version supports continuous development of UDL theory and practice through interaction with the UDL community worldwide. This presentation is a snapshot in time, showing the current state of UDL as we, and our contributors, see it. Inevitably, it will begin to change the moment it is launched. By its nature, the medium of print implies a kind of permanence and authority to whatever ideas are placed onto the page and reproduced. The malleability of digital media reflects a more realistic view of reality—a constantly changing flow. We think of *Universal Design for Learning: Theory & Practice* as a "digital river" that is both consistent (UDL itself as the subject, the water if you will) and changing (the water as moving and continuously replenished). The flow also reflects the dynamic, changeable nature of learning; the river changes as we come to it at different times and for different purposes.

Finally, the digital version enables us to seek your help to improve and grow this publication, enabling it to "learn." Just as expert learners are striving to learn and refine ideas, so, too, do we seek to improve this publication. With our current contributors, we have begun an interchange within the UDL community. They have taught us a great deal as we prepared this publication. We ask that you share your ideas, research, practices, lessons, feedback, and helpful resources so that we as a larger community can keep improving this publication. Throughout the text we offer links to community conversations about UDL, and the opportunity to give us feedback and to submit your own work for possible inclusion in ongoing revisions. We look to you as expert learners, and we hope you will share your challenges and your successes. As a community, we can transform the way we practice education for the good of all.

Expert Learning

The word "expert" probably conjures up a person who has mastered a particular skill or domain of knowledge, a professional, or a highly skilled amateur who can perform at a high level. But if we think a moment, we realize that expertise is never static.

Developing expertise in anything is always a process of continuous learning—practice, adjustment, and refinement.[1] In the context of UDL, we focus on learning expertise: the lifelong process of becoming ever more motivated, knowledgeable, and skillful.

The goal of becoming an expert learner in this sense applies to people of all ages and situations. All participants in any educational environment should be learning, growing, and improving. Thus, when we speak of expert teachers or expert learners, we do not mean that they necessarily know more than other teachers or learners. We mean they are people who continually develop in the context of their professional community, the classroom, informal settings—indeed, wherever learning takes place.

For the purposes of this book, we define expertise not as a destination—signifying the mastery of content knowledge and skills—but rather as a process of becoming more expert on a continuum of development. Expertise looks very different from person to person because each of us has different proclivities, opportunities, rates of development, and domains of engagement.

FIG. 2.1. Expert learning occurs everywhere and at all levels of proficiency.
© 2013 GETTY IMAGES

Everyone can become an expert learner because everyone can develop the motivation, the practice, the reflection, the self-efficacy, the self-regulation, the self-determination, the executive functioning, the comprehension, and the situational awareness that help to make experts what they are.

In educational settings, the goal of developing expertise is shared by all participants: students, teachers, and all of the personnel in the system itself. If everyone is focused on developing expertise as a learner, the context is suffused with great models. Continual improvement, engagement, and growth are available to and expected of everyone. This emphasis on process does not negate the importance of mastering specific content and skills, but it does require us to consider these kinds of mastery in a broader context. The ultimate goal of our efforts as educators is to engage, challenge, and support each learner to become the best s/he can be. Mastery of specific content and skills serves as grist for the mill, the practice ground for developing oneself into someone who wants to learn and knows how to learn continuously throughout life. Viewing education this way profoundly changes the way we go about it. We no longer hold narrow views of what it means to succeed. Mastering content and skills or reaching particular standardized milestones are not the only measures of being a successful learner. *Learning* expertise cannot be measured simply by evaluating competencies and outcomes at a single point in time because learning is a process of continual change and growth.[2]

To enable everyone to develop learning expertise we need to design learning environments that are smart and flexible enough to support this ongoing, continuous development at every level. For students, the focus of learning is the general curriculum; for educators, the focus is on teaching about learning; and for the system as a whole, the focus is on fostering collaboration and community to maximize learning opportunities for all.

> We define expertise not as a destination but rather as a process of becoming more expert on a continuum of development.

In this chapter you'll first read about expert learners, then expert teachers, and finally expert systems. We separate these for the purpose of study. However, in reality they interact so closely that they are not functionally separable. By the end of the chapter it should be clear that in order to have expert learners, teachers, and systems, all three must work together as a flexible, supportive community.

LEARNING EXPERTISE IN ACTION

While mastery of particular skills or content knowledge is not the end-goal of becoming an expert learner, we can come to understand what learning expertise entails by studying those who have achieved mastery in a domain. We begin by looking outside of traditional education settings to a youngster with a great deal of expertise.

Australian teen Feliks Zemdegs may look like a typical high school student, but to millions of people around the world who are engaged with the addictive puzzle called Rubik's Cube he is already a legend. Feliks is the reigning world champion at "speed cubing."[3] For most people, solving a Rubik's Cube even once can be a daunting challenge. But for expert "Cubers," solving the puzzle is almost automatic. The

VIDEO 2.1

Watch Feliks Zemdegs on YouTube solve the Rubik's Cube in world-record time.

▶ http://udlvideo.org/ch2/1

thrill of competition comes in solving it the fastest. Watch Feliks solving the Cube during a competition (Video 2 .1). It won't take long—about 5.6 seconds![4]

Domain experts like Feliks make whatever they are doing look simple, almost effortless. But watching Feliks at work can be deceiving. We see a performance: a snapshot of expertise at an advanced stage of development. That expertise did not come quickly, nor was Feliks born with it. He had to become an expert at learning to get there. How did that expertise develop?

We reviewed interviews with and articles about Feliks to get a sense of his particular path. In April 2008, Feliks, then 12 years old, came across several videos on YouTube of people solving the Cube quickly. He thought it would be "pretty cool to try it." He bought a Cube, then found an online tutorial. By following the tutorial, he was able to solve the puzzle. His enthusiasm grew as he joined the online community of Cubers sharing videos, strategies, and tips. Before long he was setting speed records—and then topping himself.

Over time, Feliks gained the confidence that he could continuously improve, noting, "Basically it just comes down to practice." With practice, he says, you can improve rapidly. In an interview with a reporter from Rubik's TV, Feliks says that it took him a year to get his speed down to 15 seconds and another year to reduce it to 10.[5] His strategies? Feliks names three or four methods that are his favorites. He's learned to be flexible enough to start his solution on any of the Cube's colored sides to give himself more options. He suggests that once you have learned to solve it, you should work to reduce the number of moves it takes. (You want to get your move count down to about 60 or 70.) He tries out a lot of different approaches, learns to be flexible about where he begins his solution, communicates with the community of Cubers, and just "plays around" with the Cube."[6]

Clearly, success at competition hasn't made Feliks complacent. Even after a win, he reviews his strategies and considers alternatives he might have tried. He is learning continuously. Feliks is expert in a domain: one where he appears to have a natural ability and proclivity. Were talent his only asset, Feliks might have been

FIG. 2.2. Speed cubing champion Feliks Zemdegs
© 2009 REBECCA MICHAEL/NEWSPIX/REX USA

a flash in the pan. As we have seen with certain prodigies, talent alone can only take you so far. Feliks is also an expert at learning.[7]

What qualities are needed to develop learning expertise? We define an expert learner as one who is purposeful and motivated (the "why" of learning), resourceful and knowledgeable (the "what" of learning), and strategic and goal-directed (the "how" of learning). Does Feliks have these qualities?

PURPOSEFUL & MOTIVATED LEARNERS	RESOURCEFUL & KNOWLEDGEABLE LEARNERS	STRATEGIC & GOAL-DIRECTED LEARNERS

FIG. 2.3. Expert learners are ... © 2011 CAST, INC.

Feliks is clearly motivated to improve his performance and to learn more effectively. His intense concentration and attention are obvious in the video—as is his delight at his success and the cheers of his colleagues after breaking yet another record. But we know that his engagement is not limited to the context of competition. He has learned to set goals and to pursue those goals. His persistence through the long hours of practice needed to develop skill was situated in a supportive social context where mentors and peers provided models, feedback, and encouragement.[8] His own developing competence also led him to persist—spending a year shaving off just 5 seconds from his time. Feliks knows how to regulate his own practice because he is aware that anxiety can interfere with his progress. He says that he practices daily, but if he is not able to do well, or he is not enjoying it, he takes a break. He also notes that in a competition his nerves can interfere with his performance. He says that he can solve the Cube faster at home than he has ever been able to do in competition.

Feliks is knowledgeable about both the Rubik's Cube and his own learning. From the earliest tutorial he watched, Feliks began to absorb information about key patterns—the starting pattern on the squares, the sequenced pattern of different solutions—essential knowledge to build on.[9] Look again at the video of Feliks and watch what he does before he actually begins to manipulate the Cube. There is a brief period of inspection. During that time, Feliks recognizes the most relevant patterns of colors in the Cube, and he understands the kinds of problems he will face in solving the Cube. He doesn't have to look at all of the squares in order to know what color they are because he is so familiar with the patterns and relationships that he can predict what is on the sides he can't even see. His self-knowledge as a learner is also continuously developing. He compares his own learning techniques with those of others, and he is always on the lookout for new approaches that might suit him. But he is also clear about those that don't work for him.

Finally, Feliks is strategic, both about the Cube and about his own learning. Once he has sized up the problem, he adopts and fluently executes a general plan of attack. As you looked at the video, you were probably first struck by how smooth and skillful his movements were. In his tips to others, Feliks mentions the need to practice and automatize both the motor movements and the mental sequences of moves.[10] But he is more than skillful; he is also strategic. He knows multiple plans of attack—general algorithms that he has learned from others or developed himself—and he can apply them fluently. His specific choice of strategies or approaches reflects both his previous experience and the local configuration of the problem.[11]

> An expert at learning is someone who is continually growing and developing through introspection and guided feedback from other experts and peers.

Feliks transitioned from being a novice to being an expert performer in a few short years, though he admits: "It's easier to learn if you start young because you have more time to work on it. People who are 18 and have jobs might not have the time." Still, his story gives us a window into how expert learning works—for him.

Designing for Variability

When we observe any expert learner we might fall into the trap of thinking that that person's approach and strategies are optimal for everyone. Even within the domain of Rubik's Cube, what is most striking about expert learners is how variable, not how similar, they are. The strategies that work for Feliks are certainly not effective for every Cuber. A quick review of experts in the field reveals the effectiveness of the diverse approaches to mastery of the Cube.[12] As is true in chess, specific strategies have names and operate effectively for Cubers of different skill levels and preferences. Some are helpful for beginners, while others require some fluency. Each method poses a particular mix of challenges and advantages. For example, some are motorically complicated (many moves) but demand very little memorization, while others are much simpler to execute manually but require a great deal of memorization. There is no one optimal strategy, just as there is no one optimal path or learning method in any subject or skill.

Selection of strategy depends upon the learner (prior experience, preferences, amount of practice) and upon the context (home, alone or with others, being filmed, in competition). A novice needs strategies to scaffold understanding and execution, and would probably not progress well in a fast-paced competitive context. Indeed, even a skilled competitor like Feliks admits that nerves can interfere in a match. An advanced player has selected the strategies that work well for him or her, using different ones in different situations. One of the better sites for learning how to solve the Cube offers the following advice about methods: "Of course, every single brain works in a bit different way, so what may be an advantage for one may be a disadvantage for others. You can just try and see for yourself."[13]

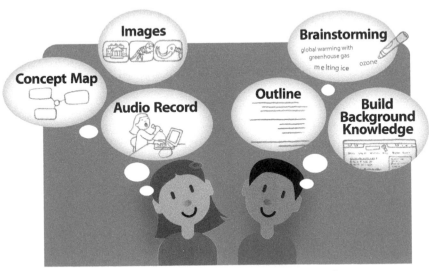

FIG. 2.4. Every learner approaches tasks with his or her own set of strategies.
ILLUSTRATION BY CHRIS VALLO © 2013 CAST, INC.

Like learners in any domain, varied Rubik's Cube players learn and operate in very different ways. The goal remains the same for everyone—to align all the colors on all six sides. But to optimize everyone's chance to do that quickly, the learning environment needs to be flexible enough for each player to employ different methods and different ways to assess how they're doing. We have already described different strategies to suit different puzzlers. But what about the Cube itself, the medium involved in this kind of learning?

Indeed, a variety of Cube designs have emerged to suit different puzzlers. Some were inspired by individuals who could not solve the traditionally designed Rubik's Cube, where faces of each "cubie" (individual small cube) are only differentiated by colored stickers. It would be impossible for a blind person to solve a traditional Rubik's Cube because the preliminary inspection would have to be visual. Absent a re-design of the Cube itself, you might say that the blind person's "disability" makes it impossible to participate in this activity. But if the Cube is redesigned to be accessible for this person, then blindness is not actually a barrier.

One approach was developed by German university student Konstantin Datz.[14] Datz created a Rubik's Cube for the blind (pictured here). Because color itself seems irrelevant for blind people, the Cube is all white with the words for each color in braille on each cubie's surface. Heralded in design circles for its beauty and simplicity, the Cube inspired one observer to note: "One of the more sensible concepts in a long time that hopefully will delight the sighted folks too! Maybe we'll learn braille in this process!"

Although beautiful, this design has several flaws both as a learning tool and as a tool to use in competition. First, the majority of potential blind users do not actually know braille![15] And for those who do, deciphering the color words would take extra time. More significantly, this Cube is designed for a single "special" population and is inaccessible to most other users. But given the extensive Cubers community, many persons who are blind want to learn, teach, or practice the Cube with individuals who are sighted. The removal of color actually makes this much more difficult, causing a

FIG. 2.5. A white Rubik's Cube with braille
© 2010 KONSTANTIN DATZ

communication barrier for no functional purpose (an "undesirable difficulty"). The white design does not take learning context—the community of Cubers—into account.[16]

A far more effective approach is to design a better Rubik's Cube for everyone. A Cube designed from the outset with more options—one whose surfaces are differentiated by both color and tactile information—is more usable for everyone. The symbols that align with colors are easy to identify through touch, supporting rapid recognition, and they provide the additional benefit of enabling users to inspect the sides of each Cube without turning the Cube to look.

We see that poor design can exclude some people from participation and restrict available paths and strategies. In the design of a Rubik's Cube, just as in any good learning design, supporting user variability is critically important. This is called *universal design* in the fields of product development and architecture. Originally formulated by Ron Mace at North Carolina State University, universal design principles aim to "create places, structures, or products that are conceived and built to accommodate the widest spectrum of users without the need for subsequent adaptation or specialized design."[17] Our educational framework, universal design for learning, echoes this core concept.

Using the example of the Rubik's Cube, we have demonstrated key characteristics of an expert learner: high motivation and engagement, extensive knowledge and ability to build new knowledge, and fluent use of varied strategies. We have also seen great variability among experts, including their reasons for playing, the ways they most easily recognize key variables, and the strategies they use to execute the puzzle and become more expert over time.

FIG. 2.6. A Rubik's Cube with different colors and textured symbols on each cubie makes the Cube accessible to a variety of players.
ILLUSTRATION BY CHRIS VALLO © 2013 CAST, INC.

EXPERT LEARNING AND THE GROWTH MINDSET

An expert at learning is someone who is continually growing and developing through introspection and guided feedback from other

VIDEO 2.2–2.6 (SERIES)
CAST Director of Research Gabrielle Rappolt-Schlichtmann explains and demonstrates the deeply contextual and social nature of learning. She cites important research and shares practical examples from her life as she and her daughter learn to ski. These rich examples illustrate the effects of physical and social context, affective states, the way scaffolds work, and other important learning concepts.

▸ http://udlvideo.org/ch2/2

experts and peers. Key to expert learning is self-knowledge as a learner. *What are my strengths and weaknesses? What is the optimal setting for me to learn? Which tools amplify my abilities and support my areas of weakness? How do I best navigate my environment? How do I best learn from peers? How can I support myself when I feel anxious about an upcoming challenge? How can I learn from my mistakes?*

Expert learners know that ongoing practice and deep engagement bring about development. They have what Carol Dweck calls a "growth mindset," seeing that they can develop their qualities and their "smarts" through effort and dedication.[18] They know how to learn in a social context, to observe others as models, to refine their approach based on feedback, and to engage deeply in their learning. And they know that learning is continuous, that there is no arrival point at which one is finally "expert" and no longer needs to practice.

Expert learners also know how to solve problems flexibly, to adapt or change course when they make mistakes, and to fine-tune their own strategies for even better performance. Dick Fosbury, winner of the 1968 Olympic Gold Medal in high jumping, startled the world with his idiosyncratic technique, later dubbed the Fosbury Flop. Fosbury had to persist against the opinion of his coaches who tried in vain to teach him the "correct" form. That form didn't work

FIG. 2.7. Dick Fosbury's innovative jumping style led to a whole new generation of jumpers who could reach higher goals by imitating his method.
ILLUSTRATION BY CHRIS VALLO © 2013 CAST, INC.

for Fosbury. Had he stayed within it he would probably never have become a great jumper. By pursuing the strategy that worked for him, Fosbury revolutionized the sport. This led to a whole new generation of jumpers who could reach higher goals by imitating his innovative method.

Learners with a growth mindset are self-aware and active learners. The UDL framework (described in Chapter 4) aims to move

Dig Deeper: Mindset and Learning

A growing body of research on mindset and goal motivation shows that the mindset with which students approach learning tasks has a critical role in motivation, behavior, and learning outcomes. Some students approach learning tasks with a fixed mindset: they believe that intelligence and ability are inherent and unchangeable. Other students approach the same tasks with a growth mindset: they believe that intelligence develops and evolves with time and effort.

When learners with a fixed mindset experience setbacks or failure, usually they are reluctant to seek help. Learners with this mindset perceive help-seeking and showing effort as demonstrating "neediness" and incompetence. Learners with this mindset feel that help-seeking and working hard reveal underlying inadequacies. Going to a teacher for help or consulting references seem to show a lack of intelligence.

In contrast, learners with a growth mindset are motivated by self-development through learning. They perceive and seek out challenges as opportunities to expand their intelligence and ability. When faced with failure, learners with a growth mindset see these events as key to the process of learning rather something to be avoided, and see effort and persistence as leading to positive outcomes rather than indicating low ability.

The great news is that mindset orientation can be trained and changed. For more information on mindset and to test your own mindset orientation, see Carol Dweck's Mindset Online at http://mindsetonline.com/whatisit/about/index.html.

VIDEO 2.7–2.10 (SERIES)
In this YouTube series, Carol Dweck, Professor of Psychology at Stanford University and author of the bestseller *Mindset*, shares insights and examples from her research of how mindset affects learning.

▶ http://udlvideo.org/ch2/7

VIDEO 2.11-12 (SERIES)
Watch YouTube footage of Dick Fosbury winning Gold at the 1968 Olympics in Mexico City with his eccentric high jumping form, as well as a tutorial on the "Fosbury Flop," which became a widespread technique.

▸ http://udlvideo.org/ch2/11

learners towards becoming purposeful and motivated, knowledgeable and resourceful, strategic and goal-directed. How do expert learners develop these qualities? What attitudes and habits indicate that learners are developing this expertise?

Some examples of learning expertise in action will shed light on this question. To illustrate, we introduce four individuals who have developed learning expertise in different ways.

Examples of Expert Learners

Mason Barney

Consider Mason Barney. We offer his story as an example of expert learning because with learning support and technology tools he overcame barriers by becoming aware of his own learning process. Early on, he had to develop determination and persistence. Over time he developed key strategies for managing challenging learning tasks as

PURPOSEFUL & MOTIVATED LEARNERS	RESOURCEFUL & KNOWLEDGEABLE LEARNERS	STRATEGIC & GOAL-DIRECTED LEARNERS
+ Are eager for new learning and are motivated by the mastery of learning itself	+ Bring considerable prior knowledge to new learning	+ Formulate plans for learning
+ Are goal-directed in their learning	+ Activate that prior knowledge to identify, organize, prioritize, and assimilate new information	+ Devised effective strategies and tactics to optimize learning
+ Know how to set challenging learning goals for themselves	+ Recognize the tools and resources that would help them find, structure and remember new information	+ Organize resources and tools to facilitate learning
+ Know how to sustain the effort and resilience that reaching those goals will require	+ Know how to transform new information into meaningful and useable knowledge	+ Monitor their progress
+ Monitor and regulate emotional reactions that would be impediments or distractions to their successful learning		+ Recognize their own strengths and weaknesses as learners
		+ Abandon plans and strategies that are ineffective

FIG. 2.8. Learners are variable, but expert learners across domains share some key characteristics. *© 2011 CAST, INC.*

well as navigating relationships with teachers to maximize his ability to succeed.

We first met Mason in 1986 when he came to CAST as a 4th grader. Mason had been designated both for special education services and a gifted-and-talented program in his school. He was bright *and* also had learning disabilities. Dyslexia made it hard to decode written text and to spell. Poor hand-eye coordination made handwriting and many sports next to impossible. Difficulties with executive function made it hard to organize and express his thoughts. And the typical school curriculum was not designed to address those differences. The result? Mason spent a good deal of time in pull-out programs, working one-to-one with a special education assistant.

At CAST, we created digital texts of Mason's school materials that could be read aloud to him using a computer or used with on-screen highlighting, a medium more supportive and flexible than the printed classroom materials he was used to. We also worked with him to organize and express his thoughts in novel ways—using pictures or audio, for example, to begin the writing process rather than insisting that he conquer the blank screen only with words. By using alternate symbols to express his thoughts, he could organize and carry out the composition process. Eventually, Mason was able to write complete essays using a computer.

Most importantly, caring instruction supported by technology helped Mason "catch fire" as a learner. He was motivated, challenged, and excited—and learned how to sustain that engagement and persist through hard times. Mason went on to finish high school, earn a bachelor's degree at Bowdoin College, and finish second in his class at Brooklyn Law School.

In college, he wrote about his experiences for George Lucas's national magazine *Edutopia*: "Now I know how much I can accomplish, and I know there is nothing I can't do just because I have a learning disability."[19] As a productive lawyer and an expert, lifelong learner, Mason continues to grow and develop his skills and strategies to optimize his performance.

Ellie Schlichtmann

The effort to become an expert learner starts early on, and a critical part of this work is developing an awareness of one's own strengths, challenges, and needs. Take the case of prekindergarten student Ellie

VIDEO 2.13–2.16 (SERIES)
Mason Barney and Anne Meyer trace some key aspects of Mason's development as an expert learner, illustrating his innovative learning strategies, and highlighting the critical importance of self-confidence and persistence.

▶ http://udlvideo.org/ch2/13

VIDEO 2.17

Gabrielle Rappolt-Schlichtmann, CAST's research director, talks with her daughter Ellie, age 5, about the ways Ellie learns, including strategies for problem-solving and persisting.

▸ http://udlvideo.org/ch2/17

Schlichtmann. In an interview with her mother, CAST's Director of Research Gabrielle Rappolt-Schlichtmann, Ellie reveals that she is motivated, knowledgeable, and strategic about her learning.

How is she strategic? She knows, for example, that she needs to stay focused in order to learn effectively. But sometimes this can be hard when there's a lot of noise, says Ellie, who was age 5 when this interview was conducted. What does she do when there is lots of noise? "I ask some people to be a little quiet, the ones that were making a bunch of big noises," she says. Ellie is already learning how to improve the conditions for learning.

When learning a new song, she employs another strategy. "Echo," she says. "It means repeating after... [The teachers] do a word and then we do it after. But if it's hard, then the teacher does it every time, [even] with us on the second time when we are echoing back." She knows that taking on small chunks of new information, such as song lyrics, and building on those are an effective way to learn.

"Ellie seeks out new knowledge, knows when to seek help, and where to find resources," says Dr. Rappolt-Schlichtmann. For example, when she's struggling in reading, she will get some support from the teachers—but just enough until she can persist on her own. "They sort of sound it out for us and then we say it after. ... They do as much as we need [for] help."

Richard Wanderman

Richard Wanderman—artist, teacher, and educational technology consultant—describes himself as "someone who never thought he could get good at anything and then spent the latter part of his life getting good at a lot of things." Traditional school was not the venue where this transformation occurred. Because he had difficulty with reading and writing, he was served a steady diet of practice in language arts sub-skills, activities that brought him face to face with his "deficits" rather than enabling his strengths.

Over time, as Richard became skilled in three other areas, each requiring very different kinds of learning, he began to experience his own competence directly, and could distinguish for the first time the difference between his learning disability and his intelligence.

First, Richard became adept at rock climbing. In that social circle, he was a good climber, teacher, and guide. He recalls this world as a

VIDEO 2.18-2.20 (SERIES)

Richard Wanderman, education technology consultant, describes how he was able to "experience" his own intelligence rather than just his learning disabilities, and to spark a sense of competence, which in turn made him want to learn more.

▸ http://udlvideo.org/ch2/18

context in which his reading and writing difficulties were irrelevant, and where he could identify himself simply as skilled. "And until I had to fill out paperwork for Eugene Parks and Recreation, there was no evidence of this other issue," he says.

Another learning experience developed due to circumstance. Being unable to afford expensive cars, Richard drove old Volkswagens that had a tendency to break down. One such occasion drove him to delve into John Muir's book on how to fix Volkswagens. He was not only able to take apart and successfully repair the engine, but also to truly read an entire book (possibly his first). The reading was purposeful because he wanted to get the car running, and the sense of competence that accrued from these experiences was significant. Reflecting back on it, he says, "I got a sense that I had a certain kind of capacity that I didn't know I had before."

When he started college at the University of Oregon, Richard was overwhelmed by the demands of traditional curriculum and was "about to flunk out," when he discovered the art program. It was "a very Bauhaus-inspired, process oriented, not-heavy-into-grades place that was full of charismatic people who were probably all LD in some way. And it was fantastic. It was probably the most important social experience of my life at that point. That was really important. I got facile with that, I got comfortable socially with that group."

Each of these experiences, and many smaller ones, gave Richard a sense that he could do more than he had thought he could. Collectively, they helped him develop strong insight into his own learning needs, preferences and strengths, and to value his abilities. "Those [experiences] allowed me to see myself as a learner," he says. "They all gave me a reference for myself and my ability to learn things that was useful going forward. I would say, that's my platform."

Rick Birnbaum

Education researcher Rick Birnbaum emphasizes the important role of affect and motivation in his learning. As a young man, Rick spent endless hours studying, trying to pursue his natural inclination for academics, but he constantly encountered difficulty with the work and the lack of support from teachers and professors. "I always felt I could do better, but I just didn't know what was in my way. So I worked like

VIDEO 2.21
Education researcher Rick Birnbaum describes the critical importance of emotional support for his success in graduate school.

▸ http://udlvideo.org/ch2/21

an animal." He would eventually finish college but felt so disheartened that he turned away from academia entirely.

He became an actor, a writer, a stand-up comic, a fitness trainer. After some time, he again attempted school, this time pursuing a pre-med program to follow his interest in science, only to be stonewalled by both the amount of time it would take him to complete assignments and by the university learning specialists who did not know what to make of him. Left with little choice, he fled.

At the suggestion of a friend, Rick then began working with inner-city kids in New York, tutoring in an afterschool program: "I understood them and they understood me. I helped them figure out how to use what they were good at. I was also giving them the one thing they really needed: someone who was emotionally involved. I let them know I was going to be part of their solution."

—

All of these expert learners personify the growth mindset. In the context of an inflexible school system and curriculum, they were marginalized. Yet each found the determination and the support to fulfill their profound commitment to learning. They became ever more self-aware as learners and ever more able to fashion or find strategies, tools, and contexts that enabled them to grow and flourish.

The strategies these learners invented out of necessity are also applicable and helpful more generally. For instance, as Mason explains, he developed his own way of reading legal cases because his slow reading pace necessitated a system that did not require him to read every word of every case. But his system of investigation is highly efficient and could benefit anyone, keeping wasted time to a minimum. What is "essential for some is good for all"—a cornerstone theme of UDL.[20]

VIDEO 2.22
Rick Birnbaum discusses how he learned to persist as a learner despite many challenges.

▸ http://udlvideo.org/ch2/22

EXPERT TEACHING

Teaching is central to everything we do as humans. We teach skills, knowledge, concepts, procedures, culture, language, expression, emotion, and values. We teach directly and indirectly. We teach the practical and the abstract. Teaching is found in all cultures, and with all peoples. Teaching is an unmistakable part of who we are.

FIG. 2.9. Expert teaching happens in a huge variety of contexts. © *2013 GETTY IMAGES*

Given that teaching is so common among humans—and that we all watch and experience a great deal of teaching in our own lives—it is understandable that those outside the classroom feel that is easy and that anyone can teach. Naively, we think that someone who knows a subject or skill should automatically be able to teach that subject or skill to others. On the flip side, we may also assume that someone who teaches a subject knows all there is to know and has nothing left to learn. But teaching is its own domain, quite apart from any content area.

Teachers need to be expert learners themselves, continuously growing and changing. Beyond that, they need to be able to model and mentor the process of learning, with all its hills and valleys, for their students. Exposing their own learning and making it explicit both in

VIDEO 2.23
CAST Research Scientist Sam Johnston explains the key qualities of a successful community of practice, as well as how and why such communities help teachers and enrich both practice and theory.

▸ http://udlvideo.org/ch2/23

action and in personal reflection might be one of the most powerful parts of teaching. How do teachers develop expert teaching practices? And what strategies and insights help them?

Analyzing a single brilliant lesson would be similar to taking a snapshot of a moment of high performance in any field of endeavor. Such moments demonstrate mastery but shed little light on learning expertise itself. When we watch skilled teachers demonstrate their craft, we see expertise in action, but not the path to expertise. We do not see the many years of practice and reflection. We do not see the failures and obstacles. We do not see their internal motivation and challenges. And we do not see the community within which the teacher is situated.

Yet these unseen aspects are at the very heart of teaching expertise. Habits of mind and habits of practice both need to be cultivated to build expertise. Habits of *mind* (such as cultivating a growth mindset, reflection, self-efficacy, self-regulation) and habits of *practice* (such as consistency, persistence in the face of setbacks, learning from errors) are critical features of expertise.

Equally important are the community and the affordances of the educational environment. People rarely, if ever, travel the journey of continuous growth and refinement on their own. Expertise develops within communities of practice or "systems" of apprenticeship, teaching, and education. Three key ingredients make up any community of practice. Members share a domain of interest where they recognize knowledge about that domain as "expertise" and they value collective competence. They are part of a community that is focused on learning from and with one another. Members discuss and engage in joint activities and share tools, resources, and ways of dealing with persistent problems. They share a common practice that they improve together. Etienne Wenger and Jean Lave, who first coined the term "community of practice" in their study of apprenticeships worldwide, were trying to capture the idea that it is the community that acts as a living curriculum for the apprentice.[21]

We interviewed a number of educators who use the UDL framework and asked them about their practices. Self-awareness as learners and models for their students is a persistent theme.

VIDEO 2.24–2.29 (SERIES)
Expert teachers from elementary to post-secondary levels share different perspectives, strategies, and techniques to engage varied learners through UDL.

▸ http://udlvideo.org/ch2/24

- **Alexis Reid** emphasizes the importance of planning for learner variability, constant monitoring of student understanding, and changing course on the fly when necessary. She subscribes to an ever-developing, changing curriculum, and remains open to changing her approach if the classroom situation calls for it.

- In a similarly self-aware way, **Allison Posey** discovered how powerful it can be for students when teachers expose some of their own vulnerabilities, leaving themselves open to falter or fail, and therefore model that taking such risks is all a part of learning.

- **Jon Mundorf** focuses on equipping his students with the ability to self-regulate and to be aware of their own learning needs and preferences, so that when they move on from his class they are equipped to appraise and appropriately respond to whatever challenges might arise. Jon is aware of and articulate about his own learning, and he quite consciously builds that self-awareness in his students.

VIDEO 2.30
Expert teacher Alexis Reid identifies a major barrier to effective teaching and suggests a solution.

▸ http://udlvideo.org/ch2/30

These teachers demonstrate some of the core qualities expert teachers share. They cultivate their own development as teachers, embrace change, and continuously appraise their own work and their students' progress, adapting on a dime when something calls for a new strategy. In a UDL context, teaching involves building engagement, knowledge, and strategies through a variety of tools and techniques, and participating actively in the larger learning community with colleagues, families, and administrators.

If the development of students as expert learners and teachers as expert learners is to be the goal for education in the 21st century, then our educational systems themselves will have to be reinvented to focus on that goal.[22] We will have to redesign, re-nurture, re-implement, and reassess our educational systems so that they are places where expert learning thrives for all participants and where the system itself is continuously improving.

> " At their best, teachers learn from their students and from each other, and students teach each other and their teachers.

EXPERT SYSTEMS: PUTTING IT ALL TOGETHER

We have seen that the fixed roles that we tend to assign learners and educators don't correspond to reality in an effective classroom. At their best, teachers learn from their students and from each other, and students teach each other and their teachers. For this kind of constructive, creative exchange to occur, both student and teacher need to be situated in systems or communities of practice that value and nurture the development of both groups' expertise. Recent research in the field of systems change confirms that making communities to support optimal student learning requires the simultaneous development of supportive communities of learning for educators, too. This requires expert systems, where expertise is valued, nurtured, and developed for educators and students alike.

Dig Deeper: Communities of Practice

A community of practice is a network of individuals who share a common area of interest, who share information about that interest, and who put that information into practice. The concept of a community of practice grew out of an apprenticeship model of learning wherein it is understood that individuals require mentoring and continuous feedback to grow in skills and mastery. This idea has been extended to academic teaching and learning environments as well as business and informal learning environments. In their 2002 book *Cultivating Communities of Practice*, Etienne Wenger, Richard McDermott, and William M. Snyder have identified seven principles that support the development and effectiveness of communities of practice:

- Design for evolution

- Open a dialogue between inside and outside perspectives

- Invite different levels of participation

- Develop both public and private community spaces

- Focus on value

- Combine familiarity and excitement

- Create a rhythm for the community

To explore more of Wenger and colleagues' work on communities of practice, see http://hbswk.hbs.edu/archive/2855.html. Also visit Wenger's site http://www.ewenger.com/theory/index.htm.

In education, we routinely refer to "school systems" and "systems change" but rarely do we examine what a system really is and how it functions. Donella Meadows, an educator and MacArthur fellow who advocated systems thinking, described a system as "a set of things interconnected in such a way that they produce their own pattern of behavior over time."[24] Our bodies are systems, our global environment is a system, our brains are systems. Each has many parts that work together dynamically. Understanding part of the system requires that you understand the whole system, and vice versa.

Consider the solar system. All of the individual elements of the system—the sun, planets, asteroids, comets, and so forth—are interdependent. They interact through dynamic tensions caused by the forces of gravity and momentum within the whole system. These forces impact all of the individual parts, holding them in position while still in constant movement. Likewise the parts impact the system as a whole. A wayward giant asteroid can have a dynamic effect on the rotational orbits of planets and other astral bodies as their gravity pulls on it and its momentum pushes against them, causing an unbalanced relationship and orbit adaptation. Understanding how a system works involves focus on both the individual components and the relationships and forces that influence and are influenced by these components.

VIDEO 2.31
Learning scientist Todd Rose explains learning progress from a dynamic systems viewpoint, showing how traditional methods of measuring progress, based on a linear model of learning, can give an inaccurate result.

▶ http://udlvideo.org/ch2/31

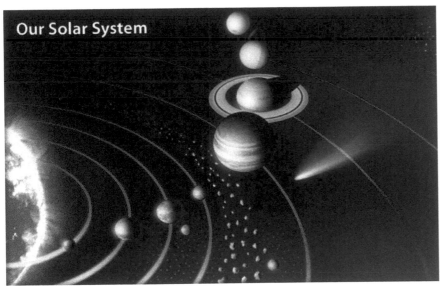

Our Solar System

FIG. 2.10. All of the elements in the solar system work in interdependent, dynamic balance. © 2012 NASA

VIDEO 2.32
School administrator Brett Boezman discusses his district's efforts to combine UDL and Positive Behavioral and Instructional Supports (PBIS).

▸ http://udlvideo.org/ch2/32

Seeing education from a dynamic-systems perspective shifts our thinking about the role of learners, educators, and the places they learn. Instead of seeing learners' qualities as static, self-contained, and stable, we understand that they change in dynamic interplay with their surrounding context. The way we conceive of individual elements in a system also impacts how we understand change and development. Like practitioners in other fields, educators are realizing that schools are complex systems and that building a culture of expertise requires consideration of whole systems, not just components.

We should note that when we talk about expert educational systems, we often draw examples from schools or institutions of higher education, such as colleges and universities. But there are many kinds of educational settings, both brick-and-mortar and online, for which the principles of dynamic systems pertain. Museums, community classes, workplace training centers, trade schools, online courses, crafts workshops, and so forth are all examples of learning environments where expert learning, teaching, and systems-thinking can take place.

In K–12 environments, one example of applied systems thinking is Positive Behavioral Interventions and Supports (PBIS).[25] School systems that adopt PBIS aim to develop positive behaviors and reduce negative behaviors in all students throughout the system. To do that, they must develop system-wide supports and interventions that extend far beyond single students, single incidents, single classrooms, or single administrators.

What is systemic about PBIS is the recognition that both the causes and the solutions for increasing positive behaviors are complex, interdependent, and schoolwide—not simple and isolated. Cafeteria workers, school bus drivers, teachers, aids, administrators, and parents all need to play complementary roles in the system in order to encourage positive behavior and reach the goal of school-wide success. No particular component is sufficient in isolation. A systemic PBIS implementation is effective only when its components work together as a whole to incent positive behaviors.

To reach the goal of expert learning, all the parts of the system must play complementary roles in support of the goal of learning expertise for all. This requires a whole system that is not only safe and positive, but of itself, as a system, encourages and is supportive of expert learning. In expert learning systems, learners can find models of expert learning everywhere; not just models of expert performance, but evolving models for the long process of developing expertise from novice to advanced practitioners. Classroom teachers in such a system model their own learning processes, including trying something new that might not work out, making mistakes, seeking help, and "thinking aloud" about their own learning.

Various personnel in an educational setting can also model their own learning and make the process explicit with others in a collaborative and supportive environment. At the K–12 level, the cafeteria worker, the bus driver, the administrative secretary, and the school principal can all be invested in developing their own expertise in the process, not just the product, of learning. And there should be ways in which the learning of every one of them is explicit and visible to every student. Likewise, in a post-secondary setting, the library, the bursar's office, and the athletic department can demonstrate ways of growing and becoming smarter—using feedback from many stakeholders to adjust performance and to improve efficiencies, for example.

Mirroring the UDL framework, an expert learning environment or system is conducive to 1) being motivated to learn, 2) becoming knowledgeable about learning, and 3) becoming strategic about learning. You might say the system, made up of learners, is itself motivated, knowledgeable, and strategic about learning!

Qualities of an Expert System

To prepare expert learners for their future, helping them become highly supportive of motivation for future learning, the learning system itself needs to be highly motivated for learning. While many goals and motives animate any school, if the top priority is developing expert learners, then members of the system, above all else, demonstrate and model what it means to be motivated by learning.

Furthermore, members of an expert learning system demonstrate that they are motivated enough to sustain the effort and persistence that learning may require, despite frustrations and difficulties, and even when additional time and resources are required. Finally, they demonstrate self-regulation about learning: setting high expectations

VIDEO 2.33
CAST Research Scientist Sam Johnston emphasizes the importance of gaining tacit knowledge, or knowledge of how to do something that can only be gained by observing others practice, giving examples from medicine, law, business and craft.

▸ http://udlvideo.org/ch2/33

VIDEO 2.34
CAST's Sam Johnston describes Donald Campbell's metaphor for distributed intelligence, wherein team members with overlapping expertise work together like the scales of a fish.

▸ http://udlvideo.org/ch2/34

for the learning system itself, measuring progress towards goals, and adjusting and improving methods and tools according to reliable feedback.[26]

When we say that an expert system encourages becoming knowledgeable about learning, we mean that the people that make up that system have a well-formed theory of how learning happens and create the conditions to enable it. Increasingly, systems are based on an understanding that learning is a socially constructed process (often experienced vicariously or with supported experimentation and feedback) rather than experienced alone through direct trial and error. In fact, a social view of learning is taking hold in many learning systems. In an effort to improve student performance and retention in higher education, curricula are being restructured around learning communities. These learning communities allow students and faculty to engage more deeply with material through their interactions with one another and through holding collective accountability for what is learned.[27]

An expert system also views intelligence as distributed rather than held within one individual human mind. Gerhard Fischer, Director of the Center for Lifelong Learning and Design at the University of Colorado, argues that intelligence needs to be distributed across individuals to examine, frame, and resolve what he calls "wicked" problems. "Wicked" problems, such as global warming, are almost always too complex to be examined, framed, or resolved by a single individual human mind.[28] These problems require "cultures of participation" where creativity is socially constructed as people share tools and resources and together find solutions.

Solving wicked problems requires a distributed intelligence as a framework for supporting the "unaided human mind." And underneath the ability to solve problems, big or small, is the need to develop tacit knowledge before one gets to advanced knowledge. Tacit knowledge comes from observing someone else performing a skill: the medical student participating in rounds; the law student involved in case studies. The shared idea here is that people solve problems together, in communities and groups.

To prepare expert learners for a future where they are knowledgeable and value new knowledge, a school system itself needs to value knowledge. That means participants in the system must have expertise in the relevant domains of our culture. Since schools are not just repositories of knowledge, but rather are institutions for teaching, participants in expert learning systems are knowledgeable about their own discipline—teaching.[29]

Staff members in expert learning systems are also knowledgeable about learners and their differences, without which the science of learning cannot be applied effectively. Members of a learning system also support the idea that developing expertise requires continuous change and progress rather than reaching a static end state. In a changing universe, members of expert school systems know that knowledge must be updated, revised, and expanded to be useful to students who will live in the future.

To prepare expert learners for their future and to help them to be strategic in their learning, expert learning systems need to help develop highly strategic learners. That means all participants behave like expert learners: they set goals and plans for new learning, adopt effective strategies and tactics for continuous learning, monitor their progress in learning, and make course corrections. But members of expert learning systems do one more thing: they model and mentor goal setting, strategies, and progress monitoring for the community to see. Where learning is modeled and mentored by all participants, the first outcome is that educational settings become effective learning communities.[30]

Getting smarter means trying new tools and techniques, monitoring their effectiveness through evidence, selecting what is of high value, rejecting what is not, taking risks, and moving on quickly when something doesn't pan out. It also means challenging—and replacing—"foundational" ideas (such as the one-size-fits-all curriculum) that no longer work. Architectural engineering provides an appropriate analogy in the area of earthquake-safe skyscrapers. Such foundations are designed not with the hope that the building will not be shaken but instead with the knowledge that the building *will* be shaken, it will move. They are designed to provide the flexibility to withstand the inevitable and speedy shock of rapid movement in the earth beneath by moving themselves.

VIDEO 2.35–2.40 (SERIES) This series of six videos covers the specific steps taken by the Bartholomew Consolidated School Corporation (BCSC) to solve diverse challenges for elementary, secondary, special education and gifted students by committing to and implementing UDL district-wide. Examples include developing a common vision, providing professional development and ongoing support, evaluating their progress and revising their approach.

▸ http://udlvideo.org/ch2/35

VIDEO 2.41 Learning scientist Todd Rose describes how sometimes very tiny "inputs" lead to large changes in dynamic systems, suggesting that huge positive shifts in schools can be catalyzed by a small individual initiative.

▸ http://udlvideo.org/ch2/41

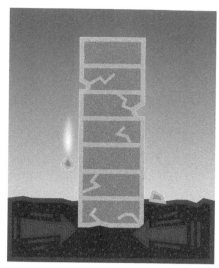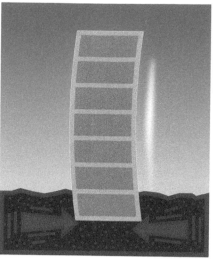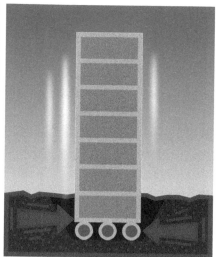

FIG. 2.11. How different building designs perform during earthquakes: A rigid building (left) cracks; a flexible building (center) sways above a fixed foundation but doesn't break; and the foundation of a base-isolated building (right) moves with the quake to prevent damage. *ILLUSTRATION BY CHRIS VALLO AND CATHY SIMON © 2013 CAST, INC.*

> " Getting smarter means challenging—and replacing—'foundational' ideas that no longer work.

In a similar way, expert learning systems of the future will need to be imbued with flexibility from the start, assuming that the learning environment and everyone in it will be in continual flux, and recognizing that change, just like variability, is the "new normal." In these settings, all participants at every level will develop and thrive as learners.

UDL: NEW THINKING ABOUT LEARNING

In this chapter, we have made the case that learning cannot be characterized as a process of absorbing factual knowledge or demonstrating skills. Rather, learning is about deepening our participation in a community of learners and thereby transforming the way we work and see ourselves as learners. A well-functioning learning community engenders continuous development in individuals and in the community itself.

Our education system does need to build specific competencies in literacy, mathematics, science, the arts, and every other content area. But in today's world, specific competencies are insufficient. Graduates of our schools, colleges, universities, and trade schools must be expert learners who are eager and ready to keep learning. This flexible, engaged readiness to learn new things is required by the changing workplace and the changing society, driven in part by communication technologies that are in constant flux, requiring that users learn new skills constantly just to keep current. The need for continuous learning is also a reflection of greater understanding about how learning works, gained from sophisticated neuroscience research.

Finally, dynamic, flexible learning environments are needed to respond to the natural variability of learners. Expert learners come in many guises, and our educational environments should nurture and validate them all. This vision is a significant shift from the traditional mentality of education systems as they currently exist. The framework of universal design for learning can enable that shift.

The Variability
of Learners

3

Experience and common sense suggest that
all individuals are unique and learn in ways
that are particular to them. And in the past
quarter century, science has elucidated the
great variability of the human capacity to
learn.

Yet our educational system is designed around the idea that most
people learn the same way and that a "fair" education is an identical
one. These ideas influence every aspect of our educational system. To
understand why we need to move away from these underlying assumptions, we turn to the latest findings on the learning brain.

From one perspective, human brains are remarkably similar. But
to neuroscientists, this similarity is an illusion—an artifact of inspecting
them from afar. Up close, individual brains are remarkably distinctive
in their anatomy, chemistry, and physiology. Like each person's finger-
prints, every brain is unique. Yet some of the differences are systematic
and predictable. Scientists often seek to uncover these systematic differences by comparing the brains of individuals from different groups,
such as people of different genders, ages, cultures, native languages, or
degrees of expertise.[1]

What they find is fascinating. Consider the brain scan in Figure 3.1.
In an experiment looking for physiological differences, researchers
explored how the brains of individuals diagnosed with autism differ
from those not diagnosed with autism. They asked both groups to

engage in exactly the same task—an intelligence measure called the Raven's Progressive Matrices—while measuring their brain activity via scanning technologies such as FMRIs and PET scans.[2] They found little difference between the two groups in most areas of the brain, but there was one area where the individuals with autism differed quite consistently from the comparison group—an area of complex visual perception highlighted in yellow.[3]

How can we interpret this difference? Many people might assume that the highlighted area would represent some kind of damage or dysfunction among individuals with autism. But the findings actually show something quite different. On this type of task, individuals with autism generally show superior performance. The scientists were not looking for sources of *dis*-ability but rather *vari*-ability. They were looking for what is different about the brains of individuals with autism who have *enhanced* abilities.

The brains of individuals with autism do show some systematic patterns that differ from the brains of those not identified as autistic. Whether that variation is a liability or a benefit depends entirely on the task being performed. On the Raven's Progressive Matrices, individuals with autism tend to perform better.[4] On a different measure of intelligence—for instance, one that relies primarily on language—individuals with autism usually underperform when compared with others.

Another interesting aspect of this study is the research team itself. One of the authors, Michelle Dawson, is herself autistic. Her colleague for the past seven years, neuroscientist Laurent Mottron, recently wrote a fascinating article in the influential journal *Nature* titled, "Changing Perceptions: the Power of Autism."[5] In addition to describing their research, Mottron explains the benefits that Dawson brings to their scientific investigations. He writes:

"Dawson's keen viewpoint also keeps the lab focused on the most important aspect of science: data. She has a bottom-up heuristic, in which ideas come from the available facts, and from them only. As a

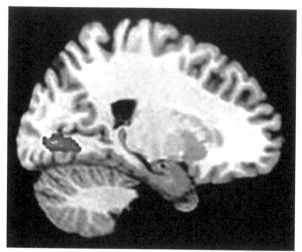

FIG. 3.1. The brain of a person with autism
© 2011 MACMILLAN PUBLISHERS LTD. REPRINTED WITH PERMISSION.

FIG. 3.2. Autism researchers Laurent Mottron (left) and Michelle Dawson
© 2011 MACMILLAN PUBLISHERS LTD. REPRINTED WITH PERMISSION.

result, her models never over-reach, and are almost infallibly accurate, but she does need a very large amount of data to draw conclusions. By contrast, I have a top-down approach: I grasp and manipulate general ideas from fewer sources, and, after expressing them in a model, go back to facts supporting or falsifying this model. Combining the two types of brains in the same research group is amazingly productive."[6]

Both the science and the scientists in this research point to the pervasiveness and the power of variability.

In this chapter we explore what is systematic and important about variability for teachers and learners. Learners are highly variable, but that variation is not chaotic. Of course, each learner is unique; but learners share common, predictable patterns of variability that are very useful to consider when designing learning environments.

THE BRAIN AND LEARNING

In the past, brain research focused on the anatomy of the brain and the functions of different regions. Whatever its value for other disciplines, such a static view of the brain has not been particularly useful in education, in part because it has little to say about how the brain learns. Now, instead of seeing the brain as a collection of discrete structures with specific functions, modern neuroscience views the brain as a complex web of integrated and overlapping *networks*. And learning is seen as changes in the connections within and between these networks.

This new view of neuroscience is deeply relevant to education, not only because it deals directly with issues of learning, but because it provides a foundation for understanding the nature and origins of learning variability. Here we provide a brief overview of how the brain actually learns. This forms the foundation for why and how we need to change our approach to teaching.

Returning to the study about the Raven's Matrices, why is it that individuals with autism differ in this particular area and not in a more distributed way? First, let's examine something fundamental about the brain that every learner shares. Figure 3.3 shows that brain matter is made up of different kinds of tissue. Everywhere around the convoluted outer edge of the brain there is a thin band of gray tissue called cortex. In contrast, most of the rest of the brain—the massive interior— is dominated by white streaks that seem to crisscross everywhere.

VIDEO 3.1
CAST Director of Research Gabrielle Rappolt-Schichtmann describes insights from neuroscience revealing overlapping, interconnected, and interdependent networks in the learning brain—and how the UDL framework aligns to these.

▶ http://udlvideo.org/ch3/1

This is white matter, or connective tissue.[7] The white color comes from myelin sheaths that are wrapped around the long connecting fibers, or axons, like insulation around a phone cable.[8] These massive white regions that seem to crisscross the bulk of the brain are composed almost entirely of the trillions of interconnections between individual neurons.

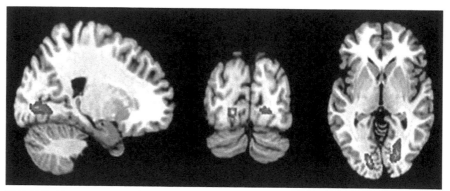

FIG. 3.3. New imaging techniques reveal different kinds of brain tissue.
© 2011 MACMILLAN PUBLISHERS LTD. REPRINTED WITH PERMISSION.

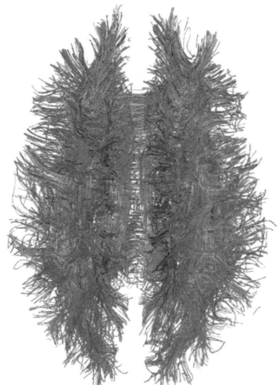

FIG. 3.4. Science reveals trillions of interconnections in the brain *© 2008 XAVIER GIGANDET ET AL., PLOS ONE*

These interconnections are being mapped with a wide variety of new imaging techniques. In Figure 3.4, MRI tractography techniques reveal the neural tracts between cortical and subcortical regions of the brain. What is most significant about our brains is not the thin band of neurons themselves but the astonishing interconnectivity between them. The human brain is, above all else, a dense, massively interconnected set of networks. The approximately one trillion neurons in cortex are linked by approximately 100 trillion connections. Just like computer networks, these multifaceted connections enable the individual components to communicate rapidly, flexibly, and along multiple pathways whether they are in close proximity or on opposite sides of the brain.[9]

All of us share this basic architecture—lots of neurons connected in huge networks. And learning actually changes the brain: the neurons don't change but their interconnections do.[10] The brain comprises massive numbers of networks large and small. Small networks are each specialized for performing certain kinds of tasks. When confronted with a specific task, such as the Raven's Progressive Matrices test, some networks are much more engaged and active than others and these active areas "light up" in images from brain scans. Because of their specialized functions, networks can be seen to engage with certain tasks reliably and predictably.

Consider, for example, the location of the highlighted area in Figure 3.1 (p. 50). Because the Raven's test demands the ability to recognize and comprehend complex visual patterns, a neuroscientist would predict that those networks specialized for visual pattern recognition would "light up" on a brain scan, indicating that this part of the brain is very active when the subject is working on this test. Where is that part of the brain? Generally, networks specialized for perception are located toward the back, or posterior, of the brain. Within that area, the networks specialized to recognize complex visual patterns are just about where the yellow highlighting is shown in the figure. Not surprisingly, given the task, the difference in brain activity between autistic and non-autistic individuals shows up here.

Individual differences often show up in this way—as differences in the activity of small, specialized networks. But how many of these smaller networks can we discern? And how many do we need to consider in being able to think about individual differences in learning?

Dig Deeper: What Does It Mean to Learn?

"Cells that fire together, wire together." This well-known axiom sums up Hebb's Theory, first posited in 1949 by Canadian psychologist Donald Hebb in his classic book, *The Organization of Behavior*. Hebb speculated that whenever people act or think in a way that makes multiple neurons fire in the brain, pathways among those neurons are formed.

And those connections get stronger and more efficient as the thoughts or actions are repeated: the thoughts and actions become learned, or memorized, with experience, and that learning has physical manifestations, not just intellectual ones. Conversely, when people stop practicing certain thoughts or actions, the brain eventually prunes the connecting cells that formed the pathways. The thoughts or actions become unlearned.[11]

THREE PRIMARY CLASSES OF NETWORKS FOR LEARNING

While thousands of networks specialized for different functions have been identified, in this book we emphasize just three large ones. These are the three primary classes of networks that comprise the vast majority of the human brain, and are significant, together, for learning. These networks are:

Affective networks that monitor the internal and external environment to set priorities, to motivate, and to engage learning and behavior.

Recognition networks that sense and perceive information in the environment and transform it into usable knowledge.

Strategic networks that plan, organize, and initiate purposeful actions in the environment.

Each of these classes (or kinds) of networks tends to be spatially distinguishable in the brain. The affective networks are buried largely in the very center of the brain. The recognition networks dominate the posterior (back) of the brain, and the strategic (motor) networks dominate the anterior (front) of the brain.[12]

Affective   Recognition   Strategic

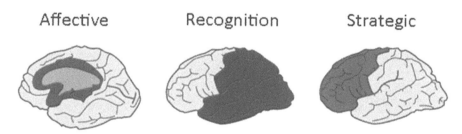

FIG. 3.5. Locations in the brain of the three network groups © 2013 CAST, INC.

Why do we focus on these three networks, rather than tens or hundreds of more differentiated models of networks that we could use? This question has important implications for the way that educators think about *any* models that are used in science or education. Briefly, like most phenomena in science, the brain is far too complex to study "as-is" (a fact that is quite obvious once you realize you are using your brain to understand *your brain*), and so we rely on models that simplify the complexity, highlighting what is relevant and ignoring what is not. When selecting a good model, we need to find a balance between the two extremes of being too complex or too simplistic.

We have chosen to focus on three classes of networks because this is the most basic way to partition the learning brain. It is possible to take a more complex model of the brain, recognizing many different networks or functions, but it is not really possible to take a simpler model that would still reveal the fundamental foundations of learning.

The division that we will follow originates in the anatomy of every animal with a central nervous system. When anatomists look at the most basic levels of the central nervous system, they differentiate three types of neurons: receptive or sensory neurons that bring information into the nervous system, motor or effector neurons that carry information out of the nervous system to stimulate muscles into action, and interneurons that represent the current state or "values" of the organism.[13] Everywhere we look in the nervous system, we can see the same three kinds of differentiation. And these all play a key role in any act of learning.

But we can look beyond neuroscience to other fields for confirmation of the importance of these three basic components of learning. For some time, educators, psychologists, and organizational theorists have pointed to the same three components in any learning organism. For example, Lev Vygotsky, a pioneering Russian psychologist of the early 20th century, described three prerequisites for learning:

- Engagement with the learning task;

- Recognition of the information to be learned; and

- Strategies to process that information.[14]

Benjamin Bloom, whose taxonomy of educational objectives is one of the most widely cited references in the educational literature, chose to divide educational objectives into three very similar areas—cognitive, psychomotor, and affective.[15] In his work on innovation in business, Clayton Christensen describes yet another three-part division in the key components of a corporation: its values, knowledge, and processes.[16]

Thus, though universal design for learning is rooted in the neuroscience of learning, the model of the three classes of brain networks

VIDEO 3.2
David Rose explains that the learning brain more closely resembles a social network, with thousands of interconnections, than a hierarchical, linear system such as a traditional school.

▶ http://udlvideo.org/ch3/2

aligns with the insights of other researchers and theorists. And it makes common sense. To learn we need to care about what we are learning and want to learn it; we need to take in and build knowledge; and we need to develop skill and fluency in our actions

Before we describe each of the three networks we offer an important caveat: any division of the brain is useful only as a model and a lens through which to study phenomena. In reality, networks always work together as one overall organism. We separate the parts only to try to understand more clearly how each contributes to learning overall and to understand learner variability. By dividing types of networks and studying the functions for which they are specialized, we can gain insights about how students learn and how they vary.

What do all three classes of networks have in common? First, networks are *specialized*. Like any complex machine or organization, the networks are composed of many different parts that work together, each of which is specialized in some way.[17] Second, networks are *heterarchical*, meaning that the flow of data, power, and influence is not only top-to-bottom, but also bottom-to-top and side-to-side.[18] And finally, brain networks are highly *variable*, both among individuals and within individuals over time and in different contexts. This broad and deep variability plays out in many ways, and it impacts and is impacted by the way we learn and teach. The environments in which we live and learn have a huge impact on how we live and learn.[19]

Through universal design for learning, we provide a structured framework to account for much of the variability of all the individuals in a given learning environment to design that environment to be flexible. A first step is exploring the characteristics of the three types of learning networks and providing examples of learner variability within them.

Affective Networks

Imagine that you are a teacher in a large urban school with a large and persistent racial achievement gap.[20] A number of strategies to close that achievement gap come to mind—providing extended-day school programs, offering intensive remedial programs in core literacies, initiating a one-to-one laptop program, and so forth. All of them require considerable investment of time and resources and generally have produced only limited success.

VIDEO 3.3
Jon Mundorf, a teacher, shares his insights on affect in the classroom and the role teachers can play.

▶ http://udlvideo.org/ch3/3

A line of work reported and replicated in the journal *Science* suggests that there may be a more efficient way to approach this problem. A simple intervention, offered three to five times a year and taking only a few minutes, has been shown to lower the achievement gap as measured by grade point averages. In the experiment, students were asked to complete a brief in-class writing assignment wherein they were prompted to reaffirm their sense of personal adequacy or self-integrity. This simple exercise resulted in a 40 percent increase in scores of African American students on tests they took afterward. That's it: no extended remedial skills training, no special course in study strategies, no reward system.[21]

This experiment has been replicated under a variety of different conditions and with a variety of students who, like the African American students in the first study, typically feel the effects of what is called "stereotype threat" or the experience of stress, anxiety, or worry that one's performance will align with a negative stereotype about a group to which they belong (ethnic, racial, social, etc.). It can be thought of as a way of measuring how context can impact educational or academic performance.[22] The positive effects of this kind of intervention have been seen among minority students who often experience stigmatization and the tyranny of low expectations. Amazingly, in a follow-up study, positive effects were still being seen up to two years after the intervention. What is consistent across these experimental interventions is the focus on affect.

A simple affirmation of learners' positive sense of self, of their value as individuals, and of the importance of their membership in a cultural tradition has repeatedly been shown to have positive effects on learning and on performance. Those effects can be seen on a test taken just a few minutes after the intervention, on cumulative grades over a month of study, or even on overall academic and health status over the span of a college career. For most of us, these results are still astonishing even though they have proven robust in multiple studies. What they show is the enormous power of affect. In the last decade, we have witnessed an extraordinary volume of theory and research—including whole new journals and major books—on the topic of affective neuroscience and its relationship to learning.[23] Where affective neuroscience once seemed "squishy" and unempirical, it is now central and dominant to the empirical understanding of

VIDEO 3.4
CAST Research Scientists Gabrielle Rappolt-Schlichtmann and Samantha Daley explain the interconnections between affect and cognition, emphasizing the importance of supporting students' positive appraisals of the learning experience.

▶ http://udlvideo.org/ch3/4

VIDEO 3.5
Harvard Graduate School of Education lecturer Richard Weissbourd reflects on the intimate connection between literacy and affect, and describes reading as a relational activity.

▶ http://udlvideo.org/ch3/5

any brain function. At the same time, we have seen a parallel growth of research within the education sciences on the power of emotion and affect in the classroom. Congruent with the renewed emphasis of neuroscientists on the centrality of affect, educators have also come to recognize the central role of engagement and motivation in any effective educational reform.

The consensus is emerging—from neuroscience, education, psychology, and economics—that our brains are not only "information processing" systems designed for objective reasoning and logic. Rather our brains are purposeful, goal-driven networks that have evolved to bias our perceptions and actions in ways that make them very much more subjective than objective. They have evolved not to mirror reality accurately, but to warp reality in ways that are self-serving and self-sustaining: some parts of reality are much more valued or important than others and our brains survive by being highly selective.

Because we tend to focus on the physical world that we can see, hear, and touch, we don't often realize that we all walk around in an emotional landscape that colors and even generates our experience. We initiate action and respond to our world based on how we feel about it, not based on a mythical, objectively measurable "reality." We appraise everything and everyone continuously. Is this good for me, bad for me, exciting, frightening, supportive, or threatening? Am I relaxed, interested, at risk? These appraisals determine at core how we function. Experiencing ourselves and our world through an affective filter, we interpret and in a sense create our reality.[24] Some learners—such as those who are often marginalized by negative stereotypes—experience the world as more threatening than those who feel themselves in the majority, often with good reason.

Recent research has suggested, for example, that middle school students with learning disabilities often view academic situations as threatening, even exhibiting physiological stress responses upon entering a room where they will be asked to read. While more successful readers tend to show mild anxiety when asked to read aloud, students with a history of reading difficulties show elevated heart rates and other indicators of stress even before being given instructions.[25]

> " A simple affirmation of learners' positive sense of self, of their value as individuals, and of the importance of their membership in a cultural tradition has repeatedly been shown to have positive effects on learning and on performance.

The parts of our brains that set "value" or priorities, that color our experience and drive our actions, are all located at the very center of the brain. As we shall describe, the affective networks are specialized, heterarchical, and highly variable. All of this impacts how students learn—and how they don't.

Affective networks are specialized

First, the affective networks are specialized. That is, like any complex machine or organization, affective networks are composed of many different parts, each specialized in some way, that work together. As an example, let's examine the parts of our brain that are specialized for one of the most basic emotions: fear. We have all had moments of being afraid when we wish we were more courageous, but fear is vitally important to our survival and even to our success. Not to fear dangerous things, such as extreme heights, large wild animals, or threatening enemies is dangerous in itself. What part of the brain is specialized for fear? Actually, there are quite a few places (fear is very important!), but foremost among them is an area called the amygdala.

How do we know that the amygdala is involved in fear? For one thing, lesions to the amygdala disrupt the normal functions of fear—animals do not fear things they should, can't learn to fear new things that signal danger, and don't recognize threats from other animals.[26] In addition, the behavioral and physiological reactions associated with fear—dilated pupils, increased sweating, racing heart rate—are also often missing. Neuroimaging tools now enable us to study which parts of the brain are most active in fear-inducing situations. The amygdala is intensely active when people or animals are confronted with fearful stimuli or are placed in fearful environments. This is one example of an area of specialization within the affective networks.

FIG. 3.6. Neurons communicate in multiple directions. *Illustration by Chris Vallo © 2013 CAST, Inc.*

Affective networks are heterarchical

The affective networks are also heterarchical. As we noted, to be heterarchical means that control and influence is not only hierarchical ("top down") but also "bottom up" and "side to side." How does that work? Let's continue with our fear example. Certain stimuli, such as unexpected noises or scary faces, can provoke powerful feelings of fear even before we have had a chance to consciously process what those noises or faces mean or what threat, exactly, is posed.[27]

Our nervous system may initiate physiological responses such as a rush of adrenaline, contraction of the large skeletal muscles, and increased blood pressure: the physiological symptoms of fear. This unconscious process of emotion is both "bottom up" and "top down"—a prime example of the heterarchical nature of emotion and cognition in thinking. These processes are "bottom up" because information travels from the sense organs up the neural system, at least as far as the amygdala. However, the processes are also "top down" because the amygdala depends on input from the cerebral cortex to evaluate information as threatening or benign. As this example of bi-directionality in the nervous system suggests, emotion and cognition are so intertwined that disentangling them is rarely practical or useful.[28]

An everyday example illustrates this bottom-up/top-down processing. Suppose you are walking in unfamiliar woods and detect a sudden movement in your peripheral vision. Almost before you are aware of the disturbance, your eyes leap to focus on the source and your body prepares for fight or flight. Seconds later you consciously register that the disturbance is a harmless squirrel. Your initial response to the noise—the physiological changes, the protective hunching of your body

FIG. 3.7. Affective response: Fight or flight   *ILLUSTRATION BY CHRIS VALLO © 2013 CAST, INC.*

and covering your head with your arms—are part of a crude defensive response mediated by rapid bottom-up processing.

It is not until almost a full second passes that conscious awareness of fear coincides with a more analytical look at the source of the noise, allowing you to consciously and strategically decide what to do. Because the amygdala is connected not only to sensory and perceptual information coming in from the environment but also connected to "higher" levels of the nervous system (like orbitofrontal cortex) that deal with planful and predictive behaviors, whether you "jump" or not in response to a sudden sound depends as much on your learned expectancies for what might happen as it does on the sound itself. If you are in an environment where dangerous things have happened to you before (or others have told you that dangerous things can happen) you will usually become hyper-alert and jumpy. Almost any unexpected sound can startle you and make you freeze.

Alternatively, if you are passing through an environment where you have learned previously that there are always loud sounds that are completely harmless and explainable then you tend to react very little to those sounds, and, in fact, become habituated to them.[29]

When faced with a potential stressor like a presentation, a recital, or an athletic competition that we expect to be anxiety provoking, we can call upon conscious techniques such as breathing, refocusing attention, and visualizing success. Teachers can help students become skillful in using these kinds of techniques to help them manage their emotional responses in stressful and fearful situations. Understanding how emotions can impact student learning can help.

An example illustrates this. Studies demonstrate the power of conscious strategies for interpreting emotional responses. Researchers recruited students who were planning to take the Graduate Record Examination (GRE) for entrance into graduate school. When participants came to the laboratory, they were presented with a practice GRE. During instructions for completing the practice test, one group of students was told that recent research had shown that feelings of arousal and anxiety during a test might actually precede better test performance. This group was instructed that if they felt anxious during the practice test they might remind themselves that this could be helpful. Instructions for the other group of students stated that people often feel anxiety during test taking but did not suggest how to reinterpret this experience.

VIDEO 3.6
David Rose talks about his own anxiety before giving talks, the strategies he uses to manage that anxiety, and what students might learn from his experience.

▶ http://udlvideo.org/ch3/6

Dig Deeper: Exercising Affect

Alfred Yarbus used a well-known painting called "An Unexpected Visitor" (Fig. 3.8) to study the eye movements of subjects viewing the image for different purposes. To experience your own affective networks at work, begin by examining the image freely. When you first direct your attention to Figure 3.8, some parts seem to "grab" your attention. But many of the factors that impact your attention are actually internal: your emotional state, your familiarity with the picture, your interest (or lack of interest) in the content or form, and your state of energy or fatigue, to name a few. More generally, we can say that memory, personality, motivation, mood, interest, and biological state all influence how you will engage and sustain interaction with the picture.

FIG. 3.8. What grabs you? © 1967 ALFRED L. YARBUS

Of course, these characteristics and states vary tremendously across viewers. A psychologist might attend to the expressions on the people's faces, while an interior designer might take more note of the room's décor. The mother of a toddler may be drawn to the child seated at the table, whereas a musician may first notice the piano. If asked to comment on the state of mind of those in the picture, everyone would offer a unique perspective.

The power of these variables to influence what we see and how we interpret the environment is exploited in the Rorschach test used by psychologists. Though not from the Rorschach itself, the inkblot shown in Figure 3.9 presents a similarly ambiguous image. Clearly, inkblots are not representational images. But when asked to describe what they see in an inkblot, most people find figures, animals, landscapes, or objects. By collecting many responses, researchers develop norms based on what people without emotional disturbances are likely to find.

The emotions and internal states experienced by individuals with affective disorders tend to strongly influence what they see in the outside world, leading to unusual kinds of responses on a test like the Rorschach. By examining a patient's responses across many different stimuli and looking for commonalities and patterns, psychologists can deduce a patient's fears, preoccupations, and desires.

From one perspective, the entire world is a Rorschach. Take any student in the classroom context, for example. At any instant, multiple facets of the classroom environment—peers, teacher, what's going on outside—compete for that student's attention. These demands in our day-to-day world require not only that we recognize objects and formulate strategies but also that we evaluate their significance and importance to us. How we do so is, in large part, a reflection of our own history of emotions and motivations. The fact that people impose their own unique interpretations on something as vaguely formed as an inkblot is another illustration of how our affective states influence how we experience the world.

FIG. 3.9. What we see and how we interpret the environment is influenced by the combination of variables that make people unique. © *1994 MARK W. MATTHEWS*

The results of this manipulation were striking. Students who were told how to "reappraise" the feelings they experienced during the test had significantly better performance on the math section of the practice GRE in the laboratory compared to students who were not told how to interpret their anxiety. Knowing how to reappraise or reinterpret the arousal experienced during testing appears to have had a dramatic effect on performance.[30]

Affective networks are variable

Of course, the kinds of reactions described above vary from person to person and within an individual over time and in different contexts. For example, there are huge individual differences in every aspect of the fear heterarchy—some students seem puzzlingly anxious much of the time, others often seem "too fearless." Some of this is conscious, some unconscious. But these differences all affect learning and performance.

In controlled studies, researchers have come up with an array of simple manipulations that foster the desired affective states in study participants. By playing happy or sad music, displaying different emotionally moving photographs, or giving different kinds of feedback to participants during a taxing task, researchers can manipulate participants' affective responses. This proves the variability of affective states in response to constantly changing surroundings and social interactions. Of course classrooms are rife with changing conditions that influence students' affective states.

Affective differences clearly exert powerful effects on learners' ability to learn. Affect can influence a learner very positively—as shown in Rosalie Fink's work on reading instruction of individuals with dyslexia—or, as is more commonly noted, negatively.[31] Students with severe affective disorders, such as schizophrenia or a history of abuse, are highly vulnerable to reading failure, in part because strong affective influences derail the work of recognition and strategic networks. More prevalent issues, such as learning disabilities, can also produce strong affective responses over time. We have talked to college students with learning disabilities who vividly describe the palpable dread with which they pick up and open new textbooks.

VIDEO 3.7
Affect is centrally important to learning. Samantha Daley suggests emotional supports and strategies that teachers can provide to reshape learning experiences into something positive for students.

▶ http://udlvideo.org/ch3/7

Naturally some effects are commonplace for everyone—anxiety before a test or a presentation is not only typical of most people but also beneficial. A certain amount of stress or anxiety can prepare us to pay close attention and to perform at our best. Understanding these differences can help teachers support learners appropriately.

Affective networks determine the emotional and motivational significance of the world around us: they motivate and prioritize what we do and what we learn, whether we are planning a summer vacation or merely gazing at a painting on the wall (see Exercising Affect, p. 62). But they do not work alone. Their work is always tightly interwoven with the other networks. Let's move on to recognition networks.

Recognition Networks

Take a look at Figure 3.10. You will undoubtedly recognize many aspects of the image—the checkerboard, the cylinder, the shadow. Your ability to recognize those things seems quite effortless—automatic—as if your brain were merely a camera. But there is something quite surprising about the image. Look carefully at the two squares marked A and B. If your brain were merely a camera you would notice that those two squares are exactly the same shade of gray. But your brain is not a camera and it actually distorts your perception of the colors of the squares. One looks white and the other looks dark grey even though they are exactly the same tonality.

In fact, your brain is so powerful at distorting the way the image appears that you are probably either contesting our assertion that the two squares are the same or else having a hard time believing your own eyes. Even those who have seen this illusion before and know full well that those two squares are identical in brightness cannot see it. (Try it yourself! Go to www.michaelbach.de/ot/lum_adelsonCheckShadow/index.html and click on question one for proof that your visual system is distorting what you see so that you interpret it incorrectly.) [32]

Edward H. Adelson

FIG. 3.10. Adelson's Checker-Shadow Illusion: Are A and B really the same? © 1995 EDWARD H. ADELSON

Just as affect can influence what we perceive in the outside world, our expectations about what we are seeing can warp what we do see. Illusions like Adelson's are great ways to illustrate the brain's dependence on and interaction with patterns when recognizing our world. The environment is comprised not of random or chaotic information but rather of predictable patterns. Humans' ability to rapidly recognize those patterns is a critical part of how recognition networks function.

Our brains, and particularly the posterior lobes of cortex, have evolved to recognize environmental patterns efficiently. They recognize the visual color patterns that signal ripe fruit, the sound patterns that signal running water, the smells that distinguish rotted food, the taste of sugar. They enable us to recognize voices, faces, letters, and words, as well as more complex patterns such as an author's style and abstract concepts such as justice. In the example of Adelson's illusion, our brains are so good at recognizing patterns from the physical world—the pattern of the checkerboard and the pattern of the shadow—that our expectancies for those patterns can actually distort what we perceive in a two-dimensional image.

Let's examine the recognition networks in a little more depth. Located in the back of the brain, recognition networks parallel affective networks in that they are specialized, heterarchical, and variable. Let's examine the significance of these qualities for learning.

Recognition is specialized

Like affective networks, recognition networks are *specialized*. In Figure 3.11 we see a very elementary example of specialization in recognition networks: recognizing words in two very distinctive ways. In this image of a brain scan, the same words have been presented orally to the brain pictured on the left and visually to the brain pictured on the right. It is quite obvious that different regions of the brain are activated for the two kinds of word recognition: auditory and visual.

Pattern recognition takes place in different areas of the brain that are each specialized in some way. It was no surprise to anyone that visual patterns of words would be recognized in a different part of the brain than auditory patterns of words—they each require somewhat different capabilities. But the specialization goes far beyond just the differences between two sensory modalities. Within each sensory modality there are striking specializations as well. Visual recognition of objects, for example, is distributed across at least thirty different areas in the brain so that elements like vertical lines, diagonal lines, color, and motion are all processed in physically discrete areas.[33] Because the specialized work of different parts of the brain is distributed, the recognition networks can operate in parallel.

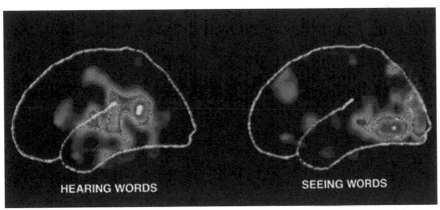

HEARING WORDS   SEEING WORDS

FIG. 3.11. Recognizing words orally and visually happens in different regions of the brain. © 1987 MACMILLAN PUBLISHERS LTD. REPRINTED WITH PERMISSION.

An analogy may clarify how this works. Think of the brain as a kitchen full of food processors. Imagine that all of the processors may be the same basic make and model but each has specialized attachments for blending dough, shredding cabbage, and other specialized tasks. They all perform the same general function—food processing—but their output is as different as pie crust is from coleslaw. By having multiple processors, a chef can be very efficient—each processor has a very specialized blade that is just right for a specific task. In the brain, specialized processing provides a similar advantage. All of recognition cortex has the same basic structure, but the tissue in each region is fine-tuned to process one type of input extremely efficiently. This works more effectively than would "all-purpose" tissue that would have to adapt to each new task or treat every task in the same way.

Why does distributed specialization and parallel processing matter to educators? First, the evidence on specialization sharpens our understanding of how complex the tasks we assign to students really are. Typically, brain images reveal that seemingly simple tasks place widely varied, distributed demands on the brain. Many of those demands are implicit and unexpected, and as educators we may not even be aware of them all. We think that the demands of any given task are focused in the area of our goal, such as mathematical computation. But within the way we present a task, we often create demands that are not relevant to the goals or purposes of the lesson or task. For instance, consider the classic case of the word problem. We think the demands of the task are about math, but there are of course also reading demands that confound our understanding of students' successes or failures.

Second, the evidence on specialization contradicts our simplified view of individual differences. We tend to think that learners differ along general dimensions such as IQ or verbal ability. But, in fact, each of the myriad small specializations are sources of individual difference. The person who has perfect pitch is not necessarily more likely to have amazing color perception or remarkable face recognition. People differ in hundreds of thousands of ways rather than in one way or even in a handful of ways.

Third, because individuals differ in many specific skills and abilities—the specializations above—it is especially important to design lessons so that systematic variability is anticipated from the outset. When that is not done, unexpected demands and difficulties are imposed on all students, and their effects are not equal. For some students, whose brains are specialized in one way, the incidental demands of a task are irrelevant. For others, the incidental demands of a task are barriers or hurdles to overcome. As a result, some students are sharply "on task" and others are decidedly "off task"—behavior that is often attributed to deliberate choice or some kind of affective interference.

It's important to remember that learners may seem "off task" but actually be pursuing the task in a novel way. When some students accomplish tasks using pathways that work for them, the learning of all students is supported. Diverse models support self-efficacy because, as psychologist Albert Bandura wrote, "If people of widely differing characteristics can succeed, then observers have a reasonable basis for increasing their own sense of self-efficacy."[34]

Recognition is heterarchical

We have seen that individual aspects of patterns, such as their color, shape, orientation, or motion are processed by separate parts of recognition networks. And these specialized processes proceed in parallel. But they do not proceed independently. Like affective systems, recognition systems are intensely interconnected and heterarchical. The naïve assumption is that recognition is primarily a "bottom-up" process. In this view, visual sensory information enters the nervous system at the retina (the bottom) and then travels up through an increasingly complex hierarchical network, eventually reaching the visual cortex where patterns in the visual information are recognized (the top).

But as we saw in the Adelson illusion, recognition is very much a "top-down" process. Our brains don't just passively receive information in that bottom-up way. Instead, our brains are constantly and persistently anticipating and predicting what patterns we will see, hear, smell, taste, or touch, and those expectancies profoundly affect what patterns we actually do perceive. To facilitate recognition, our brains consistently make use of higher-order information such as background knowledge, context, previous experience, and overall pattern.

Now it is possible to understand the checkerboard illusion—a great example of the heterarchy at work. The illusion shows how powerful the top-down expectancies can be in the network. You have lived in a culture where you have a great deal of experience in the patterns created by checkerboards, cylinders, and their shadows. As a result, your brain (not your eye) expects that shadows will change the luminance of any object. This is a classic finding in neuroscience, whereby the brain is projecting a three-dimensional space and makes use of past knowledge about the effects of shadow on luminance to actually change what you perceive through your retina. In other words, our expectations about what we perceive literally determine what we do perceive. Perceptual distortions can be highly adaptive. Our ancestors did not fail to recognize a lion when they saw it hiding in the shadows even though its coat was not as yellow and luminous as it looked in the sunshine. Their brains (but not those of their cave mates who have no descendants) distorted what their eyes perceived, to our eventual benefit!

Heterarchical processing is also critical for modern-day literacy development. Consider learning to read. The common assumption used to be that reading was mainly a bottom-up activity. The letters are recognized by their features, synthesized into words and sounds, and then analyzed for meaning. But research has shown that it is easier and faster to recognize letters in the context of words than to recognize them in isolation, a phenomenon termed the word superiority effect.[35] The word superiority effect occurs because familiarity with the larger pattern (the word) constrains the bottom-up process of individual letter recognition, reducing the number of features that need to be examined based on expectation. That is why proofreading is so difficult. We miss errors because word expectancies are so powerful that they influence how we see individual letters, especially if we wrote them. Use of context and meaning to predict what is coming next is another example of top-down processing in reading.

Smoothly functioning recognition networks take advantage of both top-down and bottom-up processes. Thus, teaching exclusively to either process does not take full advantage of what we know about the learning brain. A positive example is the recent truce in the "phonics wars."[36] Most programs have adopted a balanced approach to reading where top-down whole language is balanced with bottom-up phonics. This balanced approach is consistent with the way the learning brain works.

Recognition is variable

The distributed nature of recognition has profound implications for the variability of learning. Were recognition the product of one homogeneous area of brain tissue, recognition abilities would vary from person to person in a limited number of ways and differences in recognition would have global effects on vision (or other senses) as a whole. Instead, because recognition is actually a coordinated act of many different networked neural modules, each very small component of recognition has the potential to vary in its functioning from person-to-person. The differences between us may affect one module, and therefore one aspect of recognition; or many modules, and therefore many aspects of recognition. But the variations are not infinite; variability is actually systematic and largely predictable.

All human brains share the same basic architecture for recognition and recognize things in roughly the same way. However, in their detailed anatomy, size, connectivity, physiology, and chemistry recognition networks are highly varied. And the impacts of that variation can only be understood in context. PET scan images usually represent averages across individuals. These averages highlight the commonalities between individuals but obscure the fact that each individual brain actually reveals a unique pattern of activity. For example, while most humans show increased activity localized to the back of the brain when they are recognizing an object visually, the exact magnitude, location, and distribution of that increased activity is variable. The active area of the cortex may be larger or smaller, more localized to the right or left hemisphere, and more widely or closely distributed. These differences manifest in the way people recognize things in the world—their recognition strengths, weaknesses, and preferences.

Specific differences in recognition networks of individual learners range from the subtle to the profound. The recognition cortex in Albert Einstein's brain was disproportionately allocated to spatial cognition.[37] He had difficulty recognizing the letter patterns and sound symbol connections required for reading, but he was a genius at visualizing the deepest fundamentals of physics. Awareness of these differences across his recognition networks could have helped Einstein's teachers shape instruction that would support his areas of weakness and capitalize on his spatial genius.

Of course we have to remember that separating recognition from the other classes of network is done for purposes of study and does not reflect how the brain works. Recognition networks are also completely intertwined with those of strategy and affect. A whole body of work focuses, for example, on perception of the steepness of hills. Research in this area focuses on both the mechanics of visual perception of this single phenomenon and also on non-mechanical conditions that affect steepness perception. Contextual factors have been shown to be a strong influence on perception. For example, individuals who have just completed a long run, are carrying a heavy backpack, or are in poor health tend to perceive hills as very steep.[38]

In education, the challenges posed by problems in recognition are often treated as less complex than those posed by strategic or affective concerns. But as we've seen here, recognition is actually a highly complex set of processes and is highly variable from person to person. This understanding may convince those who create learning environments to embed maximum flexibility so that flexibility so that no learners are constrained in their learning opportunities.

VIDEO 3.8
Learning scientist Todd Rose describes research involving dyslexic astrophysicists, showing that a weakness in the context of reading became a strength in the context of scanning the sky for black holes.

▸ http://udlvideo.org/ch3/8

Dig Deeper: Exercising Recognition

Let's return to "An Unexpected Visitor." This time, try to identify as many objects in the image as you can.

Probably you will identify many objects: chair, table, piano, people, pictures on the walls, and others. And you could also identify parts of objects: eyes, frames, table legs, or doorknobs. Some of these objects are partially hidden; others are at odd angles or clustered in poor light, yet your recognition networks are so powerful that you recognize them essentially instantaneously. This is the heterarchy at work. We have experience with three-dimensional objects viewed from many angles and partially hidden, and we recognize them because they are familiar patterns that conform to our expectations. We have the same benefit of top-down processing seeing them in a painting.

We can do more than just recognize many objects at the same time; we can recognize the same object in a number of different ways. For example, even out of context we recognize the shape in Figure 3.13 as a chair.

This is remarkable given that this particular representation does not show the features we usually associate with chairs, such as four legs and a seat. You might also categorize the chair not only as a chair but also as the chair from "An Unexpected Visitor." You can recognize and distinguish this specific chair from all the other chairs you have ever identified. Without necessarily being conscious of it, you also recognize the chair as a member of the category "furniture."

FIG. 3.12–3.13. Even with minimal details we can recognize objects. © 1967 ALFRED L. YARBUS

Strategic Networks

Imagine that you are a four-year-old youngster and your teacher offers you a marshmallow. But, before you eat it, she makes you a better offer. If you can wait for just a few minutes while she goes and gets another one, you can have *both* of them to eat. Here's the hard part: to enjoy both of them you will have to wait and *not* eat the first one until the teacher comes back with the second. That one delicious marshmallow will be sitting right in front of you during the whole time the teacher is out of the room. Can you wait?

Columbia University psychologist Walter Mischel first conducted this experiment, and it has become a classic.[39] Some children at this age do very well, and invent interesting strategies to help them succeed (such as covering their eyes so that they can't see the marshmallow or holding their hands together tightly so they don't inadvertently reach out and take it). Some just can't wait.

Even though very simple, this task demands a great deal. It requires a wide variety of motor acts and skillful movements: being able to reach out, grasp the one (or two) marshmallows, carry them to your mouth without dropping them. Prior to the motor movements, a wide range of capabilities (both physical and mental) have already come into play: setting a longer-term goal (acquiring two marshmallows), formulating a plan for reaching that goal (waiting, adopting various strategies to manage the wait), actualizing those strategies and tactics, and monitoring progress (continually checking to see that the teacher hasn't returned yet, to see that one marshmallow remains, to check if your hand is reaching for the marshmallow in spite of your intentions). All of these activities, both mental and physical, are what we mean by acting strategically.

FIG. 3.14. The marshmallow test *ILLUSTRATION BY CHRIS VALLO © 2013 CAST, INC.*

You Tube

VIDEO 3.9
This Ignitermedia.com film shows young children employing strategies (with varying degrees of success) to resist eating a single marshmallow in order to obtain a second.

▶ http://udlvideo.org/ch3/9

(It is important to remember that we are focusing here on the strategic aspects of this task. But like almost any learning task, the "marshmallow task" requires all three networks working together: recognition networks are critical in recognizing that the white object is a marshmallow in the first place, and affective networks are critical in evaluating, monitoring and regulating how important and motivating that marshmallow actually is at the moment.)

Strategic networks are specialized

Strategic networks allow us to plan, execute, and monitor all kinds of purposeful acts in our environment. They range from the most elementary motor act—a purposeful step, the blink of an eye, a grasp of a marshmallow—to a fluent and complex skill—a spoken sentence, a dance, a basketball shot, a smooth reach to bring a marshmallow to our mouths—to acts of enormous planfulness—playing chess, practicing piano, applying to a college, building a school, waiting a long time to get two marshmallows.

To accomplish this range of capabilities, the strategic networks are highly specialized in several ways. The most familiar is specialization for various body movements. The "map" of this specialization is illustrated in the weirdly distorted homunculus of the primary motor cortex.[40]

Hand movements are specialized in one part of the motor cortex and foot movements in a different part. The diagram also shows that there is a much larger allocation of cortex, in controlling our hands or our mouth, than in controlling our feet or back. The motor cortex specializes to devote more computing power to the kinds of movements that require the most skillful and exacting control. During the last decade we have learned a striking thing: that the proportion of motor cortex devoted to any specific type of movement is altered by learning. An expert violinist, for example, will have a huge area of motor cortex devoted to controlling the very fine movements of the left hand that are critical in playing the violin.[41] Years and years of practice have "shaped" the motor cortex distinctively so that it has the power and flexibility it needs to play the violin. This kind of "plasticity" of the brain has been one of the most dramatic discoveries in neuroscience, revealing that the brain's ultimate

VIDEO 3.10
David Rose explains the role of strategic networks in planning, initiating, and executing purposeful movements, from the simplest to the most complex.

▶ http://udlvideo.org/ch3/10

specialization depends not only on genetic factors—the brain you were born with—but also very much on experiential factors—the brain you learned with.

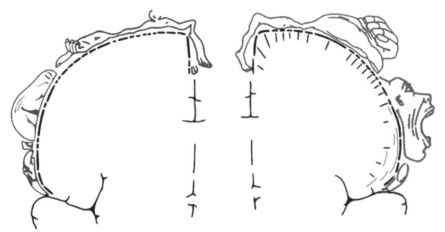

FIG. 3.15. Brain network specialization is illustrated in the weirdly distorted homunculus of the primary motor cortex   *PUBLIC DOMAIN IMAGE SHARED VIA WIKIMEDIA COMMONS*

Strategic networks are heterarchical

Consider the marshmallow task with which we began this section. In the end, the task is completed with one seemingly simple action: reaching out to grasp one (or two) marshmallows. Accomplishing this simple action clearly requires at least one area of specialization—the part of the motor cortex with which we control the muscles in our arm and hand, enabling us to reach out to grasp the marshmallow. But it is obvious that this simple act is embedded in a much larger, heterarchical network required for strategic action.

At the lowest level are the networks that actually stimulate muscles to action. This area is often called the primary motor cortex. In a company that made shoes, this would be the unit that actually produces a finished shoe, stitching it together from the various parts and shining it up for sale.

At a slightly higher level are areas that coordinate those simple muscle movements into complex and skillful actions. This part of strategic networks sequences and coordinates a large number of simple movements into an effective series of actions that accomplish goals such as speaking, walking, jumping, dancing, or playing

VIDEO 3.11

David Rose describes a dramatic shift in the way neuroscience understands brain plasticity. Far from being "a given," the brain changes in measurable ways with particular activities and contexts.

▶ http://udlvideo.org/ch3/11

basketball. In our shoe company analogy, this would be the unit that specialized in coordinating the materials and steps needed to produce the shoes—making sure all the materials are available, sequencing the manufacturing steps in the right order, routinizing an assembly process, inspecting the results. In the marshmallow task, this is the level at which the acts of reaching out, grasping, and bringing to the mouth are all coordinated and initiated. In many ways it is like middle management.

Finally, at the highest level, there are networks for executive functions. These areas are specialized for setting broad or longer-term goals for action, making plans for effective strategies, monitoring progress toward goals, and making course corrections as needed. In a shoe company, the executives may know little about how to stitch a shoe together. Their role is to anticipate demand (e.g., make boots in time for winter, sandals in time for summer) and prepare the company for meeting those demands: set up production goals, allocate resources, develop strategies for new kinds of shoes, and monitor progress.

To return to the marshmallow task, let us summarize strategic networks with a look at the heterarchy at work. To an observer there is one set of behaviors. The child reaches out to grasp one or two marshmallows to end the task. But that action is embedded and accomplished in a rich network of both higher order (executive) functions and lower order (muscle control) functions. What research shows, for example, is that the actual reaching out is very different depending on the goal (to eat it or to put it away in a pocket) and also on the target (the reaching is adjusted in advance for the weight of the marshmallow). The reaching itself would change as those variables change. Thus even simple reaching behavior is highly variable depending on context.

It is important to understand how richly complex the control of something as simple as reaching for a marshmallow really is. For one thing, it helps to remember that one individual child's reach can be very different than another's in lots of ways. From a developmental perspective, infants, toddlers, and elderly people may lack coordination to reach effectively. Motivation and affect also influence this seemingly simple motor act: in a high-stakes job interview, our nerves might make us clumsy enough to spill our coffee. Some, such as children with cerebral palsy, have trouble at the "bottom" of the heterarchy—they may have difficulty with the motor demands of reaching and grasping. Others, such as children with attention difficulties, may have trouble at the "top" of the heterarchy—they have difficulty inhibiting the reach for the first marshmallow in order to wait for the second one.

Strategic networks are variable

Given the persistent variability among networks and students, It's no surprise that an individual student's deficits and strengths can affect very specific aspects of strategic skills. For example, a student may be skilled at making a plan but have difficulty self-monitoring when executing the plan. Another might be an expert at finding information but have difficulty organizing and keeping track of that information.

Recent brain imaging experiments provide a novel illustration of individual differences in strategy. When two individuals are confronted with the same problem but solve it using different cognitive strategies, brain images reveal two very different patterns of activity. This parallels the differences across individuals seen in scans taken during recognition and affective tasks.

Differences in strategic networks manifest themselves in various ways in the classroom. For example, early learners differ dramatically in their ability to acquire and automatize routines such as forming letters, typing, spelling, and multiplying. And students differ in their ability to enact higher-level strategies such as planning, organizing, monitoring progress, devising alternative approaches, and seeking help when needed. Much of this variation falls loosely under what teachers and clinicians cluster as strengths and weaknesses with executive functioning and includes abilities such as reasoning, logic, and hypothesis testing.

These organizational skills impact elementary reading at the level of individual letters, causing some students to make impulsive guesses rather than carefully inspect each letter. At the paragraph level they may become distracted by certain details and progress through the text erratically, negatively impacting their reading comprehension. On the other side, reading comprehension can be enhanced when we are intensely interested in the subject matter or feel that the content is critically important in some way.

Dig Deeper: Exercising Strategy

Look at "An Unexpected Visitor" again and ask yourself this question: What kind of a room is pictured? For this question, you probably glanced at the image and recognized it effortlessly as a parlor or living room. Without being aware of it, you used your strategic networks extensively to figure this out. You identified the goal of the task, came up with a plan to achieve it, executed your plan, evaluated the outcome, and all the while avoided distractions that might carry you off track.

To see a change in your own search strategy, examine the picture with this question in mind: What are the material circumstances of the family? Did you notice yourself employing yet another search strategy? Where did you look? You may have looked in some of the same places, at the objects in the room or the people's faces, but for a different kind of information. And you may have looked at new places that you hadn't examined before, such as people's clothing.

FIG. 3.16. What kind of room do you see? © *1967 ALFRED L. YARBUS*

FIG. 3.17–3.19. Eye movement patterns when participants were asked to examine the painting freely (left), estimate the family's material circumstance (center), and remember the characters' clothes (right). © *1967 ALFRED L. YARBUS*

Alfred Yarbus's eye movement studies show different patterns of visual search based on different search goals. He established that patterns of eye movement vary remarkably depending on the task at hand. The images shown above represent the eye movements of the same individual looking at the same image, yet each one is different. Why? This viewer inspected the image with different goals each time. According to writer Sasha Archibald, Yarbus asked the subject to:

1) examine the painting freely,

2) estimate the material circumstances of the family,

3) assess the ages of the characters,

4) determine the activities of the family prior to the visitor's arrival,

5) remember the characters' clothes, and

6) surmise how long the "unexpected visitor" had been away.

Each instruction required a different viewing strategy, and each new strategy resulted in a different pattern of eye movements.

To see these images and to learn more about the Yarbus study, see Sasha Archibald's 2008 article "Ways of Seeing," available at www .cabinetmagazine.org/issues/30/archibald.php. In the original study, Yarbus juxtaposed "An Unexpected Visitor" with the eye movement maps. In the images shown here, Archibald combined the painting and the eye movements. The images are used with permission.

Even a process that seems simple—such as searching an image for a particular purpose (see Exercising Strategy)—involves complex, layered processes in the brain. At a minimum, strategic action involves these steps:

- Identify a goal

- Design a suitable plan

- Execute the plan

- Self monitor

- Correct or adjust actions

This same discrete set of actions can be applied to almost any mental activity which is why the strategic network is so crucial to teaching and learning. Many students—young and old—face challenges when internally organizing or preparing for action. Knowing the importance of these skills for learning and processing can help teachers remember to explicitly teach and reinforce organizational skills.

Dig Deeper: Connecting Social Engagement and Academic Engagement

In his explanatory model of student departure (drop-out) from college, sociologist Vincent Tinto explains the difference between social engagement and academic engagement. He considers how each contributes to student persistence in school. Applying his model to the student population in two-year urban institutions (students who spent little time on campus and were learning in traditionally structured programs with little active learning amongst students themselves), Tinto found that academic engagement enhanced social engagement and vice versa, but that academic engagement was a more important predictor of persistence.[42]

However, in two-year urban institutions where students shared a core set of courses with an underlying collaborative pedagogy that required them to be responsible for one another's learning, Tinto found that social engagement fostered academic engagement. Tinto also found that if you hold everything else constant, students more often leave college because of loneliness or isolation than they do because of poor academic performance.[43]

As noted at the beginning of this section, it is critical to remember that separating the networks as though they functioned independently is a device for study rather than a reflection of how things actually work. Breaking them into categories can help us understand the complex processes and factors that go into learning. But of course, these networks are all part of an overarching network in which affect, recognition, and strategic functioning are interrelated and simultaneous.

VARIABILITY: IMPLICATIONS FOR EDUCATION

Once upon a time, developmental and cognitive psychologists believed that certain capacities and qualities resided entirely within an individual. These innate, personal characteristics could be enhanced by education, it was thought, but that didn't change the idea that certain people were inherently dull or bright, good or poor at understanding abstract ideas, "good" at learning or learning disabled. People were labeled accordingly. The source of those differences was generally thought to be biological: first the brain, then the genes.

That way of thinking isn't a thing of the past; it still fuels much of conventional thinking in education today. But such conventions are rapidly being eclipsed by dramatic new discoveries and ideas in both neuroscience and genetics. Recent research tends to reveal that none of these qualities or abilities resides entirely within an individual—neither in their brains nor in their genes. Nor are they static and fixed. Personal qualities and abilities continually shift, and they exist not within the individual but in the intersection between individuals and their environment, in a vast, complex, dynamic balance. Each individual varies over time, and responses across individuals to the same environment also vary.

We now understand from scientific research that brains and even genes are highly responsive to their environments. Individual differences in our brains are not innate or fixed, but developed and malleable, and context has a huge impact. This is the best news yet for educators who have the opportunity to provide environments that facilitate positive growth, or learning, for all students.

VIDEO 3.12
Mason Barney, a successful lawyer with learning disabilities, and Todd Rose, a learning scientist, discuss the situational, contextual nature of "disability." Variability is the rule, and "disability" is context dependent.

▸ http://udlvideo.org/ch3/12

❝ Personal qualities and abilities are not fixed; they continually shift as individuals interact with and their environment.

This modern view also reframes our understanding of variability. We are steadily moving away from the vision of the normal curve, where "average students" can be counted upon to experience curriculum and to act in an "average" way. We now know that variability is the rule both within and between all individuals. The rest of this book is about how we can respond to that variability as a natural thing—as an asset, not a liability.

Brain imaging technologies and neural networks are certainly not the first things that come to mind when we consider what it takes to develop expertise in learning, teaching, and educational systems. But we do not need to have a degree in neuroscience nor use brain-scanning instruments to reap the benefits of understanding the learning brain. As science continues to reveal the fundamental nature of how the learning brain works, we can use the framework of the three classes of learning networks—affective, recognition, and strategic—as a helpful way to think about how to design learning environments that take into account the tremendous variability of individuals.

One of the most important revelations emerging from brain research is that the notion of broad categories of learners—smart/not smart, disabled/not disabled, regular/not regular—is a gross oversimplification that does not reflect reality. By categorizing people this way, we place an undue burden on individuals to adapt themselves in all their wonderful diversity to inflexible learning environments. We should instead be expecting more of our learning environments. Chief among these expectations is that our learning environments be designed with a deep understanding and appreciation for individual variability. That is a fundamental premise of universal design for learning and the educational systems made with UDL principles in mind.

Universal Design
for Learning

Those who wish to transform and improve education can learn a lot from Global Positioning System (GPS) devices. Think of how, in a few short years, GPS's have utterly transformed navigation for driving, flying, boating, and even walking.

They provide continuous progress monitoring, feedback, and course corrections. They offer a wide variety of choices for how to enter information and receive feedback; more importantly, they often suggest multiple routes to take, giving the traveler options. Some respond to changes in traffic patterns and suggest alternatives to escape a jam. And, in most cases, the GPS is very accurate, leading to the desired outcome for almost every user, on almost every trip.[1]

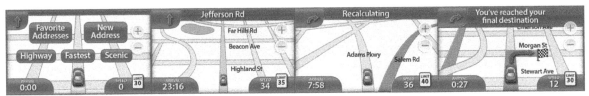

FIG. 4.1. A GPS can monitor where you are in relation to your destination and adjust for ways to get there. *ILLUSTRATION BY CHRIS VALLO © 2013 CAST, INC.*

VIDEO 4.1
The goal of education, says David Rose, should not be to try to standardize kids but rather to optimize diversity, which research shows is more powerful than homogeneity.

▶ http://udlvideo.org/ch4/1

Education needs this kind of innovation—emphasizing flexibility and individuality—to remake the way teaching and learning happens. We believe universal design for learning (UDL) is that transformative innovation. The three principles of UDL can help us meet the challenges and take advantage of the opportunities inherent in the great variability of students, offering paths for those currently disenfranchised and developing the talents of all.

Of course education is vastly more complex than simply driving to a particular destination, so this analogy can only be taken so far. Still, the GPS has more to teach us as we think about transforming education, especially as we ponder two fundamental questions: What is our destination and how do we plan to get there?

First and foremost we need to be clear about what we want to achieve. What is the goal of education in today's world? We have argued that the goal of education goes beyond the mastery of knowledge and skills to the mastery of learning itself. Education should help novice learners develop into individuals who are *expert at learning*—individuals who know how to learn, who have already learned a great deal, and who are eager to learn more.[2]

To reach this goal for all learners, there is not one fixed route. British educator Ken Robinson, who writes and lectures frequently on arts and creativity in education, eloquently expresses the aspiration to help all learners meet high standards by whatever route is most effective for them as individuals: "Education," he says, "doesn't need to be reformed—it needs to be transformed. The key to this transformation is not to standardize education but to personalize it, to build achievement on discovering the individual talents of each child, to put students in an environment where they want to learn and where they can naturally discover their true passions."[3]

The call for effective personalization has intensified, in part because of the urgent demands of the global society and the increasing diversity of our students, and in part because of the emergence of technologies that seem to hold the promise of a new kind of education.[4] But the devil truly is in the details. How can we transform our education system into one that holds all learners to high standards, responds to each individual's passionate interests, and appropriately supports and challenges each student? How can we design learning experiences so that the routes to success are as varied as learners themselves?

LESSONS FROM THE LEARNING SCIENCES

First we need to incorporate what learning and education science have revealed about the nature of learning into a newly conceived and designed education system. Two key concepts emerge:

- Learner variability is systematic and to a large degree predictable.[5]

- Learner capacities are context-dependent.[6]

These scientific findings go against the grain of traditional approaches to education reform, many of which are rooted in misconceptions. To the degree that learner variability has been considered in theory, it has generally been treated categorically via describing and labeling different "kinds" of learners as belonging to distinct groups.[7] To the degree learner variability has been addressed in practice, customization has tended to be offered either according to those categorical groups (e.g., solutions for students with "learning disabilities" or who are "gifted") or taken to the other extreme, treating every learner as an individual case.[8]

Both of these approaches to variability are flawed. Putting learners into categories is a flawed approach both because it grossly oversimplifies and distorts the reality of those learners' experience (thereby leading educators to make groundless assumptions about the best way to teach them) and because it implies that learners in one category are somehow different from those in another category. Addressing each learner "on the fly" as a unique case, aside from being impractical, also misses an important aspect of learner variability. Variability is largely systematic and predictable across the three classes of learning networks (affect, recognition, strategy). That predictability can be used as a basis for designing flexible options that will reach most learners.

Perhaps the biggest misconception underlying many reform efforts may have been treating individual learners as separate from their contexts or environments, gauging ability/disability or strength/weakness as a learner as if these qualities resided wholly, and unchangingly, in the learner. To illustrate this error, consider T.V. Raman, a research scientist at Google who leads a team of engineers in building innovative user

VIDEO 4.2
CAST Director of Research Gabrielle Rappolt-Schlichtmann explains that we cannot separate learners from the many variables in their contexts.

▶ http://udlvideo.org/ch4/2

FIG. 4.2. Google engineer T.V. Raman, a pioneer in customizing technology for blind users
© 2009 PETER DASILVA/THE NEW YORK TIMES/REDUX

interfaces, including highly efficient eyes-free interfaces. Raman, who is blind, can solve the Rubik's Cube in 24 seconds—provided he is using a Cube that offers multiple representations, with squares differentiated by texture as well as color.[9]

Were we to evaluate Raman's "internal capacity" to solve a typical Rubik's Cube without considering context (the design of the Cube itself), we would likely say he has a "disability." With the universally designed version, that same evaluation would rate him as brilliant and highly skilled. This simple example makes it abundantly clear that it is impossible to assess a learner's capacity without knowing the affordances of the learning context.

Dig Deeper: "Essential for Some, Good for All"

An extensive review of schools across Ontario's six regions produced the unexpected finding that strategies originally targeted at one or a few students with special needs turned out to be useful for many other students. This finding emerged repeatedly: often enough so that personnel from the project began characterizing the theme as "essential for some, good for all."[10]

This insight parallels those from the universal design movement in architecture and product development. For example, before 1993, individuals with hearing impairments could only obtain captioned television content by purchasing a set-top captioning box for about $100. When technology advanced, enabling captioning capacity to be included within the electronics for approximately .03¢ per television, the Federal Communications Commission mandated that every television have the appropriate chip.[11] As we well know, caption use is nearly ubiquitous. People learning English, couples going to sleep at different times, people working out in gyms or languishing in the waiting rooms of noisy airports—all benefit from captions. Captions: Essential for some, good for all.

FIG. 4.3. Captions benefit the whole population in a variety of ways. *ILLUSTRATION BY CHRIS VALLO © 2013 CAST, INC.*

Over and over we see that capacities that seem to reside within the individual vary over time and in different situations. Take the seasoned, highly talented major league pitcher who told a reporter after a particularly tough baseball game, "Look, I didn't have my curve ball today." No one in the press room needed further clarification. They instantly understood what he meant. Sports fans understand that you can't separate a player from his context. The pitcher had successfully thrown countless curve balls, but the conditions that evening interacting with his own internal state led him to "lose" it for that game.[12]

Or consider these examples, familiar to many parents: a child recites the alphabet at home but cannot do it again the next day with his teacher. Or a student struggles with a math problem when the example being used is apples and oranges but shows fine math skills when the example relates to sports.

These two insights from the learning sciences—the predictable, systematic variability and context-dependency of learner characteristics—strengthen the argument for UDL as a framework for education design. Being able to largely predict specific types and ranges of variability in learners enables us to build corresponding kinds of flexibility into learning tools and experiences, thus making customization at the point of instruction feasible. Realizing that learner capacities are context-dependent boosts our confidence that a well-designed, flexible curriculum can have a profound positive impact on learning. In universal design for learning, we build upon the model of the learning brain wherein we consider the natural variability across affective, recognition, and strategic networks and design flexibility into curriculum to meet this variability.

These concepts defining the networks—affective, recognition, and strategic—may still seem abstract. However, if you step back and consider the UDL as a way to shift your understanding of how all people learn, then UDL becomes a broad framework made up of principles, with related guidelines that provide a systematic means by which we move to the practical. UDL is not a prescriptive checklist or formula with set methods and tools to be applied in every situation. Such an approach would be to substitute a new set

VIDEO 4.3
UDL is a transdisciplinary and translational framework where researchers and practitioners focus on common areas of interest, says Gabrielle Rappolt-Schlichtmann.

▸ http://udlvideo.org/ch4/3

FIG. 4.4. "Look, I didn't have my curve ball today."
ILLUSTRATION BY CHRIS VALLO © 2013 CAST, INC.

VIDEO 4.4
Rachel Campbell, a Language Arts teacher from Indiana, explains that classes offering multiple options for all require few modifications for individual students.

▶ http://udlvideo.org/ch4/4

of rigid practices for the old. The UDL framework is translational—a means for translating research and innovation into practice. From the principles we derive guidelines for creating and choosing tools, methods, and practices, whose specifics depend upon context: learners' developmental levels, varied schools and communities, and the proclivities of teachers who are doing the teaching, among many other variables.

UDL can help us reshape teaching and learning by guiding the design of an entirely new system with flexibility at its core. New media have shattered the old model of basic skills. The idea that mastery of print and text-only related skills (decoding, comprehending, and writing text) defines the full extent of literacy has lost credibility. The digital environment, with its connectivity, multimedia, just-in-time communications, distributed authoring, wisdom of the crowd, and many other qualities, has opened the door to a broad palette of communication skills and options, most critically perhaps, the opportunity for learners to act on materials—to understand them by changing them and making them their own.

In the following sections we describe the UDL principles as they have grown and developed over the past ten years and offer new on-the-ground examples from educators who have been putting these principles into practice. (We invite you to share your comments and reactions, your ideas and experiences on UDL Connect at http://community.udlcenter.org. Your feedback and your expertise will enrich this ever-changing resource, this "digital river," to the benefit of the entire educational community.)

UDL stems from a broad base of research in how the brain learns (as reflected in the affective, recognition, and strategic networks) and a similarly broad base of educational research in the core components of effective teaching (as reflected in optimal techniques for building engagement, knowledge, and skills).[13] Other factors feeding into the framework are rapid developments in digital technologies; our own work with individuals, educators, and schools; and the concept of universal design in product development and architecture.

In this context we developed the three UDL principles to guide the design, selection, and application of learning tools, methods, and environments. Although the principles have undergone considerable

VIDEO 4.5
David Rose describes the link between the brain's primary neural networks and the UDL principles.

▶ http://udlvideo.org/ch4/5

elaboration and revision since their inception a decade ago, they remain fundamentally the same:

- Provide multiple means of engagement (the "why" of learning)

- Provide multiple means of representation (the "what" of learning)

- Provide multiple means of action and expression (the "how" of learning).[14]

Dig Deeper: Unpacking UDL

By "universal" we mean every learner—not just those traditionally seen as belonging in the middle of the bell curve (the mythical average student) or just those traditionally seen as belonging "in the margins." The goal of UDL is to make sure everybody has the opportunity to develop into an expert learner.

By "design" we mean that UDL is intentional, purposeful, and planned. The variability of learners is a given and types of systematic variability are predicted at the very beginning (when a curriculum or lesson is being designed). The needs of all are considered then and there, minimizing the need for retrofitting and subsequent accommodations.

By "learning" we mean that all individuals are challenged and supported in meaningful ways to grow toward expertise as learners. UDL is not intended to make learning easy; indeed, learning should always be appropriately challenging, offering up what Robert Bjork calls "desirable difficulties." It does not contain unnecessary and irrelevant barriers to learning that are actually caused by inflexible media and methods, but it does contain appropriate challenges in the areas germane to the learning goal.[15]

With UDL, we start with high standards for all and apply flexible means so that each learner finds appropriate learning challenges and supports. In fact, the UDL framework helps educators to maximize desirable difficulties and minimize "undesirable difficulties." In other words, with UDL we create learning contexts that optimize opportunity for all.

VIDEO 4.6

Dr. Paul Yellin observes that learners who understand their own strengths and weaknesses are able to be strategic in their approach to learning, aligning tools and techniques to the goal of the learning task and using scaffolds when appropriate.

▶ http://udlvideo.org/ch4/6

These principles, based on the three-network model of learning, take into account the variability of all learners—including learners who were formerly relegated to "the margins" of our educational systems but now are recognized as part of the predictable spectrum of variation.

Both our own research and the research we draw upon to derive guidelines and checkpoints for UDL includes the full spectrum of learner variation. A core tenet of UDL is the understanding that what is "essential for some" is almost always "good for all." Let's take a more in-depth look at each of the principles.

ENGAGEMENT: THE "WHY" OF LEARNING

With UDL, our aim is to enable all learners to become expert. In the all-important affective domain, expertise involves developing interest, purpose, motivation, and, most importantly, strong self-regulation as a learner. What researchers call "self-regulation" is the ability to set motivating goals; to sustain effort toward meeting those goals; and to monitor the balance between internal resources and external demands, seeking help or adjusting one's own expectations and strategies as needed.

Universal Design for Learning

Affective networks:
THE WHY OF LEARNING

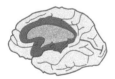

How learners get engaged and stay motivated. How they are challenged, excited, or interested. These are affective dimensions.

 Stimulate interest and motivation for learning

Recognition networks:
THE WHAT OF LEARNING

How we gather facts and categorize what we see, hear, and read. Identifying letters, words, or an author's style are recognition tasks.

 Present information and content in different ways

Strategic networks:
THE HOW OF LEARNING

Planning and performing tasks. How we organize and express our ideas. Writing an essay or solving a math problem are strategic tasks.

 Differentiate the ways that students can express what they know

FIG. 4.5. The brain networks ©2013 CAST, INC.

Within the UDL framework, it is important that learning environments support the development of affective expertise for all. Since individuals vary a great deal in the affective resources they bring to any one learning task, this requires providing options that adjust demands and provide support as needed. What kinds of options? From both research in the learning sciences and evidence from pedagogical practices, three broad kinds of options emerge: options for recruiting student interest, options for sustaining effort and persistence, and options for developing the ability to self-regulate.

It is critically important to design learning contexts that offer flexibility in the domain of engagement so that each student can find a way into the learning experience, remain persistent in the face of challenge or failure, and continue to build self-knowledge. We know that what sparks learners' interest and keeps them engaged differs radically from person to person. Some individuals are highly engaged by spontaneity and novelty; others may be put off or even threatened by spontaneity, preferring predictable routine and structure. A particular subject or activity inspires passionate interest in some people and bores others to tears. Their histories as learners also exert strong influences on learners' optimism and confidence about engaging with new ideas and disciplines.

Students, in interaction with their contexts, vary systematically along largely predictable dimensions in affect. They vary in what they find engaging, including, for example, the amount of choice they find optimal; what they perceive as relevant, interesting, and valuable; and what they perceive as threatening. They vary in the reasons they persist and in their ability to persist, including their ability to formulate goals, their comfort with collaborative environments, their optimal level of challenge and support, and the types of feedback they find most helpful. Finally, students vary in their ability to regulate their own learning, including their beliefs about personal effectiveness, their coping skills and strategies, and their ability to monitor personal progress and make adjustments. These kinds of variability are not fixed "traits" within students but rather emerge and change depending upon the learning context.

Variability demands corresponding flexibility in the learning context if each student is to find an inviting, appropriately challenging, and supportive experience. A universally designed learning environment is planned around learning goals and the

VIDEO 4.7
The ties between emotion and learning are always critical, not just in cases of extreme anxiety or engagement, says CAST Research Scientist Samantha Daley.

▶ http://udlvideo.org/ch4/7

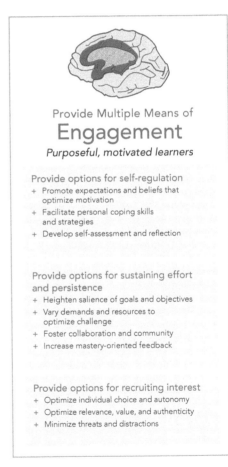

Provide Multiple Means of

Engagement

Purposeful, motivated learners

Provide options for self-regulation
+ Promote expectations and beliefs that optimize motivation
+ Facilitate personal coping skills and strategies
+ Develop self-assessment and reflection

Provide options for sustaining effort and persistence
+ Heighten salience of goals and objectives
+ Vary demands and resources to optimize challenge
+ Foster collaboration and community
+ Increase mastery-oriented feedback

Provide options for recruiting interest
+ Optimize individual choice and autonomy
+ Optimize relevance, value, and authenticity
+ Minimize threats and distractions

FIG. 4.6. The affective areas of the brain and the UDL Guidelines for Engagement. ©2013 CAST, INC.

predictable range of variability. Teachers take advantage of the built-in range of options in order to calibrate learning for each student. Fortunately, the flexibility in a given lesson need not cover every type of variability; rather it should be specific to the particular goal of a lesson. In that context, the variability that is most germane to the goal can become the focus for providing particular kinds of flexibility. An example from one of CAST's research projects illustrates some UDL approaches to support engagement.

Engagement in Practice: The iSolveIt Project

In the iSolveIt project CAST is exploring ways to address the pervasive problem of failure in algebra. Success in algebra has been linked to success in postsecondary education and the workforce.[16] Yet efforts to improve algebra performance have been largely unsuccessful. Most programs focus on describing and calculating, not on the underlying thinking that is essential to truly understanding and applying algebra.[17]

Even students with previous success in math may struggle with algebra as it is often the first course that requires abstract reasoning. Students with a history of math failure face a steeper challenge. Those who have not mastered—let alone automatized—basic computations usually find the computational demands of algebra a barrier.[18] Even more significant than competence issues are confidence issues. Past experiences of repeated failure in math tend to lead students to see themselves as inherently "poor at math."[19] This in turn raises their sense of threat when faced with algebra, narrowing the available mental resources to engage in new kinds of reasoning, and leading to failure in this important arena.[20]

CAST's iSolveIt project is a proof-of-concept project focused on the development and formative research of two prototype games. iSolveIt is aimed at helping students overcome the typical barriers to algebra by decoupling algebraic reasoning from calculation and symbolic components of algebra. The environment will eventually include a growing collection of tablet-based puzzles that have been designed using the principles of UDL and enable active, open exploration of differing aspects of algebraic reasoning. They provide multiple entry points into the experience, allowing students to start from their strengths or level of comfort. By teaching algebraic reasoning skills in a context that does not appear to be math-specific, puzzles offer greater flexibility for addressing affective barriers to learning (e.g., math anxiety).

Algebra is not an extension of arithmetic—it is, in a real sense, a different way of thinking that moves away from the "one right answer" that is prevalent in elementary arithmetic. iSolveIt puzzles are designed to support multiple pathways to solve a problem, and many have more than one correct solution. We feature two sets of puzzles: Math-Squared and MathScaled.

MathSquared is somewhat "math-looking" in that the puzzles use the basic math operations of addition, subtraction, multiplication, and division and require logic and problem-solving skills. Each puzzle is a grid of blank boxes. The size of the grid determines which numbers are used in the puzzle. For example, a 3x3 puzzle uses the numbers 1, 2, and 3. A 4x4 puzzle uses the numbers 1, 2, 3, and 4. These numbers are used once in each row and column, much like the rules of Sudoku. The boxes are grouped into cages, distinguished by a thick line surrounding the caged box or boxes. Each cage has a hint containing a target number and operation as a clue to which numbers belong in the boxes. For example, the target might be 4 +, indicating that the numbers in the boxes must add up to 4. The goal of the puzzle is to fill each box in the grid with a number without repeating numbers in rows and columns.

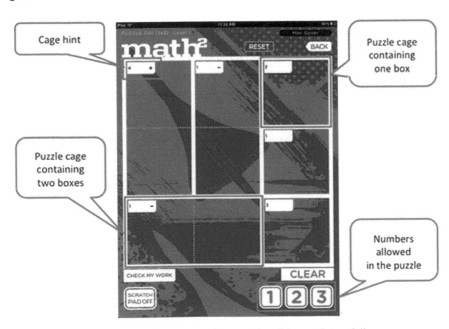

FIG. 4.7. MathSquared puzzle supports logic and problem-solving skills ©2013 CAST, INC.

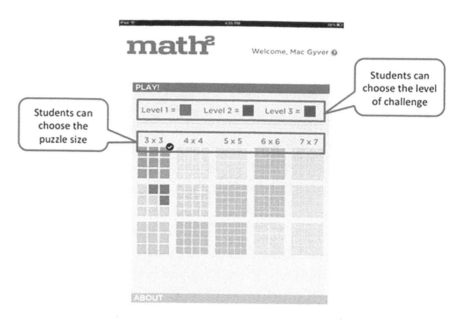

FIG. 4.8. MathSquared options for recruiting interest include choice of puzzle size and challenge level. *©2013 CAST, INC.*

The puzzles can be solved using different strategies, supporting the flexibility and logical thinking that is an essential component of algebraic reasoning. Determining the possible number combinations is a skill frequently used in solving algebraic equations.

MathScaled is based on a balance scale format, which is often used in algebra and pre-algebra classes to support understanding of equations, especially variables and equalities. Students frequently misinterpret an equals sign (=) to mean "the answer is." For example, when given the problem 3 + 2 = ___+ 1, a typical response is 5 instead of 4. The goal of the puzzle is to balance the scale using all of the shapes given in that puzzle. Balance scale puzzles help students to develop an understanding of equality that is important in solving algebraic equations. In addition, the weights used in MathScaled represent variables. Many students find variables threatening but are comfortable trying out different weights to balance the scales. Teachers can use MathScaled to help students with the algebraic concepts of equality and variables.

While all three UDL principles are essential to the design of the iSolveIt puzzles, here we highlight features flexibly designed for multiple means of engagement, thus specifically addressing the "affective hurdle" for those learning the reasoning skills needed for algebra. We

VIDEO 4.9
CAST researchers Boo Murray, Garron Hillaire, and Mindy Johnson present the ISolveIt iPad apps, puzzles designed to help students develop algebraic reasoning skills.

▶ http://udlvideo.org/ch4/9

illustrate three key areas: options for recruiting interest, options for sustaining effort and persistence, and options for developing the ability to self-regulate.

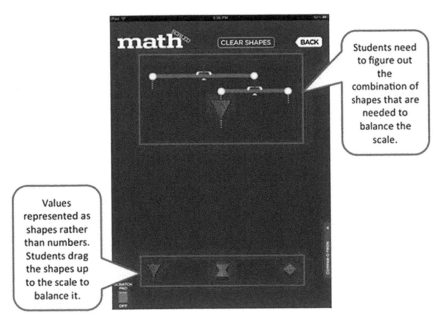

FIG. 4.9. MathScaled supports students' understanding of variables and equalities.
©2013 CAST, INC.

Options for Recruiting Interest

As distinct from a traditional piece of curriculum, the iSolveIt puzzle format and the iPad platform itself signal a sense of fun, and invite students to engage. Each puzzle can be solved in many different ways (e.g., different orders of moves) and many have more than one correct solution. This can intrigue students, engender support for exploration and inquiry, and help students move away from arithmetic thinking (one right answer) to the more flexible thinking needed for success in algebra.

Equally important, players can always select the level of difficulty and can easily move among the different levels to find puzzles that provide the right level of challenge at any particular moment. Because there is no lockstep progression, students can choose whether to move systematically forward at a mastery level, jump ahead to try something a lot more difficult, or drop back to a familiar level to explore.

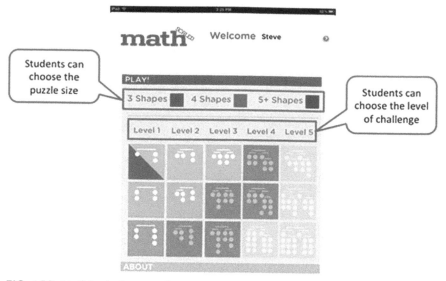

FIG. 4.10. MathScaled options for recruiting interest. ©2013 CAST, INC.

The pilot study shows that students do take advantage of these options. A graphic representation tracks the level choices of 66 students as they move from puzzle to puzzle. Clearly students choose a great variety of pathways!

Student interest in the puzzles can evolve over the course of the school year because they are not tied to specific curriculum and can be revisited again and again. Thus as students become familiar with the games, they can increase the challenge levels, and extend their thinking and application into mathematical reasoning. This is especially promising if a teacher provides guidance in making the bridge from the puzzles to algebra, such as during a group activity with discussion and collaborative solving.

Appreciation for multiple pathways was expressed by students in the pilot study. Said one student: "I think that they would help me by not just finding one way to an equation. But those puzzles helped me to actually use my brain to think of multiple solutions. I can use multiple ways." A second student noted: "It kind of helped me think of different ways to do it other than just the first answer that comes into my head. It kind of helped my brain want to do more puzzles like this. I just feel like it's all connected."

Options for sustaining effort and persistence

Good puzzles present a perplexing task that is not readily solved. At the same time they are designed to be fun and engaging, so that the puzzle solver will work to figure the solution. In math, students often give up on challenging problems that they would be able to solve with some effort.

Puzzles that are not focused on math can be an engaging way to develop persistence, even among students with math anxiety or negative impressions of their own math ability. When undertaking a puzzle, people expect to make mistakes, learn from those mistakes, and try new strategies. Embedded hints and supports also encourage trying again.

For example, in MathSquared players can open the "cage hint" for more explicit help on the math operation being used. The fact that multiple pathways, logically different and all viable, can lead to success also encourages persistence. In the words of one student in the pilot study: "There wasn't really anything that wasn't really fun. The process of figuring it out and messing up. Sometimes you get aggravated because this doesn't fit. All of it was fun, but you have to work your way up to getting all of it correct. It was work, but it was fun, kind of like a math class."

Options for developing the ability to self-regulate

In both iSolveIt puzzles, the open choice of levels puts self-regulation front and center. At any moment during a session, the player can change levels, up or down, based on what s/he is experiencing. To aid self-monitoring, the puzzles offer different kinds of feedback. In Math-Squared, the Check my Work button highlights logical conflicts (rather than "wrong" answers), leading students to work to solve the logical conflict.

In MathScaled, one or more balance scales can be "unlocked" so that adding weight to one side or the other shows immediately whether the scale is balanced or not. Students "guess and check," moving weights around and observing the results as they work. They can also self-monitor using a sandbox-like area called the "Compar-O-Tron" where they can explore and record relationships between weights, referring to these visual cues as they work on the puzzle. The iSolveIt puzzles provide examples of digital interactive learning environment designed using UDL principles. We have highlighted how these puzzles can help overcome affective barriers to the study of algebra.

VIDEO 4.10
Students' self esteem improves when they can manage their own behavior. Educator Judith Schoonover shares a program that lets students create their own behavior improvement "buttons," leading to increases in self-efficacy.

▶ http://udlvideo.org/ch4/10

❝ Studies in education indicate that confidence to learn challenging tasks increases when learners sense that there is more than one pathway to competence.

VIDEO 4.11
How can teachers manage students' appraisals of the learning environment? Research scientist Gabrielle Rappolt-Schlichtmann explains.

▸ http://udlvideo.org/ch4/11

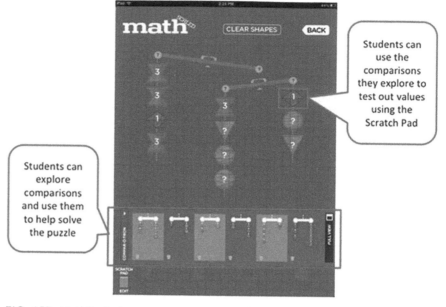

FIG. 4.11. MathScaled supports encourage students to explore and self-monitor using a sandbox-like area called the "Compar-O-Tron." ©2013 CAST, INC.

VIDEO 4.12
TED-Ed Catalyst Logan Smalley says that technology at its best can "reach out" to students in the margins, enhancing engagement.

▸ http://udlvideo.org/ch4/12

This example illustrates using UDL in context—the context of the lesson goal—to focus on the relevant aspects of learner variability and determine the key kinds of flexibility needed in the learning environment. Thus a teacher beginning to work with the UDL framework need not attempt to apply all principles at all levels for every lesson. The UDL principles offer a field of ideas to be used selectively according to the teaching and learning context.

Of course, support by teachers can amplify the effectiveness of goal-setting and self monitoring for students. Working in groups and using think-alouds, teachers can model the thinking that goes into setting goals, working with logic, and relying on feedback to change strategies. Further, teachers can tie back to specific algebraic concepts such as factoring, equalities, and variables.

REPRESENTATION: THE "WHAT" OF LEARNING

Addressing learner variability in recognition networks is the focus of the next UDL principle in our discussion. Expertise requires much more than just engagement. It requires constructing knowledge by perceiving information in the environment, recognizing predictive patterns in that information, understanding and integrating new information; interpreting and manipulating a wide variety of symbolic representations of information; and developing fluency in the skills for assimilating and remembering that information.

Learners' ability to perceive, interpret, and understand information is dependent upon the media and methods through which it is presented. For learning environments to support varied learners in all of these recognition processes, three broad kinds of options for representation are needed: options for perception; options for language, mathematical expressions, and symbols; and options for comprehension. A learning context with these options presents few barriers, regardless of the variations in biology and background of the students. Further, it provides a rich field of exploration where redundancy across media and overlap in shades of meaning offer maximum opportunity to build knowledge.

One simple example is the use of media. Take the case of printed materials. Individuals with sensory disabilities (such as blindness) or learning disabilities (such as dyslexia) or those for whom the textbook is written in a foreign language may require different representations of information in order to access and understand content. These learners struggle—or outright fail—if they are compelled to use a printed textbook which is incapable of providing basic supports such as text-to-speech or a readily available glossary. The medium itself is a barrier. Providing content in multiple media supports those who require it (essential for some) but also supplies a rich cognitive learning environment where varied options and interactivity create a more nuanced experience, enabling learners to explore the content from multiple points of view (good for all).

Learners may also struggle due to a lack of needed background knowledge or contextual understanding. For example, learners from a different culture might not understand a math word problem that situates the question in a story about NFL football or a science passage requiring some understanding of geography. In these cases, the representation—absent appropriate scaffolding—gets in the way of the learning objective so that what the learner knows about football becomes confused with what they are learning about math.

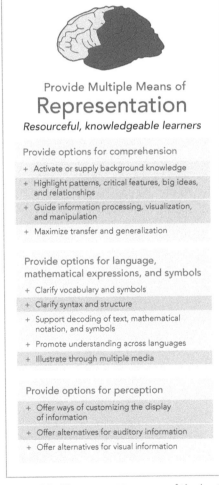

Provide Multiple Means of
Representation
Resourceful, knowledgeable learners

Provide options for comprehension
+ Activate or supply background knowledge
+ Highlight patterns, critical features, big ideas, and relationships
+ Guide information processing, visualization, and manipulation
+ Maximize transfer and generalization

Provide options for language, mathematical expressions, and symbols
+ Clarify vocabulary and symbols
+ Clarify syntax and structure
+ Support decoding of text, mathematical notation, and symbols
+ Promote understanding across languages
+ Illustrate through multiple media

Provide options for perception
+ Offer ways of customizing the display of information
+ Offer alternatives for auditory information
+ Offer alternatives for visual information

FIG. 4.12. The recognition area of the brain and the UDL Guidelines for Representation. *©2013 CAST. INC.*

VIDEO 4.13

Matt Roberts, an Indiana math teacher, provides examples of the multiple ways he presents math problems to try to engage more of his students.

▶ http://udlvideo.org/ch4/13

VIDEO 4.14

Educator Fran Smith offers a variety of ways for vocational students to "show what they know," revealing many more abilities than standardized assessments could.

▶ http://udlvideo.org/ch4/14

No single medium works for every learner, nor does it for every subject. Printed text may be a suitable medium for reading literature, but print has been shown to be a notoriously poor vehicle for teaching science and mathematics whereas dynamic interactive media can demonstrate directly how things work. To promote understanding of information, concepts, relationships, and ideas, it is critical to provide multiple ways for learners to approach them.

As we have seen elsewhere, learners in their contexts vary systematically and widely in all dimensions of recognition. They vary in their background knowledge and in their ability to access and activate that knowledge, their facility with finding and using patterns critical to understanding, their approaches to encountering new knowledge, and their ability to generalize and transfer knowledge. They vary enormously in their knowledge of vocabulary, their fluency in decoding symbols—from letters and words to mathematical symbols—their comprehension of the structure of languages, and their familiarity with multiple languages. And they vary in their preferences and abilities to perceive and work with different media. Of course this variability is context-bound; it emerges in interactions between learners and the learning environment.

Variability derives from a multiplicity of factors including biology, family context, cultural background, history with schooling, socioeconomic status, moment-to-moment internal and external changes, and,

FIG. 4.13. No single pathway works for every student.
ILLUSTRATION BY CHRIS VALLO © 2013 CAST, INC.

most importantly, the context in which the learner is functioning. We have already seen that whatever variability seems to be within the learner is functionally expressed within specific contexts which determine whether a trait, a mood, or an effect of history becomes disabling, neutral, or advantageous with regard to learning.

To illustrate the importance of context, let's consider the story of David and Ruth Rose. Ruth, a singer and musician, has perfect pitch.[21] Whenever she hears a note, she instantly knows exactly what note it is. Growing up in a musical family, her vision of family life featured singing together, in harmony, with her husband and children. Alas, David's biology did not cooperate. His pitch could only be called approximate. So, from Ruth's point of view, David has a disability when it comes to music, and many musicians would agree. But even when a characteristic seems so clearly to be a negative, context is everything. Were David to try to sing in a choral group he would probably be seen as challenged. But in the context of church, where neither the organ nor the voices of the parishioners are tuned accurately, David can participate with gusto, while Ruth is so pained by the inexact pitch that she hears a cacophony instead of a melody and cannot comfortably join in. In this context, Ruth's perfect pitch could be seen as disabling, certainly of her engagement with singing in church.

Not surprisingly, variability in recognition networks is systematic and largely predictable. In a predominantly print-centric classroom, only certain kinds of variability are supported: facility with letter recognition, word decoding, reading fluency, and comprehension. In such a classroom, a student with linguistic challenges would likely be identified as having some form of learning disability. But as classrooms increasingly expand the palette of options for representation and alternatives to printed text proliferate it becomes easier to see that a learning problem, formerly seen as residing in the student, is really a context problem, residing in the interaction between student and learning environment. The relatively recent term "print disabilities" more accurately reflects the true source of the problem in the intersection of the learner and the context—i.e., the intersection between the learner and the medium of print.[22]

VIDEO 4.15
You might think that perfect pitch would always be a positive attribute, but context matters. David Rose shares an amusing story of one context in which his wife's perfect pitch is actually disabling.

▶ http://udlvideo.org/ch4/15

VIDEO 4.16
As teacher Jon Mundorf illustrates, UDL levels the playing field without lowering standards.

▶ http://udlvideo.org/ch4/16

FIG. 4.14. David and Ruth Rose: Is perfect pitch an ability or disability? ©2013 CAST, INC.

VIDEO 4.17
Educator Libby Arthur shares a creative approach to multiple means of representation, including experiential lessons and an engaging simulation.

▶ http://udlvideo.org/ch4/17

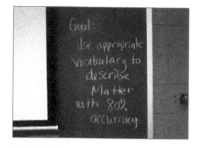

VIDEO 4.18
In Dana Calfee's experience, designing the classroom environment with UDL principles helps students feel in charge of their own learning.

▶ http://udlvideo.org/ch4/18

VIDEO 4.19
Learners' affective states greatly impact their ability to act on and express what they know, says CAST Research Scientist Samantha Daley.

▶ http://udlvideo.org/ch4/19

What do we mean by an expanded palette? Technology options are among the most obvious. Digital content can be designed to maximize opportunities for becoming expert "readers" of content in many media. Simple media options such as text-to-speech, animations to show processes, or images to expand on verbal ideas are a start. Representing content in multiple ways also means making explicit some aspects of content that are often implicit, such as the structure and key information in a legal database or highlights and annotations by the author or another expert in a text. These alternatives act as maps or signposts for readers seeking meaning and help learners understand essential ideas. Teachers practicing UDL have further expanded the idea of multiple means of representation to include different lesson formats and types.

A palette of representation options also broadens the kinds of expertise students can bring to their learning. When content is represented through two or more mediums of text, image, video, or audio, learners' strengths and interests in all of these media become potential avenues for success and engagement. In this kind of rich context, a student's preference for graphical representations can become an avenue for developing expertise that can extend from one subject area across the curriculum. Additionally, in an environment offering alternatives, rich supports, and extensions for learning, difficulty with one particular medium need not hold learners back.

Transforming the school experience to meet learner variability requires the realization that no one means of representation is optimal for all students, all subject areas, nor all circumstances.

ACTION & EXPRESSION: THE "HOW" OF LEARNING

To complete our approach to helping all learners become expert learners, we turn to the strategic network and its associated principle: provide multiple means of action and expression. Under this principle we support the development of expertise in executive functions such as goal setting, monitoring one's progress and adjusting approaches as needed, strategy development, and managing information and resources.

Also important for strategic expertise is providing options for expression and communication including multiple media, multiple tools for construction and composition, and support for the development of fluency through graduated support in practice and performance. Finally, in keeping with this principle, it is important to provide options for physical action such as varied response methods and access to a variety of tools and assistive technologies. Options in these areas enable all students to develop strategic expertise.[23]

Learners differ systematically in the ways that they function strategically. Expert learners need to be able set appropriate goals and monitor their progress towards those goals. This involves setting a goal at an appropriate level of difficulty and being flexible with strategies (trying a different approach when one method is not working). These skills develop as learners mature in age as well as in skill level with a particular discipline or subject.[24] Novices don't really know what is involved in being an expert, so they might approach learning through trial and error, persevering with an unproductive strategy or trying various other approaches that might be "off track."[25] Students who have difficulty with organization and planning, or who have never been taught those strategies, may not even know that goal setting is an option. And without models, guidance, and feedback they have little understanding of whether they have succeeded or failed. It is foundational to starting students on the road to expertise to provide models and examples and to offer guides and supports for setting and pursuing goals.

With access to models of variability in action and expression, more students are able to serve as models for one another on how to achieve a goal. The more difficult the task, the more we must learn it through interactions with others rather than on our own through trial and error.[26] Studies in education indicate that confidence (i.e., self-efficacy) to learn challenging tasks builds when learners have alternative examples of how to become competent and a sense that there is more than one pathway to competence.[27]

Learning scientist Todd Rose addresses the systematic variability in students' working memory, or the ability to hold and manipulate information in your mind. He cites research showing that, in a classroom of 13-year-olds, the natural variability in working memory ranges from that of a typical 8-year-old to that of an adult.[28] A mismatch between what a curriculum calls for the learner to know and what the learner actually knows increases the learning challenge by orders of magnitude. Because current research has yet to be applied widely in schools, educators have few systems in place to offer options in the classroom to

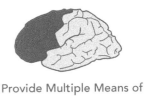

Provide Multiple Means of
Action & Expression
Strategic, goal-directed learners

Provide options for executive functions
+ Guide appropriate goal-setting
+ Support planning and strategy development
+ Enhance capacity for monitoring progress

Provide options for expression
and communication
+ Use multiple media for communication
+ Use multiple tools for construction
  and composition
+ Build fluencies with graduated levels
  of support for practice and performance

Provide options for physical action
+ Vary the methods for response
  and navigation
+ Optimize access to tools and
  assistive technologies

FIG. 4.15. The strategic area of the brain, and the UDL Guidelines for Action & Expression ©2013 CAST, INC.

☐ **VIDEO 4.20**
Samantha Daley discusses ways that educators can help learners through progress monitoring, feedback that focuses on process rather than outcomes, and setting effective goals.

▶ http://udlvideo.org/ch4/20

support working memory. Some suggestions include something as simple as putting a learning goal on paper or in assignment documents so that students don't have to keep the goal in their minds while working on learning tasks.

Mason Barney, introduced in Chapter 2, became extremely goal-directed at an early age out of necessity. The area of expression was particularly challenging for him. Handwriting was not viable. The writing sample shown in Figure 4.19 is from Mason's early elementary school days, and it shows his motor

Dig Deeper: Diverse Presentations

In his course on UDL at the Harvard Graduate School of Education, David Rose asks different students to take notes during class and to post those notes where all can view them. The differing media and style of notes illustrate the very diverse ways that students express what they are learning. The diverse presentations provide other members of the class an opportunity to expand their understanding. The examples in Figures 4.16–4.18 are actual notes taken during David's lecture about perfect pitch.

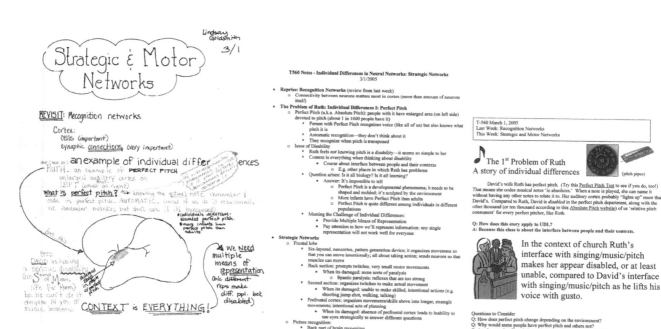

FIG. 4.16–18. Handwritten, typed, and multimedia notes *STUDENT SAMPLES REPRINTED WITH PERMISSION*

deficit, his humor, and his highly insightful thinking. Now a mid-career professional, Mason says he still avoids handwriting whenever possible and his spelling remains poor if he is writing or spelling out loud. But because he encountered barriers in his learning contexts from an early age, Mason developed strong determination to find alternatives to forge his own path.

VIDEO 4.21
Drawing on personal experience, learning scientist Todd Rose argues that "skills" and "challenges" are not innate but rather exist in the interaction between the individual and the environment. He draws profound implications for the design of teaching tools and strategies.

▸ http://udlvideo.org/ch4/21

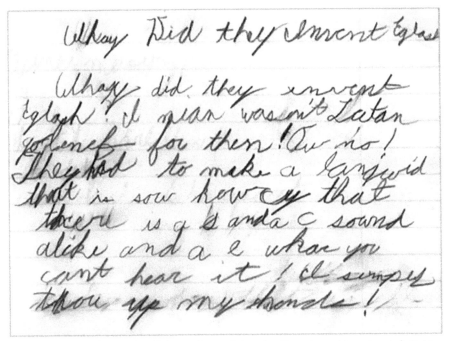

FIG. 4.19. An early sample of Mason Barney's handwriting shows his motor deficit, his humor, and his highly insightful thinking. ©2013 CAST, INC.

VIDEO 4.22
In 1998, young Mason Barney shared his understanding of his own strengths and weaknesses.

▸ http://udlvideo.org/ch4/22

At CAST, Mason learned touch-typing on the computer. But this was only the beginning. To overcome his spelling difficulties he identified certain key words he used frequently and made himself learn to type them automatically by repeating them over and over until his "finger memory" knew the words. He called his technique "brute repetition." Some of these he cannot spell orally or in handwriting but he can reliably type them. For words he used frequently that were too long to learn, he typed them consistently incorrectly and embedded a rule in his spellchecker to correct them. Mason's learning environments did not offer him options, so he had to blaze a trail and come up with them himself.

VIDEO 4.23
In a 1995 interview, young Mason Barney reflects on some key skills learned at CAST.

▸ http://udlvideo.org/ch4/23

VIDEO 4.24
Mason Barney describes his tactics to learn to spell certain words, and to develop "work-arounds" for words he finds too difficult.

▶ http://udlvideo.org/ch4/24

VIDEO 4.25
Authentic assessment, offering multiple means or choices of expression and format, is the rule at Libby Arthur's Indiana school.

▶ http://udlvideo.org/ch4/25

VIDEO 4.26
Katherine Bishop's students came up with their own ideas for multiple means of expression including writing a play, writing jokes, and others.

▶ http://udlvideo.org/ch4/26

Many teachers are actively building in options for action and expression for their students. Some of these options originated as responses to students "in the margins" who were not adept at traditional modalities of expression, but they have all rapidly developed into beneficial tools for all learners, promoting creativity, engagement, and higher quality compositions. These expanded expression options also reach into pools of talent that were previously not tapped or appreciated in school. Drawing, speaking, dance, drama, humor, videography, and many other kinds of expression are increasingly being adopted as legitimate avenues for demonstrating knowledge. In addition, many rubrics for interpreting and evaluating them are being developed as part of school assessment.

Some of these options, but not all, are technology based. Expert teacher Katherine Bishop has been offering her students options for constructing, composing, and expressing knowledge for some time (Video 4.26). She is careful to teach them how to use the tools she offers, such as PowerPoint, Keynote, iMovie, and others. She was surprised and gratified to see that after her students used the options she offered for a while, they started coming up with their own ideas. Her encouragement of their approaches ratcheted up their engagement even more.

At the level of physical action we can learn once more from students who have traditionally been seen as "in the margins." Solutions provided of necessity for them have proven repeatedly to be extremely beneficial for all learners. An example is speech recognition software (a tool that translates speech into text). For someone who cannot physically handwrite or type, this tool may be the only avenue for navigating an online environment or putting his or her ideas into text. But of course it is also a wonderful tool for anyone who needs to capture ideas quickly. Speech recognition software is used widely in fields such as medicine and law because of its efficiency and accuracy and because it eliminates extensive typing and associated repetitive stress injuries.[29]

Learner variability in strategic learning makes it crucial to supply options for action, expression, and executive functions. The more we can bring research on this variability into the classroom via the translational framework of UDL, the more we will reach and engage all learners.

PUTTING UDL PRINCIPLES INTO ACTION

Implementing UDL in classrooms, schools, and districts may seem challenging at first. But expert teacher Libby Arthur offers a perspective on UDL that makes it "relatively simple" to do. She explains this in the context of describing how she would approach professional development for UDL: "I would also tell any teacher that implementing the UDL principles is relatively simple. If you just think, *how am I going to present this lesson in a variety of modalities* and *how am I going to keep my students engaged in a variety of modalities*, and *how am I going to assess in a variety of modalities*, it's really not that difficult." Libby is describing a shift in mindset that forms the foundation for applying UDL.

VIDEO 4.27 Indiana educator Libby Arthur shares her ideas about implementing the UDL principles.

▸ http://udlvideo.org/ch4/27

Dig Deeper: The Common Core

To enable learners to build expertise, we need to ground goal-setting in the context of high standards for all learners. In the K–12 realm, the Common Core State Standards—published in 2010 by the Council of Chief State School Officers, an organization representing the top education officials in all 50 states—have emerged as a widely accepted framework for determining the skills and content knowledge students need to learn. (Notably, these Standards include few goals squarely centered on affect, an area that in our view needs development.)

The authors of the Common Core took care to differentiate learning goals from means, noting that the Standards are not a curriculum but rather "a clear set of shared goals and expectations for what knowledge and skills will help our students succeed." They noted that local educators would have to decide how the Standards are met, adding, "Teachers will continue to devise lesson plans and tailor instruction to the individual needs of the students in their classrooms."[30]

The Common Core Standards do not prescribe the means for reaching those standards, and they are deliberately worded to afford flexibility for different learning contexts. Like the GPS, the Common Core Standards leave room for individualization—a good model for goal-setting for all educational environments, including post-secondary and informal settings.[31]

VIDEO 4.28
UDL expert Jon Mundorf suggests a simple way to understand and apply UDL. His interpretation enables Jon to orient his classroom culture toward predictable variability.

▶ http://udlvideo.org/ch4/28

Applying the UDL principles can help us as educators to persist and progress in our teaching. With a UDL mindset, when something isn't working, we don't immediately think that we as teachers or learners are deficient—lacking intelligence, attention, effort, or motivation. Nor do we assume that an approach is all wrong if it doesn't work the first time. Monitoring progress and making adjustments are a normal part of our work as both learners and teachers—and a natural way to grow. As we move away from a factory model of education, we embrace a dynamic model that celebrates human diversity and variability. The work we do will have different features—still recognizable but now premised on a more accurate, scientific understanding about how best to teach and learn.

The UDL Guidelines: A Framework for Implementation

In earlier chapters, we established the need for universal design for learning (UDL) to support expert learning, teaching, and systems, and we presented a scientific rationale for the UDL principles. Now we turn to the practical application of those principles.

The practice of UDL—indeed, the practice of any high-quality teaching—makes effective use of scaffolds. Scaffolds are temporary supports, usually provided by an expert or teacher in a domain, that enable novices in that domain to build knowledge or skills efficiently and enthusiastically. Scaffolds, essential at the beginning, should be gradually reduced as the novice develops independence or fluency. While it is true that novices can often learn from open exploration or trial and error, most human cultures have employed scaffolding as a means to optimize learning.[1]

Guidelines are one of the most common kinds of scaffolds. When used well, they are effective in any field because they draw attention to relevant and productive practices, and they steer us away from strategies or practices that have already proven ineffective. Guidelines are instructive rather than prescriptive; they are not as rigid as a template or checklist but rather suggest strategies and means for implementation.

In the field of UDL, guidelines are particularly important because expert implementation of UDL can take many forms. Given its nature as a translational framework from research to practice, there could never be one instantiation that would represent expert UDL practice

VIDEO 5.1
Boston educator Alexis Reid uses the UDL Guidelines as a blueprint for developing her teaching practice at all levels.

▶ http://udlvideo.org/ch5/1

VIDEO 5.2

Instead of attempting to apply every guideline, New York City teacher Lindsay Tavares first selected ones that aligned with her current resources, then expanded her repertoire over time.

▸ http://udlvideo.org/ch5/2

VIDEO 5.3

Science teacher Dana Calfee found that UDL aligned closely with her teaching philosophy while also giving her "something to shoot for."

▸ http://udlvideo.org/ch5/3

VIDEO 5.4

Encountering alternate pathways and needing to select ones own strategies for learning can help students develop their self-knowledge as learners, middle school teacher Rhonda Laswell explains.

▸ http://udlvideo.org/ch5/4

definitively. First issued in 2008 and again with revisions in 2011, the UDL Guidelines are designed to help educators (novice and expert alike) consider the key sources and types of expected learner variability germane to a particular learning goal and to select or design flexible curricula that help all learners progress towards that goal.[2]

How do the UDL Guidelines help in the design of optimal learning environments with many different paths and options? First, they provide a framework for thinking systematically about individual variability as it relates to learning. The Guidelines draw on learning science research to reveal the primary dimensions along which students are likely to vary. They provide scaffolds for remembering who and what to consider in the design of high-performance learning environments. Second, the Guidelines provide concrete suggestions (in the form of "checkpoints") for how to address systematic variability among students. Those suggestions are the result of a multiyear review of thousands of research articles that identified specific experimentally validated instructional techniques, adaptations, and interventions.

Altogether, the Guidelines and checkpoints articulate how teachers can improve instruction by building flexibility into the learning environment. For example, students differ in the amount and types of choice they want. Some students want lots of choice, others do better with only a few options, while still others prefer someone else to choose for them.[3]

We don't even have to know our particular students to plan for the range of variability in a given dimension because it has been shown to characterize populations of learners: it is predictable and systematic. When we plan to teach, we know that if we only give students one level of choice not all students will get "hooked" on learning. So we need to offer some students a direct assignment, others a few options, and others a wide open palette. We know that building flexibility into learning environments is essential for student engagement and success; the Guidelines help us apply that concept in specific situations and for specific reasons.

At the highest level the Guidelines are organized around the three principles of UDL:

- Provide multiple means of engagement

- Provide multiple means of representation

- Provide multiple means of action and expression

Those who have worked with earlier versions of the Guidelines will note that we have placed the highest-level learning goals at the top of our graphic: those focused on self-regulation, comprehension, and executive functions. By placing these prominently at the top we emphasize the learning expertise that is the goal of UDL. The middle level remains the same: highlighting specific strategies for building towards high-level expertise. The bottom level emphasizes the importance of removing unnecessary barriers to learning.

Each of the nine Guidelines emphasizes areas of learner variability that could present barriers, or, in a well-designed learning experience, present leverage points and opportunities for optimized engagement with learning. Under the Guidelines we suggest specific

VIDEO 5.5
Corie Williams, middle school Science teacher, relies on the UDL guidelines to vary her instructional methods from day to day, thus engaging all learners.

▸ http://udlvideo.org/ch5/5

Universal Design for Learning Guidelines

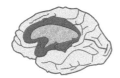

Provide Multiple Means of
Engagement
Purposeful, motivated learners

Provide options for self-regulation
+ Promote expectations and beliefs that optimize motivation
+ Facilitate personal coping skills and strategies
+ Develop self-assessment and reflection

Provide options for sustaining effort and persistence
+ Heighten salience of goals and objectives
+ Vary demands and resources to optimize challenge
+ Foster collaboration and community
+ Increase mastery-oriented feedback

Provide options for recruiting interest
+ Optimize individual choice and autonomy
+ Optimize relevance, value, and authenticity
+ Minimize threats and distractions

Provide Multiple Means of
Representation
Resourceful, knowledgeable learners

Provide options for comprehension
+ Activate or supply background knowledge
+ Highlight patterns, critical features, big ideas, and relationships
+ Guide information processing, visualization, and manipulation
+ Maximize transfer and generalization

Provide options for language, mathematical expressions, and symbols
+ Clarify vocabulary and symbols
+ Clarify syntax and structure
+ Support decoding of text, mathematical notation, and symbols
+ Promote understanding across languages
+ Illustrate through multiple media

Provide options for perception
+ Offer ways of customizing the display of information
+ Offer alternatives for auditory information
+ Offer alternatives for visual information

Provide Multiple Means of
Action & Expression
Strategic, goal-directed learners

Provide options for executive functions
+ Guide appropriate goal-setting
+ Support planning and strategy development
+ Enhance capacity for monitoring progress

Provide options for expression and communication
+ Use multiple media for communication
+ Use multiple tools for construction and composition
+ Build fluencies with graduated levels of support for practice and performance

Provide options for physical action
+ Vary the methods for response and navigation
+ Optimize access to tools and assistive technologies

FIG. 5.1. The UDL Guidelines © *2013 CAST, INC*

VIDEO 5.6

Variability is the norm, and there is no single way that works for every learner. Rhonda Laswell articulates her practice of removing curricular barriers by aligning the curriculum to students.

▸ http://udlvideo.org/ch5/6

practices for implementation—multiple checkpoints. These checkpoints are not meant to be exhaustive. They are examples that have emerged from research and practice to date upon which will be built a growing collection of new checkpoints and new ways to design flexibility into learning experiences. This collection will provide ever more powerful models for educators at all levels of the system.

An alternate way to consider the Guidelines is to look at some key questions that each one answers (Fig. 5.2). When planning a lesson or unit, consider these questions to ensure that the environment is flexible and inclusive of all students. (For a comprehensive presentation of the Guidelines and their research basis with a rich palette of references, examples, and discussion, see www.udlcenter.org/aboutudl/udlguidelines.)

Key Questions

THINK ABOUT HOW LEARNERS WILL ENGAGE WITH THE LESSON:

1. Does the lesson provide options that can help all learners regulate their own learning?

2. Does the lesson provide options that help all learners sustain effort and motivation?

3. Does the lesson provide options that engage and interest all learners?

THINK ABOUT HOW INFORMATION IS PRESENTED TO LEARNERS:

4. Does the information provide options that help all learners reach higher levels of comprehension and understanding?

5. Does the information provide options that help all learners understand the symbols and expressions?

6. Does the information provide options that help all learners perceive what needs to be learned?

THINK ABOUT HOW LEARNERS ARE EXPECTED TO ACT STRATEGICALLY & EXPRESS THEMSELVES:

7. Does the activity provide options that help all students act strategically?

8. Does the activity provide options that help all learners express themselves fluently?

9. Does the activity provide options that help all learners physically respond?

FIG. 5.2. Key questions to use to consider the UDL Guidelines *© 2013 CAST, INC*

THE AFFECT PRINCIPLE

Reframing Attention and Engagement in the Classroom

Using the affect principle as an example, let's explore how the UDL Guidelines can reframe how we approach classroom practice. The Guidelines offer structure and specific, practical examples for how to provide options to meet learner variability. They guide educators in what to attend to and what is important to vary in order to provide an engaging experience for all learners.

By highlighting predictable variability and suggesting ways to address it, the Guidelines enable us to see things differently—to see variability instead of disability, to see curriculum as the problem, not learners. In this way the Guidelines provide a new lens for viewing the classroom and the curriculum: one that enables teachers to reframe how they see their practice and to make constructive changes. To illustrate how strongly preparation can affect what you **see**, we offer an exemplary video experiment.

If you were a recent psychology major, you may have already seen the two videos we have linked to in the margin. They come from one of the most famous, and most startling, experiments in perception ever conducted. You can participate by viewing the Videos 5.7 and 5.8.

These videos demonstrate the general phenomenon known as "inattention blindness."[4] That moniker suggests a disability or limitation in perception—as though we are "blind" when we don't notice a gorilla walking across the screen while we are looking at it. Closer scrutiny in a subsequent experiment showed that everyone actually "sees" the gorilla, but they do not pay attention to it.[5]

The videos, then, actually demonstrate the power rather than the limit of human perception. Humans are able to focus their attention (and thus information processing and memory) on whatever is most important or valuable at the moment. We miss the gorilla only because counting how many times the ball is passed is more important to us—at least the first time we watch.

VIDEO 5.7
Participate in a classic experiment in selective attention.

▶ http://udlvideo.org/ch5/7

VIDEO 5.8
View a group of subjects participating in the selective attention experiment, with explanation. http://udlvideo.org/ch5/8

FIG. 5.3. Sixty percent of participants who did not report seeing the gorilla spent an average of 25 frames (about one second) fixated on it.
ILLUSTRATION BY CHRIS VALLO © 2013 CAST, INC.

The whole experiment depends, of course, on what is actually important. For most initial viewers, the instructions by the experimenter (a person of authority) determine what is important: "count the passes." Because of this, a large proportion of new viewers does not perceive or recognize the gorilla. But in any given audience many people do notice the gorilla: in the original experiment, fully half the participants did.[6] People who have seen the experiment before tend to see the gorilla during subsequent viewings because, for them, the instruction to "count the passes" is already known to be a trick or manipulation. They don't attend to the stated purpose but instead concentrate on the arrival of the gorilla, ignoring the ball tosses.

Subsequent experimenters have shown that a wide range of individual differences, from age to expertise in basketball, affect the phenomenon. Actual percentages of perception of the gorilla range from nearly 0% (young children) to 100% (experts who have seen it before) with all kinds of intermediate percentages due to individual differences in working memory, motivation, previous history, and so forth.[7]

The experiment is a powerful demonstration of human variability: in this case the variability that is evident in attention or "engagement." What we "see" and learn from is not differentiated just by our visual or perceptual systems but by our affective systems: by what is engaging to us. And that is differs greatly from one person to the next.

Because motivation is so essential to learning (and so easily thwarted in poorly designed learning environments) UDL calls for providing "multiple means of engagement." The Guidelines articulate three different aspects of engagement that need to be attended to in instructional design. Looking at our own teaching through the lens of these Guidelines can shape how we see our practice. We highlight the three affective Guidelines here.

The first engagement Guideline focuses us on the real goal of education: developing learning expertise. In the affective realm, expert learners can set difficult goals for themselves and muster the effort to sustain their effort to achieve those goals even when conditions frustrate engagement and achievement. That is what we mean by "self-regulation." This Guideline gathers a number of techniques

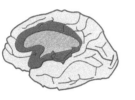

Provide Multiple Means of

Engagement

Purposeful, motivated learners

Provide options for self-regulation
+ Promote expectations and beliefs that optimize motivation
+ Facilitate personal coping skills and strategies
+ Develop self-assessment and reflection

Provide options for sustaining effort and persistence
+ Heighten salience of goals and objectives
+ Vary demands and resources to optimize challenge
+ Foster collaboration and community
+ Increase mastery-oriented feedback

Provide options for recruiting interest
+ Optimize individual choice and autonomy
+ Optimize relevance, value, and authenticity
+ Minimize threats and distractions

FIG. 5.4. Detail of the UDL Guidelines and related checkpoints for Engagement © 2013 CAST, INC

presented in the literature—options, because none will work for everyone—that can help develop self-regulation among highly variable students. This self regulation is the hallmark of expert learners, not learners who do well only in highly structured learning environments.

The second engagement Guideline addresses the sustainability of engagement. In the gorilla experiment, the task requires sustained attention to the ball passes. In fact, the experiment works because most participants are familiar with the difficulty of maintaining attention and effort: They "dig-in" with sustained effort and never consciously perceive the gorilla. If the experiment were to continue for an hour, we suspect that most people would see the gorilla because their engagement would flag considerably. This Guideline and its checkpoints suggest a number of options that research and practice have highlighted as fruitful ways to help students in sustaining their engagement.

The third engagement Guideline emphasizes options that a teacher can use to recruit engagement. In any task some things are more attention-grabbing or immediately interesting than others. For example, were it not for the directions given by the experimenter, the gorilla on the basketball court would capture most people's attention because novel, unexpected events are very powerful ways to recruit engagement in humans. But even novelty elicits different responses in different people. Some people find novelty highly stimulating and engaging while others find it frightening or annoying. Thus it is important to offer a range of options along the dimension of novelty in any learning situation.

Research has demonstrated many other factors that recruit our attention, either positively or negatively, and these are reviewed in the checkpoints. For example, in educational settings it has been often shown that authentic tasks can stimulate engagement. But the UDL Guidelines remind us that options are needed: what is authentic for one student may be quite inauthentic or foreign for another.

THE RECOGNITION PRINCIPLE

Recognition and Design of an Online Learning Tool

How can the UDL Guidelines help us design learning experiences that will be flexible enough to reach varied learners? According to the recognition principle, we provide multiple means of representation. Let's explore how this might work in the domain of music, specifically, Bach's

VIDEO 5.9

Listen to a single representation of Bach's "Toccata and Fugue in D Minor."

▸ http://udlvideo.org/ch5/9

"Toccata and Fugue in D Minor." First, please listen to the opening of the piece (Video 5.9).

We may or may not find this piece appealing. But without some musical training we probably have a somewhat superficial experience of it. We can hear the melody and notice changes in pitch. We may know something about the era during which it was composed. But we probably don't really *comprehend* the music deeply. We don't really understand the structure, themes, variations, and progressions, or how Bach used those elements to create emotionally satisfying music. If we played it many more times, or studied written resources on it, we could learn more about the piece, but this would be a lengthy process.

Perhaps an alternate representation can help. Here is the written score for the opening of the piece:

FIG. 5.5. A piece of the written score of Bach's "Toccata and Fugue in D Minor"
© 2007 ALL MUSIC SHEETS

For some readers—especially musicians, composers, or musical historians—this visual representation of part of the music provides an alternative path into the heart of it. But for most readers the visual score adds little. Decoding it requires a level of musical literacy and fluency that is beyond most non-musicians.

Now let's view a very different representation of this same piece. In this version, musician, educator, and programmer Stephen Malinowski exploits the power and flexibility of multimedia to make this music more accessible by making it more comprehensible.[8] He himself had found musical scores, especially of orchestral works with many parts, difficult to access. So he developed alternative ways of representing the music. In his own multimedia program, Malinowski creates visual scaffolds (or visualizations, if you will) for the listener. Through this carefully designed visualization of music he helps listeners "organize their musical experience so that things which might not be noticed … under normal circumstances (due to lack of experience or inattention) are obvious and have the effect the composer intended."[9] These visual scaffolds help viewers listen more effectively to the music and more readily discover its structure and, perhaps, its beauty.

To begin, play the opening of the piece in the format Malinowski designed (Video 5.10). The opening of the fugue presents the theme, or pattern of notes, that will be developed throughout the piece. See if this multiple representation of the theme in both visual and auditory modalities makes its pattern easier to recognize. Is the musical structure more vivid, more accessible, more understandable? The piece quickly becomes much more complex. Fortunately, Malinowski, a consummate educator, has more scaffolds in mind than merely adding a visual track to guide listeners. Onto his visual track he layers other kinds of representations to scaffold listeners' experience of music. Watch (and listen) to the next selection (Video 5.11). This takes the opening of the fugue a bit further.

In his visual representation, Malinowski uses color, location, and shape to draw attention to a critical feature of the fugue form: repetition of its theme. With Malinowski's scaffolding, we can more easily see (and then also hear) that the pattern of sounds shown in purple at the beginning of the passage is the same as the pattern of sounds that is shown in dark blue shortly thereafter. He uses color to represent the different "voices" in the music (soprano, alto, tenor, bass), location (high or low) to indicate pitch, and length of blocks of color to

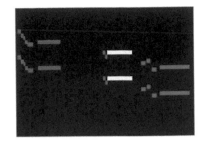

VIDEO 5.10
Watch and listen to a multimedia version of the Bach fugue created by composer, inventor, and software engineer Stephen Malinowski.

▸ http://udlvideo.org/ch5/10

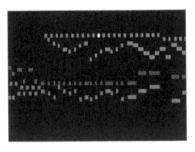

VIDEO 5.11
Watch and listen to a more complex section of the fugue.

▸ http://udlvideo.org/ch5/11

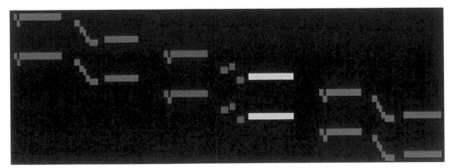

FIG. 5.6. Malinowski uses color, shape, location and highlighting to show critical features of the music. © 2005 STEPHEN MALINOWSKI, MUSIC ANIMATION MACHINE

indicate duration of notes. By using color, location, and shape in this way, Malinowski makes it easier both to recognize the similarity in the patterns and to distinguish them from each other so that the music isn't just a jumble of sounds. Finally, and of critical importance, Malinowski uses highlighting synchronized with audio to show you what is being heard at any given moment.

With his Musical Animation Machine, Malinowski aims to help people *learn* to listen. In an interview he notes the following:

> One of the things about a musical score is that if there's something in there that you're not perceiving, because it requires more attention than you're giving it, it gives you another way in to hear something. I've had people say, about pieces of music they've loved and known all their life, that after watching one of my videos they see something in it that they'd never heard before and now they hear it every time they listen to that piece of music. It's part of the education. People don't realize that when you're listening to a piece of music you're learning how to hear it, how to make sense of it. And when a piece of music is unfamiliar and you don't like it, you don't like it because you can't hear it; you don't understand it and it's not music to you.[10]

Malinowski's visual scaffolds don't make music less interesting, original, or engaging. Quite the opposite: they draw listeners deeper into the music, making it both more comprehensible and more satisfying.

Recognition, Learning Design, and the UDL Guidelines

UDL aligns with Malinowski's work in that his goal is to help listeners become ever more expert at the process of hearing, understanding, and appreciating music. Most educators face the same challenges that Malinowski did: helping students develop learning expertise by constructing scaffolded learning experiences to teach their students how to listen (or read, speak, write, draw) more effectively and how to comprehend and compose new, difficult, even beautiful things. But we don't have the decades of time to prepare that Malinowski took. So we try to save a lot of time by learning from the practice of others and by using research-based scaffolds—in this case the UDL Guidelines.

Malinowski's innovations exemplify many of the UDL Guidelines for excellent learning design. To illustrate this, we highlight the links between the Music Animation Machine and the three guidelines associated with the UDL principle of providing multiple means of representation.[11] They move from high-level cognitive functions down to basic perceptual considerations. Under each one are checkpoints suggesting specific kinds of flexibility that are needed to address systematic learner variability (Fig. 5.7).

The Guideline "provide options for comprehension" addresses the fact that people differ systematically in their ability to construct meaning by combining information from various symbols and information. It addresses variability in learners' prior knowledge and experiences, ability to recognize critical features and patterns, approaches to processing and integrating new knowledge, and ability to transfer and generalize knowledge. These kinds of variability require flexible representations that can address learner differences and scaffold deep understanding. Malinowski, as an educator, wants to ensure listeners really "get" music in a way that is meaningful to them. Here he needs to guide the construction of meaning so listeners will understand in a deep way and will construct usable knowledge about music.

Malinowski's rendition of the fugue ties in with the middle two checkpoints under this top Guideline: highlight critical patterns, critical features, and critical relationships; and guide information processing. The software's colors and animation highlight patterns, critical features, and relationships between the "voices" in the fugue. And white highlighting guides both visual processing (by locating the viewer in the graphic) and auditory processing (by synchronizing the visual and auditory representations) of the music. The net effect is that the listener's/viewer's attention is guided to focus on the music's most relevant aspects.

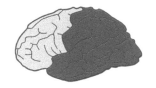

Provide Multiple Means of

Representation

Resourceful, knowledgeable learners

Provide options for comprehension
+ Activate or supply background knowledge
+ Highlight patterns, critical features, big ideas, and relationships
+ Guide information processing, visualization, and manipulation
+ Maximize transfer and generalization

Provide options for language, mathematical expressions, and symbols
+ Clarify vocabulary and symbols
+ Clarify syntax and structure
+ Support decoding of text, mathematical notation, and symbols
+ Promote understanding across languages
+ Illustrate through multiple media

Provide options for perception
+ Offer ways of customizing the display of information
+ Offer alternatives for auditory information
+ Offer alternatives for visual information

FIG. 5.7. Detail of the UDL Guidelines and related checkpoints for Representation © 2013 CAST, INC

Provide Multiple Means of
Representation

Provide options for comprehension

+ Activate or supply background knowledge
+ Highlight patterns, critical features, big ideas, and relationships
+ Guide information processing, visualization, and manipulation
+ Maximize transfer and generalization

FIG. 5.8. Malinowski's design aligns strongly with two of the comprehension checkpoints. © 2013 CAST, INC

We highlighted the first checkpoint shown in Figure 5.8 in a lighter tone because Malinowski himself did not provide background knowledge for listeners, and this is one way his animation could be improved. To better understand this composition, it is important to know that a fugue is a musical composition built on a theme that is introduced at the beginning and then repeated in different voices and contexts throughout the composition.[12] While viewing Malinowski's animation, we can activate this background knowledge to better comprehend the music: the short theme (highlighted in different colors) will appear many times, each time in a different voice (different tonality and pitch), and in different musical contexts (the background notes and chords are different). Malinowski uses color and spatial scaffolding to help with recognizing the theme and assist in perceiving the music, even as it gets more complicated. Look at Figure 5.9 and see if you can spot the theme (played down very low by the pedals of the organ, highlighted in green).

For most listeners, as the piece becomes richer and more complex, the color and shape (multiple representations) of the theme begin to stand out clearly and the structure of the piece as a whole begins to make sense. You may notice that Bach embraces variability. While the theme always maintains the same basic pattern, it sounds a little different each time as Bach plays with its musical properties. At one point, he even writes it upside down!

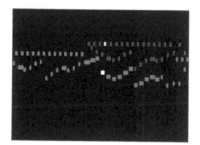

VIDEO 5.12
Experience Malinowski's multimedia scaffolding of complex musical themes.

▶ http://udlvideo.org/ch5/12

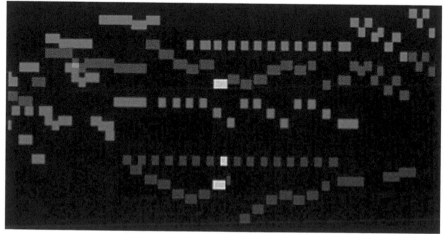

FIG. 5.9. Malinowski uses color and spatial scaffolding to help with recognizing the theme and patterns in the music. © 2005 STEPHEN MALINOWSKI, MUSIC ANIMATION MACHINE

At times as educators we need to enhance a given resource by providing background knowledge, as we've done in this case. An example comes from classroom teacher Dana Calfee, who provides multiple options for comprehending science vocabulary in part by making explicit links to students' background knowledge (Video 5.13).

The next Guideline—"provide options for language, mathematical expressions, and symbols"—addresses the fact that people differ systematically in their ability to recognize or understand various forms of symbolic representation. This is not an issue of perception (e.g, perceiving symbols) but of decoding meaning (e.g., understanding what letters, words, or numbers represent). To address the range of variation in people's ability to understand symbolic representation, this Guideline recommends that educators provide options for language, mathematical expressions, and symbols.

For Bach's fugue, Malinowski does not have to deal with verbal language or mathematical expression. But to address his audience's variability in ability to process musical symbols, he does need to provide alternative representations of musical notation and of the sounds themselves. By providing notation in a more accessible way he promotes understanding across languages. He uses his beautiful graphical system (including color, location, shape, and highlighting) to clarify the syntax and structure of the music and to illustrate that structure through multiple media.

VIDEO 5.13 In her Science class, Dana Calfee teaches vocabulary as a "foreign language" that students don't just memorize but rather learn to use. Here she describes techniques for linking words with familiar concepts and engaging students with active exploration.

▶ http://udlvideo.org/ch5/13

Provide Multiple Means of
Representation

Provide options for language, mathematical expressions, and symbols

+ Clarify vocabulary and symbols
+ Clarify syntax and structure
+ Support decoding of text, mathematical notation, and symbols
+ Promote understanding across languages
+ Illustrate through multiple media

FIG. 5.10. UDL checkpoints for providing options for language and symbols   © 2013 CAST, INC

VIDEO 5.14 Mollie Fountain's Social Studies students had difficulty understanding latitude and longitude. Her engaging hands-on activity with plenty of scaffolds brought much better results.

▶ http://udlvideo.org/ch5/14

VIDEO 5.15
Katherine Bishop's students came up with their own ideas for embedding varied media in their Keynote presentations.

▸ http://udlvideo.org/ch5/15

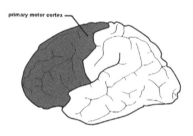

VIDEO 5.16
David Rose explains how functions of the brain's frontal lobes align with the three Strategic UDL Guidelines.

▸ http://udlvideo.org/ch5/16

VIDEO 5.17
A soccer coach demonstrates passing the ball, showing the components of a complex fluid skill. [Vid5.17_YouTube_Logo.tif

▸ http://udlvideo.org/ch5/17

The Guideline that suggests we "provide multiple options for perception" addresses variable abilities and preferences in perception, including different abilities to perceive content in different media. This Guideline highlights the importance of providing varied media to meet diverse learners' perceptual preferences and needs. Malinowski offers audio and also visual representations both to make the music more accessible and to make it more comprehensible. He explicitly provides options for the second checkpoint—visual alternatives to the patterns that are usually available only through sound. This is effective for sighted individuals, but for those who are blind, the additional visual information does not have pedagogical value.

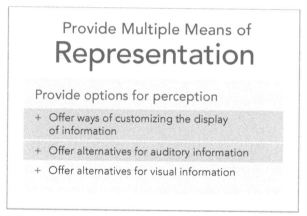

FIG. 5.11. UDL checkpoints for providing options for perception
© 2013 CAST, INC

An interesting challenge would be to provide an auditory or tactile equivalent to the visualizations themselves. Although customization of display was not built into his rendition of the Fugue, its format being digital video in a web browser fulfills the first checkpoint as well. Users can adjust the sound volume and the size of the video display on their screens.

By focusing on links between the Representation Guidelines and Malinowski's pedagogical designs, we have illustrated how the Guidelines can be applied. Now we will draw connections between the Guidelines and the learning brain by exploring the Guidelines under the Strategy Principle (providing multiple means of action and expression) in relation to neuroscience.

THE STRATEGY PRINCIPLE

The Neuroscience of Strategy

The UDL Guidelines, like the principles, are derived from research in the cognitive and affective neurosciences. To see this connection explicitly in relation to the Strategic Guidelines, we start with a diagram (Fig. 5.12) illustrating the lateral surface of human cerebral cortex.

The left half of this diagram shows the frontal lobes. Decades of neuroscience research have demonstrated that this area is the locus of our abilities to act skillfully and strategically. The frontal lobes can be articulated into different regions, each of which contributes to strategic skill in a progression of functions from back to front.

At the front of the frontal lobes, in what is commonly called executive or prefrontal cortex are the networks that provide "executive functions," underlying the especially human ability not only to be skillful but to be goal-directed and strategic in our actions.

Just behind that, in what is sometimes called secondary motor cortex, are networks that coordinate simple movements into elaborate and fluent skills that are the hallmarks of human ability. At the rear of the frontal lobes, in what is called primary motor cortex, lies the neural networks that are most directly involved in producing simple voluntary motor movement. Prefrontal cortex allows us to set goals for ourselves, to choose effective strategies rather than impulsive or reflexive responses, and to monitor our progress while changing courses of action as needed.[13] Each of these three specialized areas within the frontal lobes is a source of individual variation. Students differ in:

- Their ability to develop competent executive functions for executing certain skills and movements (their ability to set appropriate goals for themselves, to choose effective strategies and skills, to monitor their own progress)

- Their abilities to learn to coordinate simple movements into fluent skills and abilities (their ability to develop fluency in skills such as writing, speaking, dancing, drawing, playing sports)

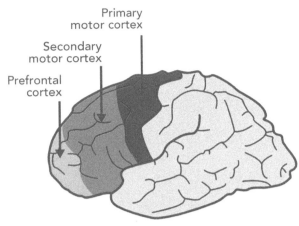

Primary motor cortex

Secondary motor cortex

Prefrontal cortex

FIG. 5.12. Each Strategic Guideline addresses specific kinds of variability linked to areas of motor cortex © 2013 CAST, INC

You Tube

VIDEO 5.18
In an interview with Charlie Rose, physicist Stephen Hawking shares insights via a synthetic speech device, illustrating variability in the motor cortex.

▸ http://udlvideo.org/ch5/18

VIDEO 5.19
Teacher Rhonda Laswell articulates the confidence she feels in UDL because it emerges from brain science and is research based.

▸ http://udlvideo.org/ch5/19

VIDEO 5.20

Gabrielle Rappolt-Schlicht-mann explains how teachers can increase the relevance of assignments and increase student engagement.

▶ http://udlvideo.org/ch5/20

- Their primary motor capabilities (their ability to move and perform basic actions).

These three areas of specialization are largely independent as sources of variability: the same student that is motorically awkward and clumsy may be highly strategic and goal-directed. An extreme example is Stephen Hawking, the physicist who has very little capacity for simple voluntary movement but enormous capacity for strategic thinking and executive functions.[14] It is also crucial to understand that the variability within each of these areas of cortex is largely systematic and predictable. That is, without evaluating a particular group of students we can estimate the kinds of variability we, as educators, are likely to encounter in a group. Planning for that range of variability with our curricular design will enable us to engage and support a majority of learners within the flexible curriculum itself.

Guidelines Aligned to Neuroscience

The diagram below illustrates the direct link between the three Strategic Guidelines and the three specialized areas of the frontal lobes. Each Guideline recommends options because there is no single tool, method, or path to success that is optimal for every student. Only

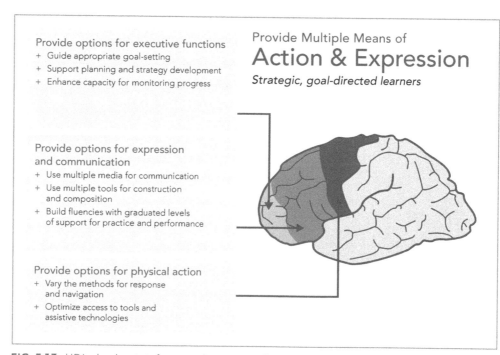

Provide options for executive functions
+ Guide appropriate goal-setting
+ Support planning and strategy development
+ Enhance capacity for monitoring progress

Provide options for expression and communication
+ Use multiple media for communication
+ Use multiple tools for construction and composition
+ Build fluencies with graduated levels of support for practice and performance

Provide options for physical action
+ Vary the methods for response and navigation
+ Optimize access to tools and assistive technologies

Provide Multiple Means of
Action & Expression
Strategic, goal-directed learners

FIG. 5.13. UDL checkpoints for providing options for strategy © 2013 CAST, INC

by providing options relevant to the learning goal and to learner variability can we create learning environments that are effective for all. The Guidelines, and the checkpoints that elaborate them, provide research-based recommendations for the kinds of options that are important to consider in relation to each aspect of learning, given the range of systematic variability we can expect.

The idea of options may make it seem that students would all be doing something different, when options actually enable all students to focus on the same learning goal together. A simple example would be the provision of text-to-speech for reading which can allow all students in the classroom to use the same social studies text regardless of their decoding abilities. While it may seem that uniformity of materials and methods would align students to the same activity or lesson, the very opposite is true. Since variability is the rule, providing only one approach automatically means that some students will be forced to work in a way that is not optimal for them. Flexible means enable the pursuit of common learning goals for all.

For each of the UDL principles, the Guidelines and checkpoints derive from the neuroscience of learning. Each Guideline helps us to understand the specific and predictable kinds of variability we are likely to encounter as educators.

WHO ARE THE UDL GUIDELINES FOR?

The UDL Guidelines were initially formulated primarily to support instructional designers who are creating curriculum: a lesson, an activity, a book or resource, an educational game or interactive activity, a scope and sequence, a full curriculum. Their purpose was to provide guidance and scaffolding that would be useful to educational designers, helping, first, to be purposeful in considering the systematic variability of students for whom curricula is being designed and, second, to consider the kinds of options and alternatives that would make their instructional designs more flexible, effective, and differentiated.

The UDL Guidelines also provide helpful scaffolds for educators in day-to-day activities. For instance, the Guidelines can inform those responsible for making instructional and curricular *choices*: what curriculum to purchase for a district, what online resource to

VIDEO 5.21
Using UDL as a means to reflect on his teaching, practice, Jon Mundorf describes how in the past he had inadvertently created barriers for some of his students.

▶ http://udlvideo.org/ch5/21

VIDEO 5.22
Educator Angela Spurgeon discusses shifting her teaching practice to offer students more effective paths to learning.

▶ http://udlvideo.org/ch5/22

VIDEO 5.23
High school teacher Libby Arthur describes a model of professional collaboration that helps teachers build UDL into their work.

▶ http://udlvideo.org/ch5/23

VIDEO 5.24
Teacher Corie Williams describes designing an exciting middle school unit bridging science, math, social studies, and language arts content.

▶ http://udlvideo.org/ch5/24

recommend to students or other teachers, what kinds of assessments to select to provide valid and accurate data for making instructional decisions. The Guidelines can help decision makers take the predictable variability in the student population into account and choose resources with appropriate kinds of flexibility to meet that variability. They can help teachers, schools, districts, and states make wise choices to serve all learners equitably.

In addition, a number of educators find that the Guidelines are important as a guide for future study, articulating the landscape of what needs to be learned about implementing UDL. They can be used to assess current practices, to stimulate discussion with colleagues, and to lead to a deeper understanding of how UDL can be effectively applied in the classroom in a practical way. The Guidelines also inform professional development and communities of practice in school districts where they have been adopted. Most importantly, the Guidelines are a learning instrument: a guide for self-reflection and the revision of teaching practices.

Designing for All: What Is a UDL Curriculum?

In 1530, Polish astronomer Nicolaus Copernicus finished drafting his theory that the sun, rather than the earth, stood at the center of the universe. He floated his idea to friends and colleagues, gauging their opinions and gathering feedback. They encouraged him to publish his work, but he resisted. He was reluctant, he said, to risk being scorned "on account of the novelty and incomprehensibility of his theses."[1]

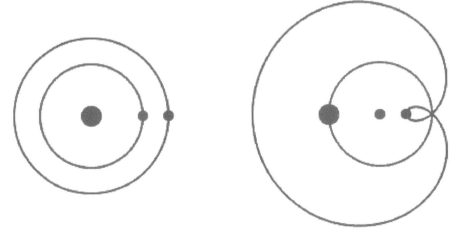

FIG. 6.1. In 1530, Polish astronomer Nicolaus Copernicus theorized that the sun rather than the earth stood at the center of the universe.

©2011 CREATIVE COMMONS ATTRIBUTION-SHARE ALIKE 2.5 GENERIC LICENSE.

He did not publish his work until right before his death, in 1543. He had good reason to worry. Copernicus knew his theory would revolutionize not just astronomy but Western society at large and that resistance to his ideas—from other scientists, from the Church, from governments, from the people themselves—would be fierce. He likely knew, too, that while it might take years for his theory to be adopted, man's understanding of the world would change forever once it was.

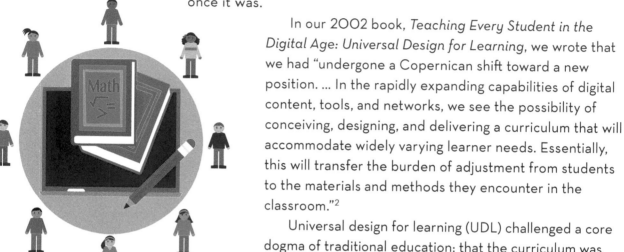

In our 2002 book, *Teaching Every Student in the Digital Age: Universal Design for Learning*, we wrote that we had "undergone a Copernican shift toward a new position. ... In the rapidly expanding capabilities of digital content, tools, and networks, we see the possibility of conceiving, designing, and delivering a curriculum that will accommodate widely varying learner needs. Essentially, this will transfer the burden of adjustment from students to the materials and methods they encounter in the classroom."[2]

Universal design for learning (UDL) challenged a core dogma of traditional education: that the curriculum was and must be at the center of the learning experience. This conviction was based largely on the fact that the predominant instructional media, such as printed textbooks and worksheets, were fixed and inflexible; anyone who could not learn from the given curriculum was labeled "disabled" or "underachieving" or "failing." The curriculum defined the learner. As we have written elsewhere, "With no obvious alternatives to print, students (and teachers) had to learn to adapt to its limits. Classrooms became textbook-centered rather than student-centered because students, rather than their textbooks, seemed more adaptable, flexible, and malleable."[3]

With the learner at the center, the curriculum is now defined, or labeled, by how adequately it can support and accommodate the diversity and variability of learners. A "successful" or "rigorous" curriculum is one that provides genuine learning opportunities for all. It is responsive and nimble enough to adjust to the needs and interests of all

FIG. 6.2. A Copernican shift in focus, from the curriculum to the learner

ILLUSTRATION BY CHRIS VALLO © 2013 CAST, INC.

users, including students, teachers, and members of the wider educational system.

In a well-designed learning environment, systematic variability is planned for from the very beginning, and diversity is expected, appreciated, and developed. Learners of all abilities and from all backgrounds are provided with optimal levels of challenges and scaffolds and are supported in developing learning expertise. This includes enthusiasm for learning as well as knowledge and skills. When students encounter difficulty, the curriculum—not the learner—is assumed to be inadequate to meet the varied and diverse needs of learners. This replaces the old practice of jumping to label learners as "disabled" or "challenged" when they encounter difficulty with a curriculum that offers limited paths to success.

VIDEO 6.1
Where is disability located? Not, as we used to think, within learners. Jon Mundorf shares his new understanding of "disability" and how it has changed his teaching.

▶ http://udlvideo.org/ch6/1

VIDEO 6.2
Grace Meo, CAST Director of Professional Development, offers an overview of the collaborative, iterative process of designing and implementing UDL curriculum.

▶ http://udlvideo.org/ch6/2

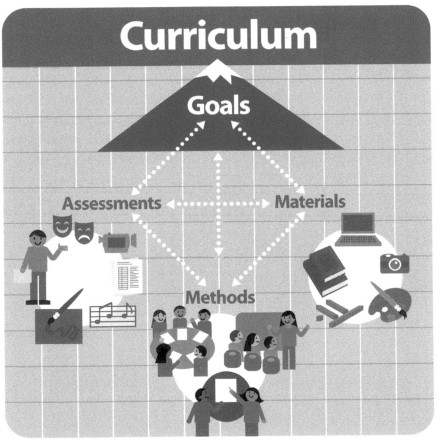

FIG. 6.3. Curriculum is the interrelationship of instructional goals, assessments, materials, and methods.

ILLUSTRATION BY CHRIS VALLO © 2013 CAST, INC.

VIDEO 6.3

After training in UDL, teacher Lindsay Tavares reflects on the reasons that her math lesson failed to reach many of her students. In upcoming videos, she redesigns the lesson using the lens of UDL and shares the results.

▶ http://udlvideo.org/ch6/3

Planning with Lindsay

Throughout this chapter, we will consider the case story of Lindsay Tavares, a public school teacher, to help us understand how to work with a UDL curriculum. Not everyone will relate to all aspects of Lindsay's story since she is just one person teaching a specific grade level (3rd) and planning in a specific content area (math). Still, Lindsay's story provides insight into how UDL can shape curriculum design and lesson planning. The principles illustrated here apply broadly.

Lindsay teaches 3rd grade in a struggling big-city elementary school. After returning from a weeklong UDL training, Lindsay reevaluates an unsuccessful math lesson on mixed numbers to see how she might be able to design the learning environment more effectively. The initial goal reads: "Students will demonstrate using quantities greater than 1 with fractions and mixed numbers by completing a whole-class circle activity and independent work in student journal pages 197–198."

In previous classes, students were asked to read two "think about it" questions on the board and cut out three paper circles while they thought about the answers. Some students had to share scissors; others did not have the fine motor skills to cut the shapes. The "think-about-it" questions posed problems, too. Some students had difficulty reading them on the board, while others could not understand the language and symbols in the questions. Many struggled with both activities. A group mini-lesson followed but many students became frustrated because they hadn't been able to create good circles or think about the questions. Behavioral problems ensued. The final part of the lesson plan called for students to paste the shapes on worksheets and fill in some answers. Many students never got that far.

Now, Lindsay will apply UDL to rewrite the lesson, making sure to plan from the start to ensure that all students are included and actually learn about mixed numbers. Follow her progress throughout the chapter.

Effective curriculum also supports teachers in their practice and continuing development.[4] In this chapter we explore this shift in thinking through the four components of the curriculum: goals, assessments, methods, and materials. This definition of curriculum is broader than a traditional one which treats curriculum as a sequence of content conveyed by a particular set of instructional materials. We emphasize the interconnectedness of these components and the importance of goals and assessment in designing effective curriculum.

GOALS

Clear learning goals are the foundation of any effective curriculum. Only by clarifying what we want to accomplish and when—in the next 10 minutes, in the next lesson, in the next year—can we begin to consider what assessments, methods, and materials will be most effective. Goals are often described as learning expectations.[5] Traditionally they represent the knowledge and skills that all learners should master and are generally aligned to standards. From a UDL perspective, affective goals such as developing enthusiasm for learning and an ability to self-regulate are equally important. In our view, affective goals should be more clearly articulated in standards, and, more specifically, included in assessment.[6] Within the UDL framework, goals themselves are articulated in a way that acknowledges learner variability and differentiates outcomes from means. Whereas traditional curriculum planning focuses heavily on content or performance goals, UDL curriculum planning aims to develop expert learners.[7] This development is an ongoing, iterative process that does not have an end point but continues throughout life. Expectations remain high for every learner, and a flexible curriculum supports progress towards these expectations in a variety of ways.

Learning to design UDL goals takes practice. Support in designing and reflecting on goals can be helpful. An online tool built to offer that support is UDL Exchange's lesson building tool (http://udlexchange.cast.org). The lesson builder provides structure and support for creating lessons based on UDL principles, including UDL goal setting. When drafting goals in the lesson building tool, users can consult tips, guides, examples, and a research base for creating UDL goals and aligning instructional goals and objectives to standards and assessments. Users can also use UDL Exchange to connect with other educators who are interested in implementing UDL principles in classroom practice.

At the risk of stating the obvious, it is worth noting that goals are not the same as standards. Standards articulate what the educational community values and, therefore, what the community believes teachers must teach and assess. Well-designed standards leave room for teachers to shape classroom goals and to individualize the means for attaining them.

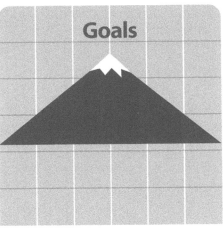

FIG. 6.4. Clear learning goals are the foundation of any effective curriculum.
ILLUSTRATION BY CHRIS VALLO © 2013 CAST, INC.

VIDEO 6.4
The central importance of the learning goal cannot be overemphasized. Grace Meo explains what clarity of goals looks like in the classroom and why goals are the guiding force in all aspects of UDL lesson planning.

▶ http://udlvideo.org/ch6/4

VIDEO 6.5

When planning a lesson the first question Jon Mundorf asks himself is "What is the point of this lesson?" Since our brains are goal-directed, a clear answer to this question is the foundation of any lesson.

▶ http://udlvideo.org/ch6/5

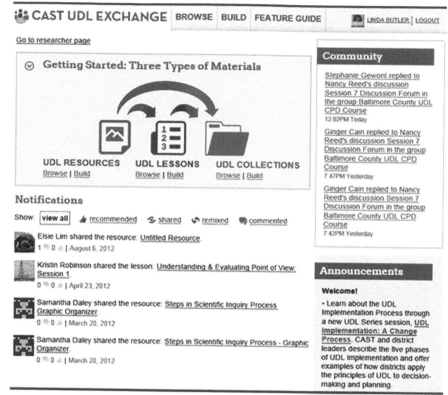

FIG. 6.5. The lesson building component of UDL Exchange enables educators to share ideas and resources. *© 2013 CAST, INC.*

FIG. 6.6. One size does not fit all. *ILLUSTRATION BY CHRIS VALLO © 2013 CAST, INC.*

Deriving clear goals from standards requires teasing out the central purpose of a standard by separating the goal from the means for attaining it and restating the goal in a way that is attainable for all students. It requires the teacher to think carefully about the intention of the standard and how flexibility can be designed around it. In short, goals do need to align to standards, but they are not the same thing.[8]

Goals from a UDL Perspective

From a UDL perspective, effective goals are goals that:

- Separate the means from the ends;

- Consider all three learning networks;

- Challenge all learners;

- Actively involve learners.

Let's consider each of these point by point.

Effective goals separate learning expectations from the means of achieving them

Partly because we have functioned for so many years with inflexible learning environments, we tend to think narrowly about goals and the ways they can be attained. When goals are too closely linked to means, some students are inadvertently excluded from working towards those goals while others are not offered an appropriate level of challenge. To engage students and enable them to evaluate their own progress, we need to express learning goals in a flexible way, offer optional paths for achieving the goals, convey criteria for success, and allow students to help determine goals.

When applying the UDL framework, goals are disaggregated from the means to achieve them so that teachers can effectively plan the remaining aspects of the learning environment, and students can see explicit and multiple pathways to success. For example, students may be asked to read *The Old Man and the Sea* and write a book report to demonstrate what they know about Hemingway's novel. If the goal in this case is not writing per se but rather demonstrating knowledge about the book, a learning goal that explicitly calls for "writing" a book report is prescribing the means by which students share what they know. This, in turn, privileges those who express themselves easily in that medium.[9]

A more effective goal would allow for multiple means of expression—e.g., "compose" a report using whatever medium works best. Students may then choose to show what they know about *The Old Man and the Sea* (including plot, characterization, setting, and so forth) using video, artwork, dramatic performance, a traditional written book report format, or other creative means.

If, in fact, the goal of our assignment is a written composition, then text must be the ultimate expression of knowledge. In this case, students can be supported in reaching this outcome. Students who find it difficult to start using text can develop their ideas in other media and then transition to text when they have clarity. Of course, spell check and other supports for writing mechanics should be given wherever appropriate.

VIDEO 6.6
Engaging students in setting goals and determining multiple pathways to reach them is rewarding and effective, according to Jon Mundorf.

▶ http://udlvideo.org/ch6/6

VIDEO 6.7
Keeping an eye on the specific goal of a lesson is important in evaluating student performance. Katherine Bishop shares a provocative example.

▶ http://udlvideo.org/ch6/7

VIDEO 6.8
Teacher Molly Fountain describes her UDL process, emphasizing the importance of goal setting and offering multiple ways to reach the goal.

▶ http://udlvideo.org/ch6/8

VIDEO 6.9

Multiple means to achieve goals need to be developmentally appropriate, according to educator Alexis Reid.

▸ http://udlvideo.org/ch6/9

Effective goals consider the learning networks

In earlier chapters, we identified three sets of networks in the brain that facilitate learning—affective, recognition, and strategic. While these networks are always operating simultaneously and in concert with each other, we often consider them separately for the purposes of thinking about curriculum. In this case, it may be helpful to ask which network-set is most relevant to a particular standard or goal as a way of understanding which aspects of a task must be held constant, and which can be designed more flexibly. Following are sample questions to help tease out these priorities:

- Is the goal for students to build enthusiasm or learn to form appropriate goals (affective networks)?

- Is the goal for students to understand specific content or to generalize knowledge (recognition networks)?

- Is the goal for students to master a skill or learn to create effective plans and manage available resources (strategic networks)?

When the true purpose of a goal or standard is understood, teachers can then think about what kinds of flexibility they can build into the learning environment to help learners reach the goal. For example, if the goal is for students to "Demonstrate competence in the general skills and strategies of writing," this goal focuses on process. Since the content is not specified and not key to this particular goal, teachers can increase engagement by encouraging students to select content of greatest interest to them and by setting the challenge at individually appropriate levels.

Effective goals challenge all learners

We know that under-challenging or over-challenging students leads to disengagement. Boredom on the one hand or anxiety on the other can lead students to feel alienated and stop investing effort. It becomes a question of balance between demands and resources. Goals must be written in ways that challenge all learners appropriately.[10]

Think about driving home from work on a quiet suburban street. What resources will you need? Since you have done it many times before, it is likely that you might just want a working car full of gas. The activity is not very challenging, and the resources you need are limited. Now think about a more challenging situation—say, driving into

VIDEO 6.10

"What would you like to do?" Asking this kind of question empowers students to take charge of their own learning. Jon Mundorf describes his collaborative goal setting process and student-led progress conferences.

▸ http://udlvideo.org/ch6/10

FIG. 6.7. What types of resources will you need in each of these situations?
ILLUSTRATION BY CHRIS VALLO © 2013 CAST, INC.

downtown Manhattan during rush hour to visit to the Empire State Building. What types of resources will you need now? How about a lookout, a good horn, and perhaps even a white flag? In other words, to successfully complete this task you will need more resources.

Similar things happen in a classroom. For some students the goal of learning algebra is like driving into Manhattan, but for others it is just like driving home. Goals should be written to allow all students to be challenged and supported in appropriate ways for them.

Effective goals actively involve learners

Ultimately, we want learners to be able to become self-directed, independent learners. Helping them understand goals and goal setting is one means to that end. One approach is to talk with students about the learning goals of the class and solicit their ideas and feedback for how to achieve those goals. Talking explicitly about the connection between goals and other components of the curriculum (assessment, methods, and materials) will make them more aware of the purposes of classroom and other learning activities.

Even more important, students can be actively involved in goal setting in their personal learning as well. If a broader goal is that all students understand the causes of the U.S. Civil War, students might be encouraged to develop their own more specific learning goals that support the broad goal, e.g., to learn about a particular figure, such as Stephen Douglas, or to understand the role of slavery in the South's agrarian economy.

Planning with Lindsay: Goals

Lindsay's first step is to rewrite her goal for the mixed numbers lesson. Originally, it stated, "Students will demonstrate naming quantities greater than 1 with fractions and mixed numbers by completing a whole-class circle activity and independent work in student journal pages 197–198."

She wants to make this goal more inclusive and reflective of what students need to learn, without unnecessary barriers. According to state standards, students have to understand quantities greater than 1 with fractions and mixed numbers. That is reflected in the first part of her goal. But the second part is too prescriptive. By specifying that all students must take part in the same whole-class activity and must complete specific written worksheets, she inadvertently built in barriers to learning for some of her students—those who had difficulty sitting and listening, and those who had difficulty writing.

Her revised version reads: "Students will demonstrate naming quantities greater than 1 with fractions and mixed numbers." She likes the new goal because it a) offers students flexibility in how to express their knowledge, b) frees her from constrained methods and means, and c) allows her to assess students in flexible ways rather than using worksheets alone.

VIDEO 6.11

Using the UDL lens, Lindsay Tavares realizes that she "boxed herself in" by embedding the means into the goal in her failed math lesson. She explains how UDL helped her create a more effective lesson goal.

▶ http://udlvideo.org/ch6/11

ASSESSMENT

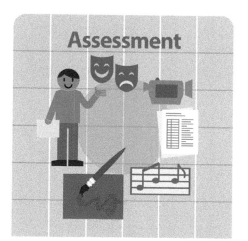

FIG. 6.8. Assessments should be designed to improve both teaching and learning.
ILLUSTRATION BY CHRIS VALLO © 2013 CAST, INC.

Assessments have many different names and purposes. In general, assessment refers to the process of gathering information about a learner's performance to make educational decisions. The two primary types of assessment are 1) formative, which is employed during instruction to gauge a learner's progress and make adjustments in teaching and learning; and 2) summative, which measures educational performance once instruction is completed, usually for accountability purposes.[11]

State-mandated summative tests—some with "high stakes" attached, such as promotion to the next grade or graduation from high school—garner the most attention. Parents, teachers, students, and policy makers all fret about the results. In general, research shows that the increased emphasis on summative assessments has had some positive effects by focusing attention on the need to raise achievement levels for all students.[12]

136   DESIGNING FOR ALL: WHAT IS A UDL CURRICULUM?

Many researchers and practitioners argue that the emphasis on summative assessment, especially in the form of high-stakes testing, has drawn attention and resources away from effective practices and forced educators to "teach to the test" rather than focus on teaching meaningful content and skills in effective ways.[13]

We believe well-crafted, thoughtful summative assessments can be important but only when used in conjunction with an array of other types of assessments designed to improve both teaching and learning. Other examples of summative assessments are unit exams and chapter summaries. The primary purpose is to capture the "big picture:" to gauge the effectiveness of curriculum materials and methods; to compare achievement levels within and across schools, school systems, districts, and states; to evaluate students' knowledge and skills for the purposes of making assignments, including promotion to the next grade or for the awarding of diplomas and degrees. This information may serve as a criterion for admittance to schools and colleges. Such summative tests are intended to provide general information about the effectiveness of teaching and learning in a particular class or district or how a particular student performs in general on specific subject matter relative to his or her peers.

In the UDL model, assessments should point primarily not at student performance but at curriculum performance. Formative assessment tends to be more immediate and informative to instruction than summative assessment because it offers the opportunity to improve teaching and learning during the course of instruction.[14]

The UDL model favors formative assessments that are planned and intentionally part of instruction—assessment by design, in other words. Where students seem to be falling down, the first place to look is to the curriculum. Is there content or a presentation that is limiting learning? How can the curriculum be improved?

Formative assessment gives teachers a concrete and visible means of getting the data they need to inform their instructional decision making. Teachers may use the results from formative assessment as the basis for coaching and goal setting with students, and for helping students build self-regulation abilities.[15] The more overt and transparent the process is, the more it will help, not only teachers, but other stakeholders such as parents, administrators, and others in the community.

VIDEO 6.12
Highlighting the importance of aligning assessments to goals, Grace Meo describes flexible formative and summative approaches.

▸ http://udlvideo.org/ch6/12

VIDEO 6.13
UDL helped Jon Mundorf move from an "autopilot" approach to assessment to a thoughtful set of approaches, tied to goals and addressing learner variability.

▸ http://udlvideo.org/ch6/13

Formative assessment may have a formal structure, such as progress monitoring, a scientifically based practice that is used to assess what students have learned and to evaluate the effectiveness of instruction. It can also be as simple as regular check-ins: "How is the student doing? How am I, as a teacher, doing?"[16]

Quick techniques such as prompting students to summarize a concept in their own words or asking students to articulate a specific question related to the instructional content can provide rich data that allow teachers to gauge their students' understanding and to develop instructional modifications. When teachers are continually evaluating learners and making decisions about instruction based on what they observe, they are rarely surprised by student performance on summative assessments at the end of a unit or year.

Most importantly, explicit formative assessment can provide a basis for individual learners to become more self-aware—more metacognitive—about their learning.[17] By modeling continuous prompts for reflection, teachers can begin to support students in monitoring their own progress. Effective scaffolding and mentorship helps students learn to assess their individual effort and persistence over time and ultimately gain a sense of autonomy over their own learning. The data collected from formative assessment can also be valuable to other teachers and parents as they work with that same learner. Intentional, ongoing assessments benefit not only individuals but also whole school communities.

Strategic Reader, a CAST prototype designed to research the impact of embedded progress monitoring measures in reading instruction, provides an example of explicit formative assessment.[18] For example, timed fill-in-the-blank maze passages are used as one measure of reading comprehension; students chose a topic from two options, read a passage with some words removed, and select missing words from a pull-down menu within a specified time frame. Upon completion of the maze, students immediately receive their scores, including feedback with the correct responses. Student scores on these maze assessments, as well as other measures, are compiled and graphically displayed for students and teachers to view.

> " In the UDL model, assessments point not primarily at student performance but at curriculum performance.

Both teachers and learners use the information from these assessments to evaluate learner strengths, challenges, and to guide revisions to instructional practice. Results from Strategic Reader showed that embedded online progress monitoring has a powerful, positive effect on student comprehension and effective teacher practice: with timely, accurate formative assessments, everyone's performance improved. CAST research continues to build on the strength of these results.

Assessment from a UDL Perspective

From a UDL perspective, effective assessments:

- Are ongoing and focused on learner progress;

- Measure both product and process;

- Are flexible, not fixed;

- Are construct relevant;

- Actively inform and involve learners.

Let's consider these point by point.

Effective assessments are ongoing and focused on learner progress

Ongoing formative assessments provide a comprehensive picture of students' performance, measuring not only their scores at one point in time, but also the evolution of their learning. They also provide teachers with a window into the efficacy of instruction, enabling them to make adjustments to keep students on track toward instructional goals.

Observing and talking to students is a direct way to learn what is working for them and what is not. Ask them what they know and what they are doing. Check to see if they understand the content, are learning the necessary skills, and are engaged in the work. Of course, there are many other ways to learn about student progress such as portfolio assessments, Project-Based Learning, and self-assessment journals. These assessments provide ongoing actionable information about students' learning.

VIDEO 6.14
Individual white boards enable students to respond to classroom questions in their own way and allows teachers to quickly evaluate the effectiveness of their teaching. Teacher Rachel Campbell explains specific benefits.

▶ http://udlvideo.org/ch6/14

VIDEO 6.15

Old-fashioned, score-based report cards provide little helpful information for students and teachers. Jon Mundorf describes a new format that conveys more specific information about student progress.

▸ http://udlvideo.org/ch6/15

Effective assessments measure both product and process

Teachers need to understand not only what students are learning but also how they are learning and under what conditions the students learn best. When teachers are able to gauge how a student's knowledge, skills, and affect change during instruction, they can also develop a good sense about what is causing the change. Teachers can do this by examining the interaction between the student and the learning environment over time, assessing not only performance but also what underlies performance. What cues does the student attend to? What strategies does the student use? What motivates the student? This interaction also involves studying the effects of different aspects of curriculum. What content areas and what kinds of activities are most engaging? What changes in content presentation are helpful? What kinds of feedback and supports help build skills?

Digital learning tools designed with UDL in mind can also help uncover what is most motivating to students. CAST's UDL Studio (http://udlstudio.cast.org), is a free online tool that supports teachers in building curriculum and digging deeper into student performance and behavior.

The analytics feature in UDL Studio enables teachers to assess the overall progress of students as well as the effectiveness of the curriculum. For example, through the use of analytics measures with a UDL Studio lesson, an instructor can see individual student responses as well as the overall the rate of learner response, where it drops, and where there is increased activity and engagement. This information can be used to revise the lesson or instruction in order to encourage continued learner effort over time.

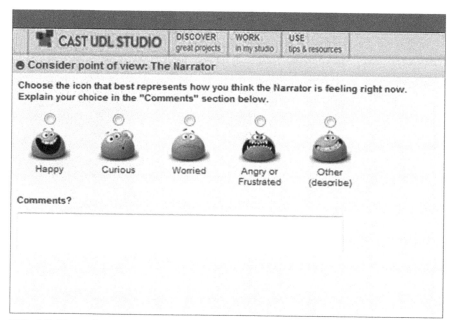

FIG. 6.9. "Rate it" assessments can be used flexibly to assess student engagement or understanding of text. © 2013 CAST, INC.

Effective assessments are flexible, not fixed

When we consider learner variation in affective, recognition, and strategic networks, we realize that in order for assessments to focus accurately on what is being assessed, they need to be adjustable to meet learner variability.[19] To get the most accurate data about what students understand and can do, assessments should not offer only one means of response but should provide multiple opportunities in varied media for learners to demonstrate skills and express themselves.[20]

Digital tools can help instructors to provide options for learner expression for open responses as well as other assessment formats for students to demonstrate skills and understanding (e.g., students may use a graphic organizer or drawing to illustrate understanding of a concept, events, or information). Furthermore, recent research provides strong evidence that creating assessments that are flexible enough to allow for customization (e.g., having context choices that place assessments within student interests, experiences, and backgrounds) increases their relevance for students, heightens student engagement, and can improve student performance.[21] When assessments are ongoing, flexible, and address learner variability, they are most able to accurately represent what learners know and can do.

Effective assessments are construct relevant

Whether formative or summative, assessments need to be on-target to measure the construct—the affect, concept knowledge, or skill—they are intended to measure. It is common for factors that are irrelevant to the goal of an assessment to interfere with its accuracy.[22] For example, requiring a response to be handwritten may conflate handwriting or spelling difficulty with lack of knowledge about a subject. Similarly, requiring students to take a test in a fixed amount of time may conflate stress-management skills with level of understanding.

The development of formative or summative assessment items is analogous to a puzzle of carefully planned components. The end goal is to infer student knowledge, understanding, or mastery of a concept by requiring the student to execute an operation on an item (write, speak, draw, manipulate, etc.). All pieces of the assessment item puzzle must be accurate and in place to truly measure student performance and to accurately measure an identified construct. The listing below

VIDEO 6.16
Poor performance on a single test does not necessarily mean that the student lacks expertise. Teacher Kate Edgren offers innovative options for more accurate assessments.

▶ http://udlvideo.org/ch6/16

VIDEO 6.17
CAST Research Scientist Tracey Hall discusses construct relevance and construct irrelevance in assessment.

▶ http://udlvideo.org/ch6/17

VIDEO 6.18
Tracey Hall highlights five parts of an assessment that are important when designing for construct relevance.

▶ http://udlvideo.org/ch6/18

VIDEO 6.19
When construct irrelevant elements must remain in test items, student supports may be the only fair approach.

▶ http://udlvideo.org/ch6/19

represents components that must be in place to accurately measure an assessment item construct:

- A student interacts with a stimulus, problem, question, or task.

- The assessment item requires action related to the construct.

- A student produces a response that is observable and measurable.

- Teacher/scorer views response and creates a quantitative score.

- That outcome/score is an indicator, by inference, of student knowledge, understanding, or mastery of the construct measured.

If a barrier exists in any component or at any step along the way, the accuracy of the measure, the measurement of the construct, will fail. In other words, you cannot infer student understanding, application, or knowledge of the construct if there is a breakdown at any point in this series. Teachers, who understand this sequence of events, may create better assessment items themselves, more clearly determine what barriers exist for students in pre-made assessment items, and learn to provide accommodations or adaptations to those items thus avoiding barriers that will interfere with interpreting actual student performance.

Because individuals are highly variable in how they learn (see Chapter 3), it would be impossible to design a "fixed" version of an assessment that would yield accurate results for every learner. It will come as no surprise that in a UDL assessment, flexibility in and options for how students interact with the material are key to reducing barriers and maintaining construct relevance.

That is, a UDL assessment provides support where needed, on construct-irrelevant dimensions only, giving all learners a fair chance to show what they feel, know, and can do. Thus if we wanted to assess knowledge about an historical period, we could provide text-to-speech support during the assessment, giving students the option to have materials and directions read aloud so as not to confound word decoding difficulties with limits in student knowledge. Were we assessing oral-reading skill, providing TTS would of course be inappropriate.

If an assessment construct is not clearly defined and construct-irrelevant factors are left unsupported, assessments cannot provide an accurate representation of all students' affect, skills, and comprehension. For example, in a traditional spelling curriculum students take a test at the end of each week on the spelling words studied. In one fourth grade classroom, a teacher gave students lined paper and asked them to number their paper from 1–20 on every other line. Once all the papers were "ready" the teacher dictated each spelling word in isolation, then used the word in a sentence, and finally restated the word alone. Students were expected to write the spelling word on the numbered lines (see Fig. 6.10).

Upon initial review, one may conclude that this student does not know initial and final consonants. She was unable to number the paper correctly, and her letters were largely indecipherable. However, she subvocalized each letter as she wrote, and the teacher, standing nearby, could tell that she had every response correct. Choosing the correct letter was not a challenge for this student. Instead, she faced extreme barriers in the tasks of physically writing text for the words, spatial relations, and page numbering and spacing requirements. These barriers rendered this method of assessing this students' skills invalid. When the teacher recognized the barriers and provided support for the construct-irrelevant factors (an alternate way for the student to express herself), the student was able to demonstrate spelling skills, and the teacher gained a more accurate picture of student skills and growth.

In addition to providing supports for construct-irrelevant factors on existing assessments, we can increase accuracy by designing assessments carefully so as to minimize construct-irrelevant aspects of the item or task. The UDL framework suggests building in supports for affective, recognition, and strategic learning, being careful not to scaffold construct-relevant aspects of the task.

For example, we might want to assess students' progress in identifying thesis statements in written essays, an applied skill. The construct or target skill is the ability to recognize a thesis statement and its component parts. The assessment task might be to highlight all parts of the thesis statements in two essays. Would it be appropriate to provide a rubric or checklist specifying the components of a good thesis statement? Would it be appropriate to provide text-to-speech support?

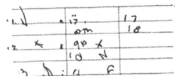

FIG. 6.10. This spelling exam does not accurately represent the student's spelling skills because of barriers in the format of the assessment that are non-construct relevant. © 2013 CAST, INC.

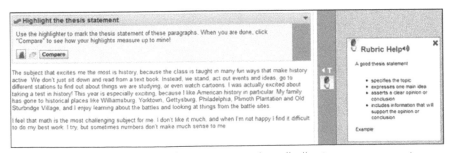

FIG. 6.11. A rubric supports working memory and recall, allowing a more accurate assessment at student skills in applying this knowledge. © 2013 CAST, INC.

Since the construct is an applied skill, it would be appropriate to provide both of these. That way, the assessment would not conflate memory of what makes a good thesis statement with students' ability to identify one in context. Nor would the assessment conflate word decoding with the targeted construct. Support using construct-irrelevant factors (working memory, recall, and word decoding) makes the assessment of the target construct more accurate.

Another example comes from UDL Editions (http://udleditions.cast.org), an online literacy environment supporting reading comprehension development. In an interactive activity engaging students with how authors create different moods, students alter text from *The Call of the Wild* to create a different mood from that of the existing passage. For a segment foreshadowing ominous events, students select one mood from three choices, then select phrases from a drop-down list displayed in the passage that best convey the mood they are aiming for. Because this assessment is focused on the construct of comprehending and applying a writer's craft, a variety of supports for construct-irrelevant factors are provided.

FIG. 6.12. Construct irrelevant supports can reduce barriers such as challenges with decoding, typing, word knowledge, and lack of background knowledge.
© 2013 CAST, INC.

Defining construct relevance and supporting construct-irrelevant factors goes against traditional thinking that in order to be fair and accurate, assessments must be uniform, unsupported, and administered identically to all learners. When we consider learner variability and the goal of construct relevance, it becomes clear that the old idea of "one size fits all" assessment cannot actually work. Inevitably, any one single version contains construct-irrelevant barriers for some students. Without supporting construct-irrelevant factors, it would be impossible to obtain an accurate impression of all students' understanding.[23]

VIDEO 6.20
Rachel Campbell used to grade writing assignments, hand them back, and move on. Here she describes her new approach: supported editing and revision, helping students take charge of their own writing progress.

▸ http://udlvideo.org/ch6/20

FIG. 6.13. Same does not equal fair in assessment. *ILLUSTRATION BY CHRIS VALLO © 2013 CAST, INC.*

Effective assessments actively inform and involve learners

Assessments should provide grist for discussion between teachers and learners—about strengths and weaknesses, ways to let learners take a more proactive role in their education, and about clarification of expectations, frustrations, and renewed purposes. This involves openly sharing feedback in a way that enables both teachers and students to evaluate their work and together figure out ways to teach and learn more effectively.

Ongoing progress monitoring provides students with multiple and varied opportunities to demonstrate skills and understanding. The data produced informs ongoing instruction. Students get timely feedback on how they are doing, their strengths, and areas that need additional work as they interact with curriculum. Teachers also get this information and are able (with students) to review learner progress and make decisions on adjustments to strategies and instructional approaches based on this data.[24]

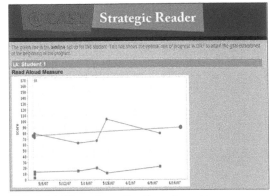

FIG. 6.14. The information from formative assessments can help students and teachers evaluate how well the student is comprehending. *© 2013 CAST, INC.*

VIDEO 6.21
Monitoring their own progress can be empowering for students, especially those previously marginal-

VIDEO 6.22
Based on her UDL goal, Lindsay relies on a variety of approaches, both during and after the lesson, to determine which students can name fractions greater than 1. With UDL, she knows more about her students and their potential for learning expands.

▶ http://udlvideo.org/ch6/22

The research project Monitoring Student Progress Towards Standards in Reading: A Universally Designed Curriculum Based Measurement System conducted by CAST has shown that when students get timely feedback on how they are doing, they are more engaged with improving their learning and more motivated to take action to improve their learning.[25] Likewise, teaching is most effective when instructors are able to obtain and act on feedback about learner progress as they are teaching because they are then able to modify instruction to react to learner needs.

Planning with Lindsay: Assessment

With a new goal in hand, Lindsay turns to assessment, an important aspect of any curriculum. She reminds herself of the goal for her third graders—"Students will demonstrate naming quantities greater than 1 with fractions and mixed numbers"—and thinks about different ways she can measure her students' progress. Originally, Lindsay called for just one form of assessment: students' workbook pages. Using the UDL framework, she identifies two problems with this. First, since the workbook pages require students to paste their shapes, those who struggle with cutting and pasting will be unable to express what they know effectively. Second, since she plans to review the workbook after school—that is, after learning has occurred—this summative assessment will be useless for guiding that day's practice. Lindsay wants to use formative assessment so she can give every student a better chance at success on the assignment.

To better monitor progress and adjust instruction, Lindsay plans to ask guiding questions while walking around the room during student activity time. This will let her see if students are having any difficulties. She hopes to head off misconceptions and provide just-in-time support for those who need it. For all students, she can make suggestions or answer questions to make their performance that much better. She keeps the summative assessment, which she expects will be more successful now, but also builds in time at the end of class for students to share what they have done. This will spark class discussion and give students the opportunity to provide peer feedback, which is engaging for most students.

METHODS

Instructional methods include the decisions, approaches, procedures, and routines that teachers use to accelerate or enhance learning. Because learners vary in the ways they become and stay motivated to learn, comprehend information, and strategically approach tasks, the UDL framework emphasizes the need to employ many kinds of teaching methods. Flexible and varied, these methods are adjusted based on continual monitoring of learner progress.

In our book *Teaching Every Student,* we identified several instructional methods that are effective for addressing learner variability.[26] Tied to the three sets of brain networks discussed in Chapter 3, these methods are as follows:

- To support diverse affective networks:

    - Offer choices of content and tools

    - Offer adjustable levels of challenge

    - Offer choices of rewards

    - Offer choices of learning context

- To support diverse strategic networks:

    - Provide flexible models of skilled performance

    - Provide opportunities to practice with supports

    - Provide ongoing, relevant feedback

    - Offer flexible opportunities for demonstrating skill

- To support diverse recognition networks:

    - Provide multiple examples

    - Highlight critical features

    - Provide multiple media and formats

    - Support background context

These teaching methods are just several examples of the range of practices needed to reach and engage all learners. This list also

FIG. 6.15. The UDL framework emphasizes the need to employ many kinds of teaching methods. *ILLUSTRATION BY CHRIS VALLO © 2013 CAST, INC.*

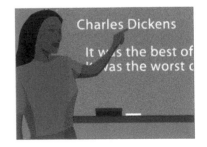

VIDEO 6.23
A single method, such as a lecture, won't reach all learners. Grace Meo describes a variety of viable methods for meeting diverse learners.

▶ http://udlvideo.org/ch6/23

provided a starting point for the development of the UDL Guide-lines (http://www.udlcenter.org/aboutudl/udlguidelines/). We invite you to look at the UDL Guidelines and to visit UDL Connect (http://community.udlcenter.org/), an online community of practice where educators share strategies for UDL implementation.

Methods from a UDL Perspective

According to UDL, effective methods are methods that:

- Can be continually adjusted to meet learner needs;

- Include all students within a collaborative environment.

Let's consider these points more closely.

Effective methods can be continually adjusted to meet learner needs

We have established that variability among learners is ubiquitous. We know that students vary in how they engage in their work, how they understand information, and how they most effectively express their learning. Because these dimensions of variability are largely predictable, we can plan for a range of interests and abilities when considering teaching methods. How can we build in multiple entry points to respond to differences in engagement? How can we scaffold background knowledge for those that need it? Are key expectations and concepts modeled for students in ways they can understand? How can we know what methods are effective for students?

Through careful monitoring of student progress, teachers can respond to students and adjust their teaching as students are learning. Based on observations, informal check-ins, and information from formal formative assessments, teachers can ask, what is helping or hindering learners during instruction? How are engagement, knowledge, and skills advancing, or not? What kinds of adjustments to instructional methods can be made to promote student learning?

For example, when formative assessments disclose that students are having difficulty with vocabulary or a key concept, teachers can take immediate action by doing a short lesson that targets the area and models strategies to support vocabulary growth. If observation

VIDEO 6.24
Offering as many different routes to learning as possible reaches more students. Teacher Rhonda Laswell finds that the UDL Guidelines make this kind of lesson planning easier.

▶ http://udlvideo.org/ch6/24

shows that some students are not engaging with class work, teachers can expand options for how students work (e.g., in small groups, pairs, or individually), thus encouraging engagement and motivation to work through challenging material.

If monitoring student performance shows that some have difficulty with weekly essays, teachers can provide models of proficient performance, or offer other options for expression such as developing a script, recording their thoughts, making a short video, or creating a drawing. Frequently assessing and monitoring student progress in engagement, understanding, and skill development allows teachers to make instructional adjustments and is itself an important method which helps both teacher and student become more expert.

Effective methods include all students within a collaborative environment

One of the ways teachers can help themselves in engaging and reaching all learners is to give students a role in teaching itself. The UDL Guidelines emphasize the importance of fostering collaboration and community in the classroom. Encouraging students to act as mentors to their peers has multiple advantages. Mentors gain confidence and reinforce their skills by teaching others, and peers benefit from individualized coaching.[27]

When carefully structured, peer cooperation can also boost opportunities for sustained engagement. Flexible rather than fixed groupings of students allow better differentiation and multiple roles. Some students enjoy having a role mentoring or leading discussions in the classroom. Others are reluctant to take a leadership role in this context.[28]

Providing multiple and flexible ways for learners to take up a role in teaching is critical for engaging the widest range of students. Creating mentoring partners, grouping students in pairs, small groups, and whole groups are classroom options; class blogs, forums, or other types of electronic discussion boards are technology tools that can be used to encourage widespread student interaction about class work when students are outside of the classroom. A student who is reticent or reluctant to lead inside the class can become a class leader of discussion in a blogging environment.[29]

VIDEO 6.25
Helping all students to grasp concepts requires "reteaching." In her Social Studies class, Molly Fountain chooses a different creative approach each time, engaging different students in different ways.

▶ http://udlvideo.org/ch6/25

VIDEO 6.26
Educator Libby Arthur finds that encouraging students to explore topics in depth and become expert—more expert than the teacher—can be highly motivating and empowering for them and for classmates.

▶ http://udlvideo.org/ch6/26

Using the method of providing varied venues for class interaction gives the widest range of students a voice and the ability to become mentors and leaders. With this range of opportunities to participate and mentor, learners take responsibility not only for their own learning but that of their peers, giving them more investment in ensuring that classroom activities are successful.

Planning with Lindsay: Methods

Having set an effective goal and chosen appropriate assessments, Lindsay considers what methods she can use that will be flexible and engaging and provide students with multiple opportunities to learn.

Her original lesson consisted of certain steps that might raise barriers to learning. She realized that thinking about questions while cutting out shapes might be challenging for many 3rd-graders, that a whole-group circle lesson depended on information presented one way, and that many students would not have the skills to complete their workbook pages.

In revising her lesson, Lindsay chooses to eliminate the paper cutting activity and start by presenting the lesson's questions and then giving a short demonstration for students to discuss. By doing this she can provide options for comprehension by activating students' background knowledge—what they already know about fractions and mixed numbers—and by highlighting critical features in the lesson. Students will then discuss their learning with peers.

Next, she elects to provide students with an activity time, which includes using fraction bars, a computer game, and the original workbook pages. Students choose two of these activities to complete. Lindsay will ask students to discuss which activities they want to do and why. This will help students with self-regulation because it will allow them to hear other students' strategies and thinking. She plans to close with an activity that involves drawing, writing, or recording about the content they learned and their learning process.

Lindsay determines that this would be a good way for students to summarize what they learned and engage in self-reflection on their learning process. A few students will share their experiences back to the whole group in a type of mini-performance.

MATERIALS

Materials encompass the media used to present learning content and the tools and media used by students while learning and to demonstrate knowledge. Within the UDL framework, materials need to be varied and flexible. For engaging with learning, UDL materials offer alternative pathways to success, including choice of content where appropriate, varied levels of support and challenge, and options for recruiting and sustaining interest and motivation.

For conveying conceptual knowledge, UDL materials offer multiple media and embedded, just-in-time supports: such as hyperlinked glossaries, background information, onscreen coaching, etc. For strategic learning and expression of knowledge, UDL materials offer tools and supports needed to access, analyze, organize, synthesize, and demonstrate understanding in varied ways. Of course, the selection of instructional materials is not about picking "the right one" but rather having options available to meet the needs of diverse learners.

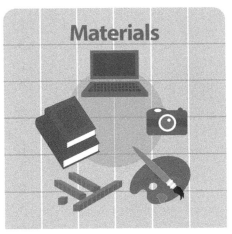

FIG. 6.16. Within the UDL framework, materials need to be varied and flexible.
ILLUSTRATION BY CHRIS VALLO © 2013 CAST, INC.

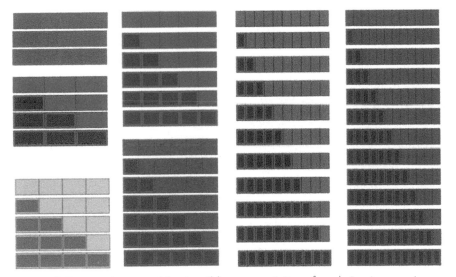

FIG. 6.17. Fraction bars provide a tangible representation of an abstract concept.
© 2013 CAST, INC.

VIDEO 6.27
Offering a variety of learning materials is one way to address the need for multiple representations of content, says CAST's Grace Meo.

▸ http://udlvideo.org/ch6/27

Materials from a UDL Perspective

According to UDL, effective materials are those that:

- Align to goals;

- Engage learners in becoming proactive.

Let's consider each of these points.

Effective materials align to goals

As we have noted, the fixed media of the past, especially print, shaped and even warped our understanding of what it meant to be an effective learner. Essentially, those people who could function well in a print-based environment were favored; we even called them "book smart." Those for whom print presented difficulties—individuals with dyslexia, say, or whose first language was not English, or those who were oriented more toward visual or auditory media—were shut out. Educational materials limited the goals of learning through contingencies and assumptions.

Planning with Lindsay: Materials

In choosing materials for her revised lesson plan, Lindsay first considers any barriers created by the materials she had originally chosen, and, for new materials, she keeps three things in mind. First, she wants the materials to help all students meet the goal. Second, she considers tech-based and nontech solutions. Third, she wants to be sure students can use the materials independently. With these in mind, Lindsay looks to the UDL Guidelines to help her choose materials that would reduce barriers for students.

To support learners who struggle with the mathematical symbols and the vocabulary in the lesson, Lindsay offers the option of using fraction bars (a manipulative; see Fig. 6.17). This provides a tangible representation students could choose to work with. Also among her choices are a computer game and the original workbook activity, offering different appeal and challenge to different learners. Some students prefer the workbook pages because the pages have a predictable, non-threatening format, while other students find using the computer to be more engaging and informative. The digital version also enables students to customize how the information is displayed.

VIDEO 6.28
Allison Posey of CAST's professional learning team makes the case for expanded use of online materials, both to address learner variability and to align with the times.

▸ http://udlvideo.org/ch6/28

VIDEO 6.29
After revising her goal and assessments, Lindsay Tavares opens the door to more varied methods and materials.

▸ http://udlvideo.org/ch6/29

New digital media provide many opportunities for teachers to reach and engage learners. For one thing, well-designed digital media are loaded with just-in-time supports—audio and visual alternatives to text; graphic organizers, checklists, and glossaries; links to background information and source material—that help learners and teachers stay focused on instructional goals. Many digital materials also have built-in options for how students interact with materials—integrated highlighting, electronic note taking, multimodal response options and work logs, as well as other supports.

Increasingly, educators are compiling collections of tools and materials that support UDL and are sharing these resources online. Two compilations of these tools and materials include the web site UDL Resource (http://www.udlresource.com/index.html) which provides links to videos and tools to support using UDL in the classroom, and the Live Binder for Universal Design for Learning (http://www.livebinders.com/play/play/421865), a compilation of resources for building understanding, practice, and implementation of UDL.

UDL Editions by CAST (http://udleditions.cast.org) is a model learning environment that engages diverse readers with flexible supports, scaffolds, and media. These materials show ideas of UDL in practice. The materials in this environment include supports such as text-to-speech, embedded multimedia glossary, background knowledge content, interactive maps, and strategy supports. Each work also includes leveled scaffolding and flexible options for students to interact with texts, including hints, on-screen coaches, and varied activities throughout that provide immediate feedback and support.

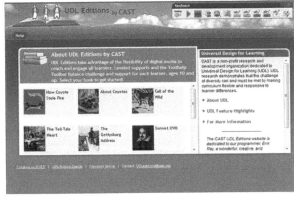

FIG. 6.18. The flexible media and educational scaffolds of CAST UDL Editions supports all learners.
© 2013 CAST, INC.

While UDL Editions shows how materials built with a UDL foundation can support learning, CAST has also developed tools that enable students and educators to create their own materials and lesson plans informed by UDL. CAST UDL Book Builder (http://bookbuilder.cast.org) is an easy-to-use online authoring tool that teachers and students can use to build supported multimedia learning materials.

UDL Studio (http://udlstudio.cast.org) guides users as they create supported multimedia instructional materials with multimodal response options and the ability to track reader progress. The lesson-building tool within UDL Exchange (http://udlexchange.cast.org) provides teachers with UDL supports as they build lesson goals, assessments, methods, and materials. These and other CAST authoring tools support the creation of effective learning environments based on UDL principles. For links to more CAST tools, see http://www.cast.org/learningtools/index.html.

Effective materials help learners be proactive

Just as educators now have many more options in the post-print age, so do learners. The days of knowledge being dispensed through one of two gatekeepers—the teacher or the textbook—are long gone. For example, students can now produce impressive portfolios of work and publish them for classmates and teachers to review and comment on. They can also conduct extensive research online and organize their work in digital notebooks. Students learning about, say, mitosis, can access high-quality, three-dimensional animations that are engaging and much more effective than flat, two-dimensional images and wordy descriptions found in yesterday's books.

New media also provide more opportunities for peer-to-peer mentoring and feedback, giving classmates a greater sense of purpose and

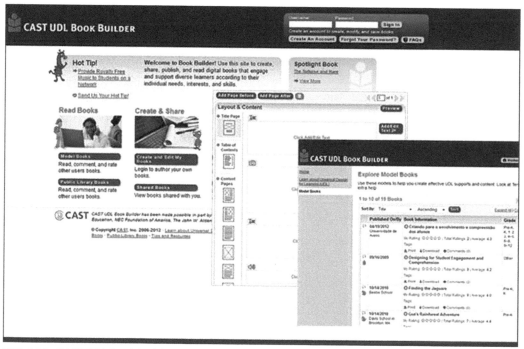

FIG. 6.19. CAST UDL Book Builder supports authors with templates, guides, and models
© 2013 CAST, INC.

responsibility. Many classes now use blogs for sharing and reflection, and students can present their work in multiple ways—by posting audio or video clips, for instance, or by writing and drawing their responses.[30] These sorts of media also provide powerful ways to monitor progress since teachers and learners can look back at entries over time and compare accomplishments before and after.

MAKING A LARGER MOSAIC

Thoughtful curriculum design and implementation are essential for effective teaching and learning, and universal design for learning provides a framework for accomplishing this. However, as we noted in Chapter 2, expertise is not a state of arrival—it's a state of becoming. Educators are learners, too, who reflect on, refine, and improve their practice. All effective teaching is both science and art, requiring practitioners to accept some trial and error, and commit to reflection and revision.

In Chapter 7, education practitioners from various levels and disciplines share some of their experiences in implementing UDL. Their stories are not meant to provide a comprehensive picture of UDL implementation but rather are pieces of a mosaic made from their particular contexts and circumstances. The larger mosaic will be crafted by the individual stories of many thousands of practitioners who take up the challenge of implementing UDL in years to come.

Learning through Practice: Voices from the Field

7

What is practice? Practice may be defined in many ways: as a place arrived at after much experience (i.e., one's professional practice); as habitual performance (i.e., common practice); and as repeated performance (i.e., practice makes perfect).[1] Those who apply theories to specific contexts are called practitioners.

Yet such a description suggests a dull and routinized picture of practice, leaving the impression that theories and ideas are largely shaped outside of practice and then applied. However, as we have learned in the evolution of UDL, the relationship between theory and practice is much more dynamic and interactive. The real world, with its messiness and complexity, is where we learn whether a theory actually works. In turn, what happens in practice shapes evolving theoretical concepts. As significant as the learning sciences are for UDL theory, practice is an essential source in the development of UDL.

Social learning theorists Etienne Wenger and Jean Lave, who coined the term "communities of practice," align with this dynamic view of practice.[2] They suggest that practice is about "learning in the context of our lived experience of participation in the world"[3] and that "knowing is a function of actively engaging in pursuits and with people that matter to us."[4] Wenger "refers not just to local events of engagement in certain activities with certain people, but to a more encompassing process of being active participants in the practices of social communities and constructing identities in relation to these communities."[5]

Communities of practice, an important vehicle for practice-based learning, are groups of practitioners that come together because they care about similar things. They bring practices to their collective learning, share them, discuss them, and work together to improve them.[6] Practice-based learning has always been essential in the professions and trades. For example, medical rounds enable experienced practitioners to hone their knowledge and skills throughout their careers while also sharing their knowledge with medical students and early-career professionals. Case-based learning and apprenticeships are essential formative tools in business and the legal professions. In crafts and trades, learners also observe one another's practices closely in order to improve.

Many of the expert learners and teachers whose stories are told in this book honed their skills in formal or informal communities of practice. For example, revisit Feliks, expert Rubik's Cube solver, as he sets a new world record. The sense of community around him is palpable—his competitors are also his teachers and vice versa. Solving the Cube in a record 5 seconds was not the result of Feliks working on his own but rather with the support of a robust community of "cubers" who shared tricks of the trade, taught each other to see new patterns and try new strategies, goaded each other to practice for hours and hours, and celebrated victories together. The "cubing" community (aided in no small part by the kind of sharing enabled by social media) has become an expert learning system.

Expert learning systems employ practice-based learning in part because they require tacit knowledge. Tacit knowledge is internalized knowledge that is not readily explained or codified but rather is exhibited through actions to achieve a goal. Tacit knowledge is often specific to a culture or community, and is about knowing *how to do* something rather than knowing *what something is*. Knowledge is gained through a process of close observation of others, tryout with feedback, and collective practice. Importantly, learners need to be able to express what they know in meaningful ways for this tacit knowledge exchange to take place. While tacit knowledge is clearly linked closely with strategic learning, affect plays an equally key role. A sense of shared experience, specific feedback, challenge and support from peers—all are essential for a successful community of practice.[7]

> ❝ Practice-based learning has always been essential in the professions and trades.

What is at the heart of UDL practice, and how is community essential? Broadly, teachers need to make sense of the curriculum—the goals, methods, materials, and assessments—they will use to support learning. While focus is often placed on the processes of setting goals, using methods, teaching materials, and conducting assessments, it is practices that teachers engage in that bring processes to life.[8] Thus, practice is a way of making sense out of processes and figuring out how processes are wielded in the context of real classrooms by teachers supporting many different kinds of learners.

Integrating UDL into curriculum practices involves planning from the outset for systematic variability among learners along key dimensions: how they perceive information, how they act on it, and how they are motivated by a task. Whether teachers are explicitly designing curriculum or choosing and assembling curricular elements, the practice of UDL rests on addressing learner variability through its three principles. How does community support "making sense" of curriculum? A community of practice brings members' experience of practice, both individual and collective, to their shared learning experience, and in this way they collectively make sense of processes, translate these into classroom practices, align new practices with existing ones, and reshape or eliminate practices that no longer allow new processes to work. In this way, the community takes responsibility for pushing practice and processes forward.

> **A true community of practice supports affective, recognition, and strategic learning in its participants.**

Teachers, of course, are learners too. Effective learning involves deep participation rather than mere performance. Practices require selective and dynamic use of knowledge—*discernment* of what is and is not useful *in context*. If we invite educators to shape practices that incorporate UDL in ways that are meaningful to them and to their students, and to communicate actively with each other, we have a good chance of enabling both of them to benefit from and to shape UDL as it develops. A true community of practice supports affective, recognition, and strategic learning in its participants.[9]

In the hope of building a foundation for a thriving UDL community of practice, we present here the voices of practitioners who, coming from a variety of teaching and learning environments, share their experiences. Our contributors include special and regular educators in K–12, college graduate and informal learning settings, teacher educators, and administrators. They share their ideas and experiences putting UDL into practice in different settings.

We have grouped their stories according to the following focus and emphasis: UDL Curriculum Design Practices, Making Instructional Adjustments with UDL, Building a UDL Culture, and UDL Professional Development. These represent a sample of the many practitioners from whom we have been privileged to learn. All make UDL their own by putting it to the test in their teaching, and each brings unique perspective and skill. We hope that their stories are kindling for reflection, conversation, and improved practice.

UDL CURRICULUM DESIGN PRACTICES

UDL emphasizes the importance of planning in advance—of designing curriculum that, from the outset, assumes and plans for the natural variability of diverse learners. Elfreda Blue, an associate professor of special education at Hofstra University in Hempstead, NY, teaches graduate students seeking certification in elementary and secondary education. She reflects on how she learned from experience the necessity of designing curriculum to meet the needs of all learners:

> *Before I began applying UDL, I remember one graduate student [who] was a shy young lady who loved students but was extremely nervous about making an in-class presentation of her final project. She begged and pleaded not to do the in-class presentation. I refused permission. When the time for her presentation arrived, she burst into tears and excused herself from the room. She needed options for expression and communication in order to successfully complete the task before her. Most importantly, she needed options for enhancing her own capacity to complete the task before her. Since that experience, I have encountered numerous graduate students who want to negotiate options for completing assignments which make room for their strengths.*
>
> *[Today] we use reflections to support expression and engagement. Learners are required to submit weekly metacognitive statements, which reflect their thinking about concepts and learning experiences. A favorite resource we use is VoiceThread*

VOICE FROM THE FIELD
Elfreda Blue—an associate professor of special education at Hofstra University in Hempstead, NY—teaches graduate students in elementary and secondary education how to apply UDL in planning to teach all learners.

(www.voicethread.com), which enables a community of individuals to contribute voice comments about an image/concept. Students can record their comments using audio, video, or typed text. For class presentations, students who are not comfortable speaking in front of others can type their comments or read them onto VoiceThread. To diminish frustration and guide thinking with written media, sentence starters are provided for those who choose to use them. What learners write is the metacognitive content that is personally relevant, reflecting changes in their thinking, nagging questions, and new possibilities they realize.

Doing reflections this way gives learners more control over the specifics of their reflection. Initial practice with both resources is incorporated into instruction to minimize threat and challenges to novice users of course resources. This experience varies the demand of metacognitive response so that learners experience varying "degrees of freedom for acceptable performance" ([UDL Guidelines] Checkpoint 8.2). They learn alternative ways of completing a specific task and are challenged in the process. By the end of the semester, more learners embrace the new resource and become avid users of VoiceThread.

The UDL Guidelines can provide a helpful framework for curriculum design. Rather than a checklist to be "completed," the guidelines are meant to be used to shape instructional goals, assessments, methods, and materials in the context of existing classroom practices. They guide; they do not dictate. Educator Allison Posey shares some examples of how the UDL Guidelines helped her in the design of a high school psychology course:

The UDL Guidelines permeate every aspect of my teaching, from how I give feedback to a student to how I plan assessments and design labs. I find that if I design a thoughtful lesson, students feel success in their learning process and take risks they may not have been willing to do otherwise. I also benefit from a well-designed lesson as it is clear to me what we have covered and what I expect from the students. I work the hardest the first time I design a lesson; then it gets much easier and I even find that I do not have to re-teach the content as often: most students get it the first time. As with every class-room, I have a diverse group of learners and our school also has a very large international population to support.

For me the most important UDL Guidelines involve the affective networks. For example, Guideline 8.4 discusses how we can give meaningful feedback to help students persist through challenges. By high school, many students have labeled themselves as "science" or "not science" students. It is difficult to break down this barrier and encourage them [to see] that it is more about the effort they put into the work that matters. By giving "growth mindset feedback," as Carol Dweck describes, and giving specific praise for the process, not just the final product, students build confidence and success toward their ability in science. I encourage students to see science as a process that they are building and learning, not just something they are "good" or "not good" at.

In terms of supporting the recognition networks (Guidelines 1–3), I aim to incorporate only material which is most pertinent towards my overarching goal. For example, consider a psychology lesson about development. I want students to know some of the most prevalent theorists and their descriptions of development (specifically, psychologists Kohlberg, Piaget, and Erikson). But I have to be specific about which parts of the theorist's research I want them to know—for example that the way a two year-old child perceives and responds to the world is very different than that of a 10-year-old child. I make it very clear from the beginning of our discussion what content students needed to know, even quantifying that there are three theorists to learn about or that there are four stages of Piaget's theory. We discuss the theories in class and I provide a PowerPoint that summarizes the main points we discussed in class and highlights the key concepts from the textbook reading. We link to YouTube videos and other online content. This provides multiple access points to the content and serves as a resource students can use on their own, outside of class, to reflect upon and study. Through supporting the representation principle, I find more students engage with the material.

> **“** I work the hardest the first time I design a lesson; then it gets much easier and I even find that I do not have to re-teach the content as often: most students get it the first time.

VOICE FROM THE FIELD
Allison Posey used the UDL Guidelines to design an inclusive high school psychology course. Allison is now a professional development associate at CAST.

The UDL Guidelines also help with strategic supports (Guidelines 4–6). I decided the most meaningful way to learn about development would be for students to consider their own developmental trajectory. The final assignment required students to map out a timeline that included Kohlberg's, Piaget's, and Erikson's theories and corresponding ages. However, students could choose how they wanted to make their timeline and they were encouraged to use their own experiences as examples to support the content from the theories.

I provided a model example from my life (supporting Guideline 5), but the students made a wide range of unique projects that went above and beyond my model example. Some students included photos of themselves as young children, and they had quotations to go with the photo to show their understanding of the theorist. Other students wrote bulleted descriptions about their developmental milestones. One student made "pop up" images to go along with the events in her life, while another student built a sort of 3D turntable for her development.

When we shared the timelines as a class, the discussion was rich with a wide variety of personal examples but also contained a lot of psychologically relevant content. It was clear that students understood the key developmental milestones outlined by the major theorists. For example, students could describe not only what Kohlberg's first level of moral development was, but they also had a meaningful example from their life to relate to, which supports the affective networks (Guidelines 7–9).

MAKING INSTRUCTIONAL ADJUSTMENTS

UDL offers educators and students an opportunity to come to know one another well so they can continually negotiate ways to balance demands and resources. In every classroom there are behaviors, beliefs, strategies, and approaches for teaching and learning at play. If you were to ask a UDL-oriented teacher, "What do you do when X happens?" he would most likely answer: "It depends." Classroom adjustments are about following learning as it unfolds and adapting teaching practices to meet learners' needs at the point of instruction.

For example, a teacher seeing a student struggle with a math problem might make a decision to pull in another student that is relatively good at math but even better at encouraging her classmate rather than pull in the top math student in the class to explain the problem in a new way to the other student. This teacher would have exhibited a deep understanding of the UDL guidelines, their interplay, and their relevance in context because she recognized that in that moment, for that student, providing an alternative for recruiting interest was more important than providing the perfect alternative representation of the math problem. Yet for UDL to be actualized, the student must decide how she will use that engagement scaffold, if at all.

The more UDL is part of classroom practices and the classroom culture, the easier it is likely to be for teachers to think in a UDL way in the moment and for students to respond to UDL approaches on offer. Students are different in how they perceive information, act on it, and become engaged in a learning environment. If systematic variability has been thought about ahead of time and if teachers can think in a UDL way to make classroom adjustments, these differences can be accommodated to advantage. When students can show the range of their variability they will explore, try out, fail, seek assistance from teachers, seek assistance from peers, and do many things in order to make new knowledge meaningful. This unpredictable variability is evidence that students themselves are engaged in sense-making by creating their own classroom practices for learning.

> " If systematic variability has been thought about ahead of time, individual differences can be accommodated to advantage.

Mindy Johnson, an instructional designer at CAST and a veteran instructor at the Boston Museum of Science's overnight program for kids, offers an example. The overnight program is designed for school groups, scouting troops, and other after-school programs. Groups spend the evening at the museum and engage in workshops and activities and then spend the night. Mindy's work as an instructor has been informed by UDL. Mindy is assigned a workshop space (typically an exhibit space in the museum) and is responsible for planning and implementing an approximately hour-long, hands-on science-related workshop with an assigned group of participants ranging in age from

6–13 and for monitoring and coordinating an assigned drop-in activity during snack time:

> Typically, the only information we're given before an Overnight is our assigned exhibit space for our workshops, approximately how many kids and how many adults we'll have in our groups, and where we've been assigned for the drop-in activities. As much as we can ahead of time, we plan for the variability we will most certainly encounter on any given evening, but we also practice UDL "on-the-fly" as circumstances arise in one of our workshops or activities that we can't necessarily anticipate.
>
> Making decisions based on this whole-group interaction and practicing UDL in the moment takes a lot of practice, experience, and sometimes trial and error. The flexibility to really get to know your participants or students isn't part of the overnight schedule, so we have to make quick decisions based on very little information. I don't purport to be flawless in my quick analysis, but I try to appraise whether a participant might benefit from one-on-one support from an adult or could succeed as a leader in smaller group situations. For the most part, I can tell a lot about learners by watching body language, paying attention to how each participant interacts with others, observing behavior when I ask questions of the group, and using varied methods for full group, small group, and one-to-one interactions within the first activity.
>
> Some examples of how I might use my knowledge of the UDL Guidelines to quickly assess and address behaviors and decisions by particular participants include—
>
> - If a participant seems shy, unwilling to participate, clings to a chaperone, or seems otherwise an "outsider" to the group, I test the waters by asking that participant a question during the group activity. If he seems receptive to participating, I might decide to have him be my "special materials helper" for the night or my partner for an activity if there are an uneven number of participants. One-on-one attention often brings these learners out of their shells, and they're much more likely to join in the group activities.

VOICE FROM THE FIELD
Mindy Johnson, an instructional designer at CAST and a veteran instructor at the Boston Museum of Science's Overnight Program for kids, shares insights into how UDL applies in an informal learning context.

> Disengagement can be a symptom of something else—fear of the unexpected, discomfort with new situations, shyness, or fear that he'll seem stupid in front of his peers.

- *If a participant seems outspoken, jumping up to volunteer for demonstrations, is unusually loud, or otherwise having challenges with impulse control, I might acknowledge her eagerness to participate, but not call on her every time I ask a question or ask for a volunteer, even if she is the only one raising her hand. I might also model or comment on models of behavior I'd prefer to see, saying something like, "Wow, I really like the way this person is sitting quietly with her hand raised to be my volunteer. When I choose my volunteers, that's what I'm looking for." When it comes to the rest of the activities, I might establish and remind all of the participants about making sure everyone gets a chance to speak and join in. In this way, the excited but a bit over-eager participant feels validated in her wonderful enthusiasm, but also has models and reminders of appropriate collaborative and group behavior.*

- *If a participant seems disengaged, bored, distracted, or distracting to others, I might go stand or sit near that participant. If he's off-task, usually just my presence can be a cue to get back on track. If he's bored, I might ask some quiet questions or point out something interesting about the activity that I haven't told the whole group. Disengagement can be a symptom of something else—fear of the unexpected, discomfort with new situations, shyness, or fear that he'll seem "stupid" in front of his peers. Providing some individual attention can alleviate anxiety, especially if [doing so is] approached in a quiet, non-threatening, non-punitive manner.*

- *For some of the activities, I have the participants create something and present it to the full group. Besides establishing the characteristics of an effective audience with the participants before the group presentations begin (e.g., actively listening with ears, eyes, and body; raising hands to ask questions; applauding at the end of a presentation), I also keep an eye on participants who might seem shy or otherwise anxious about standing in front of the whole group to present. I always let the participants know that it* is absolutely not a requirement for any of them to stand in front of the audience during these presentations, but I do encourage it.

- *However, if a participant seems particularly averse to the attention, I might ask her privately if she minds if I tell the audience that she was part of creating the project during her group's presentation, or I might ask if she'd like to sit more toward the front of the audience during her group's presentation so that if they have questions only she can answer she'll be right there to help out. Speaking in front of groups is difficult for a lot of people, but it's also a time to receive acknowledgement from your peers of your hard work and effort. Trying to find creative ways to allow participants to enjoy the benefits of this acknowledgement without increasing threat or anxiety is difficult, but well worth the effort made when a proud smile creeps over that person's face."*

Even in a formal classroom, UDL enables educators to reconsider curriculum regularly, based on learner progress and feedback. Alexis Reid teaches grades 4–6 at Kingsley Montessori School in Boston. She first learned about UDL while earning her MA in Applied Developmental and Educational Psychology at Boston College. She shares her insights from putting UDL theory into practice:

Following student assessments we were able to have conferences with students to present the data collected and discuss students' own individual goals (both academic and social) and [we also] keep a record for both teachers and students to monitor progress. Student self-assessment is one of the capstones of our work. Through this process, students identify their comfort level with different content, discuss needed or desired challenges, and [determine] next steps within the curricular unit. Furthermore, we teachers are able to acknowledge student goals and compare them to our observations and intended curricular goals through the scope and sequence of our curriculum. We are able approach each curricular unit through the lens of what our students need to provide a differentiated approach to meet their needs within identified conceptual units."

VOICE FROM THE FIELD
Alexis Reid, who teaches grades 4-6 at Kingsley Montessori School in Boston, shares the importance of student progress and feedback in UDL-based teaching.

BUILDING A UDL CULTURE

In many schools and districts, building a UDL culture may begin with one person—a teacher, perhaps, who has learned about UDL and hopes it can transform the way education is practiced in meaningful ways. In other cases, schools or district administrators may decide that UDL should become an institutional initiative. In either case, building a collaborative culture of educators is essential to the effective implementation of UDL.

Veteran special educator Katherine Bishop works closely with her colleagues to ensure that students at Lake Park Elementary in Oklahoma City participate in the general education curriculum while receiving all the services and supports they need. Since 2003, she has been applying the principles of UDL to her instructional planning and practice:

> *UDL is still a fairly new concept in my district as well as state, and I'm continually challenged to find ways to help my colleagues incorporate UDL into their classrooms. I work collaboratively with my fellow teaching colleagues in professional learning communities where we are able to build on each other's strengths to provide a learning environment that every student needs and deserves. We use our professional learning community to help us reflect on our teaching and to explore new ways to address learner variability. Our professional learning community provides us with the structure to make sure that we are incorporating UDL from the very beginning of our planning to the assessment stage. Professional learning communities provide the needed support for all learning environments.*

> *For example, just recently, as we reflected on various ways to incorporate the principles of UDL, we realized that we tended to provide students with the opportunity for multiple means of expression in only a few subject areas. That reflection prompted us to make a concerted effort to provide opportunities of expression in other subject areas as well.*

Key to building a UDL culture is securing the necessary resources and agreement to support UDL implementation across stakeholder groups. Practitioners need to feel that UDL is something that they

VOICE FROM THE FIELD

Katherine Bishop, a special educator at Lake Park Elementary in Oklahoma City, works closely with her colleagues to build a professional learning community that supports UDL's aspirations to provide greater learning opportunities for all.

can manage to do within existing constraints. If UDL implementation is a priority then opportunities need to be made for it. It can't be just added on to existing demands.

Candyce Engquist Rennegarbe, a faculty member at Tacoma (WA) Community College, has managed the college's UDL Project since 2007. Here she describes critical planning elements for a new UDL project:

> *By far, strong administrative support is the most important element. Our Vice President of Academic and Student Affairs has supported this project with funding and personal support since we started. He has used Achieving the Dream funds and reserve funds; no major grant funding has been accessed to fund this project. We give release time to a faculty member to be the Project Manager as an affordable way to make sure there is sustained leadership. In addition, we also found that voluntary participation by interdisciplinary faculty members is critical. We have also secured stipends for faculty and mentors and have involved the instructional research department from the beginning. We have a strong cross-disciplinary advisory team (Dean/VP of Instruction, Access Services, E-Learning, Developmental Studies, Professional Development, Student Services, Faculty), and strong support for building technology resources on campus.*

VOICE FROM THE FIELD
Candyce Engquist Rennegarbe, a faculty member at Tacoma (WA) Community College, has managed the college's UDL Project since 2007 and knows the importance of securing resources and administration support.

Another post-secondary instructor, Liz Berquist of Towson University's College of Education in Maryland, shares ways of incorporating the UDL mindset into her instruction of pre-service teachers and student teachers in Baltimore County and Baltimore City public schools. She emphasizes the importance of modeling UDL for other teachers:

> *I have found that when teaching pre-service and in-service teachers about UDL it is essential to model UDL. Teachers are the toughest audience—and rightly so! If a teacher educator does not model and practice the framework that they are presenting, pre-service and in-service teachers will find it difficult to buy in! In order to encourage people to think outside the box, move out of their comfort zone, and try something new, we need to demonstrate that the alternative framework being presented is useful and beneficial. The best way to demonstrate UDL's power is to let students experience it themselves.*

VOICE FROM THE FIELD
Liz Berquist of Towson University's College of Education in Maryland shares the importance of modeling UDL instruction for preservice teachers and student-teachers.

UDL PROFESSIONAL DEVELOPMENT

An essential part of building a UDL culture is providing effective professional development and training so that staff can grow as a team in their knowledge of and experience with UDL. Rather than "one size fits all" professional development—or "one-off" workshops—the best professional development approaches foster the kinds of sustained and vibrant communities of practice discussed in the opening paragraphs of this chapter. Here is how Bartholomew Consolidated School Corporation (BCSC) district in Columbus, Indiana has done this through its UDL professional development as described by the district's current special education director, George van Horn, and its former UDL coordinator, Loui Lord Nelson:

> BCSC serves approximately 11,000 students in a diverse community 35 miles south of Indianapolis. In 2002, the district began experimenting with UDL as a practical means to address the needs of all learners in an inclusive environment. What began as a special education initiative is now applied across the general curriculum.
>
> UDL provides a framework within which schools can investigate or build any curriculum. The curriculum is not altered; rather, it is enhanced through the teacher's application of the UDL principles. Because UDL aligns with BCSC's beliefs in providing a structure for clear instructional practices while addressing a specific instructional goal, we have adopted UDL as the instructional framework for curriculum and instruction throughout our district.
>
> In an effort to expand support for teachers and the implementation of UDL, BCSC has identified a district leadership team for UDL. This team, structured as a professional learning community (PLC), consists of secondary department chairs, PBIS coaches, ICT facilitators, literacy coaches and math coaches. This PLC receives ongoing training from the UDL Director and provides support to teachers across the school corporation. The staff members involved in the PLC provide building-based, in-class support to teachers for the implementation of UDL.
>
> In addition, self-identified and principal-identified UDL leaders have emerged in each building. Some of these leaders are

VOICE FROM THE FIELD
George van Horn, special education director for Bartholomew Consolidated School Corporation in Columbus, IN, describes the need for a deep commitment to providing PD and training to teachers over time.

special education teachers but most are not. UDL is equally applied at the high school level and the elementary level and those teachers who focus on the three principles when designing their lessons share that their lessons are more interesting and engaging. They feel confident they are reaching more students as proven by student outcomes.

While it is possible that the application of UDL corporation-wide could have taken less time, BCSC is confident that the time spent defining how students are supported, collecting specific data to investigate accompanying questions, and taking the time to understand how the needs of individual students often overlap with the needs of their peers helped teachers and administrators understand the necessity for UDL.

In a different kind of setting—the California State University (CSU) system—Emiliano Ayala and Brett Christie are leaders in UDL implementation as Project Director and Project Coordinator, respectively, of the Ensuring Access through Collaboration and Technology Project (EnACT). Funded by the U.S. Office of Post-Secondary Education, EnACT provides sustained, robust support for post-secondary faculty throughout the CSU system to improve teaching and learning through UDL.

Both Dr. Ayala and Dr. Christie have rich experience in instructional design, the use of educational technology, and effective undergraduate teaching practices. In UDL, they both report finding a framework that better informs their work in terms of how to meet the needs of diverse learners. They write:

The EnACT grants were designed strategically to address the issues of scalability and sustainability. To this end, we crafted a model of faculty professional development that could be adopted by any institution of higher education (IHE). We wanted to avoid the utilization of or need for unique campus-based strengths or personnel, which would limit the implementation and success of our faculty development model. Capitalizing on our relationship with the CSU Faculty Development Council, Dr. Christie provided us access to 23 campuses, where we have supported direct UDL training and information dissemination. UDL has been well received by the CSU Faculty

Development Council, which spearheads faculty development activities across the CSU.

Recognizing that "one shot" faculty development activities would not likely lead to substantive UDL course changes, we coupled UDL training with the creation of Faculty Learning Communities (FLC). Thus, after receiving UDL training and related resources, small groups of faculty from various disciplines met regularly on their respective campuses to explore and implement UDL changes to selected courses. These professional learning communities were instrumental in helping faculty apply UDL to their courses.

Based on our evaluation data, the formation and support of our campus-based FLC groups remain one specific practice that was lauded by our project faculty. Specifically, while stand-alone UDL workshops were generally seen as positive contributors to UDL implementation, after participation in FLC meetings all project faculty (100%) agreed or strongly agreed that coupling UDL workshops with FLC participation significantly enhanced their understanding and efficacy of UDL implementation. Evidence shows that FLCs increase faculty interest in teaching and learning and provide safety and support for faculty to investigate, attempt, assess, and adopt newer methods. The process includes frequent seminars and activities that provide learning, development, scholarship of teaching and learning insight, and community building. Thus, FLC members work together to reflect on their teaching and provide critical feedback to each other when attempting to infuse UDL into their courses.

In scaling our efforts, faculty participants have often requested models or examples of how other faculty members have implemented UDL into their courses. In support of this need, we developed numerous online video case stories that feature faculty exemplars and student reactions to UDL-inspired course changes. Finally, in support of broader dissemination (scale), our project web site, UDL-Universe, offers all our project resources which are structured so that faculty developers can implement UDL on their respective campuses. Embedded in *this structure are information, resources, and faculty developer "tips" that draw on our project highlights, experiences, and successes.*

Project personnel have supported the development of numerous research-based tools that support faculty in implementing UDL at the post-secondary level. One key tool is the UDL Syllabus Rubric. While universal design for learning often focuses on in-process course delivery, assignments, and assessments, syllabi can provide a larger context for how and where UDL can strengthen our teaching effectiveness.

A well-designed syllabus establishes clear communication between instructor and students and provides the necessary information and resources to promote active, purposeful, and effective learning. Thus, we see syllabi serving as road maps that define the content and context of learning. In order to support faculty [in learning] how to frame a course with UDL principles in mind, EnACT~PTD constructed, evaluated, and revised a UDL Syllabus Rubric.

This rubric and its elements are based on multiple years of research on UDL and course design and delivery. In our development and evaluation efforts, we included extensive input from both instructors and students. As a result, the UDL Syllabus Rubric reflects elements that are considered important to all stakeholders. Faculty are encouraged to use the UDL Syllabus Rubric as a way to reflect upon their current syllabus design and move toward adopting strategies that result in a syllabus that better communicates to and supports all learners.

VOICES FROM THE FIELD
University educators—Emiliano Ayala, an associate dean of the College of Professional Studies at Humboldt State University, and Brett Christie, Director of the Center for Teaching and Professional Development at Sonoma State— discuss the importance of ongoing, sustained professional development in the UDL implementation efforts in that system.

LET'S HEAR FROM YOU

We have offered a sampling of the practices with which educators throughout the educational landscape are now experimenting. The contexts and practices discussed are disparate—necessarily so, since education is a process which, involving highly variable people with variable needs and circumstances, is necessarily diverse, even messy. However, as we have emphasized throughout this book, such variability and diversity is an asset—not a liability—in building strong educational environments as long as we design those environments and curricula to leverage these strengths.

In other chapters, we have drawn connections between UDL theory and practice. In doing so, we've considered some of the ways in which educators, students, and other stakeholders in teaching and learning make UDL meaningful in the context of their classrooms, schools, and communities. Making UDL meaningful includes determining how it is to be interwoven with effective practices already in use and with the people who use them. And because what is meaningful is determined by context, no two implementations of UDL will look the same. Much like our lived experience in the world, practices also change, and so how UDL looks in a given setting is likely to vary over time.

Some of the contributors to this chapter have initiated online conversations through UDL Connect. We ask you to share your own experiences in the online forum, joining a budding community of UDL practice. You can also add your reflections and work to a growing collection of examples and ideas from the field. Visit http://community.udlcenter.org/ to join UDL Connect. Your feedback will influence the future of UDL and may be featured in future revisions of this book.

Afterword

Just as we were finalizing this first edition of this book, *The Economist* newsmagazine featured what it called the arrival of "the long-overdue technological revolution" in education. "At its heart is the idea of moving from 'one-size-fits-all' education to a more personalized approach ..." wrote the editors, "while the job of classroom teachers moves from orator to coach."[1]

The magazine highlighted numerous advances in current educational technology:

- Wireless devices that are both powerful and portable;

- Teaching programs with built-in progress monitoring capabilities that enable content to be tailored on the fly to suit individual needs;

- Systems to gather and crunch data that can be used to support decision making;

- Game technologies to make instructional presentation more engaging and rewarding;

- Increased access at all socioeconomic levels to state-of-the-art devices such as iPads and high-speed Internet service.

Interestingly, the report falls into a familiar pattern of education reform reportage: treating new and dazzling instruments of change as the change itself, as though personalization and flexibility is primarily a technical question, one of means more than methods or motivation. What's missing is a focus on people and process.

We, like the magazine's editors, are optimistic that new technologies will help improve teaching and learning for all people. In fact, *Universal Design for Learning: Theory & Practice* is filled with examples of how technologies can support a revolution in the way education is practiced. But the instruments of change will only be effective when they are deployed as part of an intentional and scientific plan. Fundamental improvements in education will happen by design, not by accident. UDL provides a structure and process for aligning change to sound, scientific education practice.

Of course, since education must be human-centered to be effective, any meaningful plan for change will begin and end with people. For that reason, *Universal Design for Learning: Theory & Practice* focuses on what we can learn from people in order to better teach and learn:

- How can we support every person in becoming an expert learner and/or an expert teacher—motivated, knowledgeable, and skillful?

- What does the natural variability of all individuals tell us about teaching and learning?

- How can we design learning environments that celebrate, accommodate, and build on the intrinsic variability of people?

- How can we create systems for education that get smarter with time by building on the feedback of individuals?

UDL recognizes that all effective teaching and learning is both science and art, requiring practitioners to accept some trial and error. For that reason, we have put forth a vision of education where those who form the heart of any education enterprise—the learners, teachers, and those who support them—have incentives and opportunities to contribute to a continual process of improvement.

We invite you to contribute to a maturing, collective understanding of UDL theory and practice. Share your stories, best practices, research, opinions, and aspirations at http://community.udlcenter.org or by email at UDLtheorypractice@cast.org. In doing so, you will help ensure that *Universal Design for Learning: Theory & Practice* evolves and improves, just as we expect education will when UDL principles and approaches are taken to scale.

Notes

Consult the References for full citations.

CHAPTER 1

1. To learn more about Apple's introduction of GUI computers, see the Macintosh 1984 page at the Obsolete Technology web site at http://oldcomputers. net/macintosh.html.

2. Microsoft's corporate goal was to put "A computer on every desk and in every home, all running Microsoft software." See Microsoft's research history: http://research.microsoft.com/en-us/um/redmond/about/timeline.

3. See the National Commission on Excellence in Education's 1983 report *A Nation at Risk: The Imperative for Educational Reform*, published by the U.S. Department of Education. For reflections on the report and its impact on U.S. education, read David Gordon's *A Nation Reformed? American Education 20 Years After A Nation at Risk* (Cambridge, MA: Harvard Education Press, 2003).

4. In 1973, Congress passed Section 504 of the Rehabilitation Act, a seminal civil rights law prohibiting discrimination on the basis of disability (29 U.S.C. § 794). Two years later, Congress passed the Education for All Handicapped Children Act of 1975, which later became the Individuals with Disabilities Education Act (IDEA) (20 U.S.C. §§ 1400 et seq.). For more information and a guide to these laws, see www.ada.gov/cguide.htm.

5. Of course, the child and the curriculum are just two definable limits on what is really a process or interaction. That is, success occurs when the "child" and the "curriculum" successfully interact. This will require that the child and the curriculum are always self-improving relative to each other. John Dewey's monograph *The Child and the Curriculum* discusses this false dichotomy between focusing on the curriculum and focusing on the child. Find it online at www.gutenberg.org/ebooks/29259.

6. See Burke (1978).

7. Rose, Daley, & Rose (2011).

8. When we talk about students "in the margins" we mean students who, during testing, would perform much higher or much lower than other students. We don't think this is the "right" way to measure learning, and we certainly don't advocate for placing students in the middle or in the margins as these "placements" are simply artifacts of the test and don't mean anything about the students' skills, ways of acquiring and expressing information, thoughts, or feelings. Students in the margins are also students who might "feel" in the margins perhaps because of how they are treated by others, because of the inaccessibility of school and curriculum, or because school simply doesn't work for them.

9. See David H. Rose and Anne Meyer's *Teaching Every Student in the Digital Age: Universal Design for Learning* (Alexandria, VA: ASCD, 2002). The book is available online at www.cast.org/teachingeverystudent/ideas/tes/.

10. The medical model is predicated on the idea that assessment measures are objective; that it is possible to evaluate a learner out of context and without input from others who know the learner; and that once you have diagnosed and labeled a condition, the diagnosis pertains over time.

11. CAST's Peggy Coyne and colleagues (2012) examined the effect of a technology-based UDL approach to literacy instruction on the reading achievement of 16 students with significant intellectual disabilities in grades K–2. During the program, nine teachers received training in research-based literacy practices and five received training in the UDL approach to literacy instruction. Coyne, et al. found that the group using UDL approaches made significantly greater gains on a standardized reading comprehension test than the group using other reading methods.

12. Martha Minow (1990) has contrasted the "abnormal persons approach," according to which individuals are classified as "normal" or "abnormal," with the "traditional rights-analysis" approach, according to which a group that has previously been the target of discrimination is provided equal treatment. Minow has proposed a third approach, the "social-relations" approach, whereby difference is viewed in the context of the relationships between individuals labeled "abnormal" or "different" and those who do the labeling.

13. To understand more about social learning, see Bandura (1977), Ryan & Deci (2000), Zimmerman & Kitsantas (2000; 2005).

14. To learn more about the neglect of emotion in education and psychological research in favor of behaviorism and cognitivism see Fischer & Tangney (1995) and Frijda (1986). See also Damasio (2003), LeDoux (1994), and Zambo & Brem (2004) to learn how cognitive science is integrating affect.

15. See Dennett (1995).

16. Davidson (2008) shows that long-term or short-term practice of meditation results in different levels of activity in brain regions associated with, for example, attention, anxiety, depression, fear, and anger, as well as the body's ability to heal itself. Davidson discusses how these functional changes may be caused by changes in the brain's physical structures. See also Lutz et al. (2004).

17. Bandura (1977) suggests that we learn everything vicariously before we learn it directly because it is the only way we can "acquire large, integrated patterns of behavior without having to form them tediously by trial and error. The harder the task to be learned, the more we must learn it through observation first. Developing a sense of self-efficacy, the perception that one can accomplish a task, is essential for accomplishing particularly challenging learning tasks" (p. 12). See also Ford (1992) and Ryan & Deci (1991; 2000).

18. Duncan (2011).

19. See "Attributes of Effective Formative Assessment," published by the Council of Chief State School Officers (CCSSO). Quotation from page 3.

20. The Higher Education Opportunity Act of 2008 states: " (24) UNIVERSAL DESIGN FOR LEARNING.—The term 'universal design for learning' means a scientifically valid frame- work for guiding educational practice that—"(A) provides flexibility in the ways information is presented, in the ways students respond or demonstrate knowledge and skills, and in the ways students are engaged; and "(B) reduces barriers in instruction, provides appropriate accommodations, supports, and challenges, and maintains high achievement expectations for all students, including students with disabilities and students who are limited English proficient." Online at www.gpo.gov/fdsys/pkg/PLAW-110publ315/pdf/PLAW-110publ315.pdf. It

21. National Education Technology Plan (2010), pp. 14-18.

22. UDL is mentioned in the appendix to the Common Core State Standards (2012).UDL is also mentioned in the U.S. Department of Education's Blueprint for Reform: Reauthorization of the Elementary and Secondary Education Act (ESEA) (www2.ed.gov/policy/elsec/leg/blueprint/index.html) and Summary of Considerations to Strengthen State Requests for ESEA Flexibility (www.ed.gov/sites/default/files/considerations-strengthen.pdf). The concept of universal design was also discussed in the 2011 Report of the Advisory Commission on Accessible Instructional Materials for Students with Disabilities (www2.ed.gov/about/bdscomm/list/aim/index.html).

23. Explore the CAST UDL Book Builder library at http://bookbuilder.cast.org/library.php. You can find books in different languages by using the drop-down menu next to "Book Language."

CHAPTER 2

1. Early ideas of expertise held that there must be some type of genetic advantage or even divine intervention that made an expert particularly skillful at his or her craft (Galton 1869/1979; Murray, 1989). As researchers tried and failed to prove this theory, new ideas about expertise formed. Expertise tends to be domain specific, and it has more to do with time spent on targeted practice rather than a genetic predisposition (Chi, Glaser, & Farr, 1988; Ericsson & Smith, 1991). Thus, although some research suggests that becoming an expert takes approximately 10 years (e.g., Chase & Simon, 1973; Hayes, 1981), other work suggests that experts are always adapting to their environment and to new circumstances, which requires them to shift and evolve over time (Ericsson, Krampe, & Tesch-Romer, 1993). See Ericsson, Charness, Feltovich, & Hoffman (2006) for a comprehensive overview of expertise development in a variety of fields, and Bloom & Sosniak (1985) on expertise development in an education context.

2. Competencies include Competency Based Education (CBE), a functional approach to education (Savage, 1993) that emerged in the United States in the 1970s. CBE "advocates defining educational goals in terms of precise measurable descriptions of knowledge, skills, and behaviors students should possess at the end of a course of study" (Richard & Rogers as cited in Weddel, 2006, p. 2). Also see Stout & Smith (1986).

3. For more on "speed Cubers," see John Nadler's article in *Time* (Oct. 9, 2007), online at www.time.com/time/arts/article/0,8599,1669535,00.html.

4. Feliks broke this record in the 2011 Melbourne Winter Open. He improved on his own record twice more, including at the Australian Nationals in September 2013.

5. What Feliks is doing is deliberate practice. He might not have reached absolute "expert" status, but he is certainly an expert at learning and improving. Ericsson, Krampe, & Tesch-Romer (1993) estimated that it took approximately 10,000 hours of specific and purposeful practice for musicians to become experts and about 2,000 to be considered an amateur. Richman, Gobet, Staszewski, & Simon (1996), among others, have estimated that this development takes upwards of 10 years.

6. In Bloom's *Developing Talent in Young People* (1985), contributor Lauren Sosniak discussed becoming engaged and motivated as the first phase of learning to become an expert. This first phase of learning, which occurs over a period of years, is generally categorized as being fun and playful rather than being rigorous and strict (discipline comes later in the process).

7. Lave & Wenger (1991) suggest that learning can be measured in terms of its usefulness. Assessing how well individuals can practice new skills and

knowledge in the contexts where they are needed becomes the measure of what has been learned. Thus, learning happens through practice and learning in a community pushes practice forward.

8. Differences in pattern perception and their effects on behavioral fluency, depth of processing, and memory are well documented as differences between novices and experts. They have been documented in many fields as disparate as chess (Chase & Simon, 1973; Gobet & Charness, 2006) and teaching (Berliner, 2001; Sternberg & Horvath, 1995).

9. There is a great deal of literature on the various types of motivation in relation to learning and how individuals motivate themselves for learning and for practice during the learning process. See Dweck (2000) and Wentzel & Wigfield (2009). Zimmerman & Campillo (2003) postulated the phases of self-regulated performance. Their three phases were the forethought phase, the performance phase, and the self-reflection phase. One important step within the forethought phase that they included, along with goal-setting, was "strategic planning." This then lead to more strategic performance and reflection.

10. The way in which motor skills become automatized relates to procedural memory—the memory of how to do things. To learn more about procedural memory and procedural learning, see Maddox & Ashby (2004), who describe the nature of the neural system that impacts procedural learning.

11. Chi (2006) summarized the ways that experts excel and some ways they are limited. She included strategy as one of the ways experts excel. Other ways they excel included generating solutions, detecting and recognizing patterns, employing qualitative analysis, monitoring, capitalizing on opportunities, and minimizing cognitive effort. Ways experts can fall short: Their expertise is domain limited, they can be over-confident, they can fail to recall surface details, they can rely too much on context cues, they can be inflexible, they can fail to relate easily to novices, and they can be overly biased.

12. Feldon (2007) summarized differences in knowledge between experts and novices including differences in types of knowledge, how experts used the knowledge they already had, and how they integrated new knowledge.

13. A great summary of these strategies can be found at http://rubikscube.info/. They include methods for beginners as well as advanced users. The beginner methods even include aspects of scaffolding.

14. Learn more about Konstantin Datz and his Rubik's Cube for the blind at www.konstantindatz.de and www.yankodesign.com/2010/03/17/color-rubik-Cube-for-the-blind.

15. In 2009, the National Federation of the Blind (NFB) estimated that the number of blind individuals learning to read braille could be as low as 10 percent.

16. Garfinkel (2011) points out that the all-white Rubik's Cube prevents blind and sighted people from experiencing the solving process together.

17. See Rose & Meyer (2002), p. 70. This book is online at www.cast.org/teachingeverystudent/ideas/tes/.

18. See Dweck (1999).

19. Mason Barney wrote about his experiences in *Edutopia* (May 1, 1998). See www.edutopia.org/leaping-over-walls.

20. The term "essential for some, good for all" was coined by the Ontario (Canada) Ministry of Education in its 2005 report on literacy and numeracy instruction for students with special education needs. A review of schools across six regions produced the unexpected finding that strategies, including UDL, that were originally targeted at students with special needs turned out to be useful for many other students.

21. Lave & Wenger (1991) argued that all learning must be situated within context, especially the social context.

22. See the white paper "21st Century Learning Environments" by the Partnership for 21st Century Skills: www.p21.org/storage/documents/le_white_paper-1.pdf.

23. For more information on systemic change, see Elmore (1996), Fullan (2002, 2007), and Hargreaves (2011).

24. Meadows (2008).

25. Positive Behavioral Interventions and Supports is described by the U.S. Department of Education as "a framework or approach for assisting school personnel in adopting and organizing evidence-based behavioral interventions into an integrated continuum that enhances academic and social behavior outcomes for all students. PBIS is not a packaged curriculum, scripted intervention, or manualized strategy. PBIS is a prevention-oriented way for school personnel to (a) organize evidence-based practices, (b) improve their implementation of those practices, and (c) maximize academic and social behavior outcomes for students. PBIS supports the success of all students." See www.pbis.org for more information.

26. Ertmer & Newby (1996) describe the ways in which expert learners are strategic, reflective, and self-regulated.

27. Price (2005).

28. Fischer (2011).

29. The "science of teaching" is not just one thing. There are numerous theories of pedagogy, the study of the process of teaching. For a list of different pedagogies, see http://serc.carleton.edu/sp/library/pedagogies.html. DuFour & colleagues (2008) explain that, "Public school educators in the United

States are now required to do something they have never before been asked to accomplish: ensure high levels of learning for all students. This mandate is not only unprecedented; it is at odds with the original goal of schools. The notion of all students learning at high levels would have been inconceivable to the pioneers of public education. If contemporary educators are to make significant progress in meeting this new challenge, they must first recognize that the institutions in which they work were not designed to accomplish the task of learning for all. They must then acknowledge the need to make fundamental changes in both the practices of their schools and the assumptions that drive those practices."

See also Fischer & Rose (2001) who explain that students do not all learn in the same fashion and students' performance depends on the context of their learning. Since a primary goal of education is to improve the functional-level performance, understanding students' learning differences can help educators teach better and improve student performance.

30. Learning communities or communities of continuous inquiry and improvement are groups in which teachers and administrators seek and share learning and then act on the results of that learning. The goal of such communities is to improve their skills as professionals (Astuto, et al. as cited in Hord, 1997). Researchers have found that as teachers engage in collaborative inquiry, they gain a shared vision and are able to use that vision to make decisions around teaching and learning (Isaacson & Bamburg, 1992).

CHAPTER 3

1. For an explanation of the challenges of group comparisons between older and younger individuals, see Samanez-Larkin & D'Esposito (2008). These researchers found there were differential patterns of activation in the two groups, but the performances on these tasks did not vary. Further, the variability that did exist in task performance were not reflected in the differences in brain activation. Therefore, this study shows some of the interesting possibilities and clear weaknesses of looking at differences between groups.

    For an example of a study looking at group differences in terms of language, in this case monolinguals and bilinguals, see Kovelman, Baker, & Petitto (2008). These researchers looked not only at group differences but also thought about how these differences can help us understand human language more generally.

2. Raven's Progression Matrices is a nonverbal metric of reasoning and problem solving. It is comprised of 60 items which are divided into 5 sets of increasing complexity. The individual taking the test is asked to look at a matrix of

geometric designs. One cell of the matrix is left blank and there are 6 or 8 options of designs to complete the matrix (Raven, Raven, & Court, 1998).

3. Souliéres & colleagues (2009) explain that they used functional magnetic resonance imaging to explore the neural bases problem solving using Raven's Progressive Matrices (RPM) for individuals with and without autism. These authors also used a visually similar pattern matching comparison task. "In the RPM task, autistics performed with similar accuracy, but with shorter response times, compared to their non-autistic controls. In both the entire sample and a sub-sample of participants additionally matched on RPM performance to control for potential response time confounds, neural activity was similar in both groups for the pattern matching task. However, for the RPM task, autistics displayed relatively increased task-related activity in extrastriate areas (BA18), and decreased activity in the lateral prefrontal cortex (BA9) and the medial posterior parietal cortex (BA7)" (p. 4082).

4. Samson, Mottron, Soulières, & Zeffiro (2011) found that people with autism have enhanced perceptual abilities in certain domains including when engaged in visual search, visual discrimination, and embedded figure detection. They also show stronger physiological engagement of the visual system. These researchers performed a meta-analysis of published functional imaging studies to determine whether autism is associated with enhanced activity during visual tasks (specifically during processing of faces, objects, and words). They found more activity in autistics compared to non-autistics in temporal, occipital, and parietal regions and less activity in the frontal cortex. They considered how autism may be characterized by "enhanced functional resource allocation in regions associated with visual processing and expertise."

   In general, studies that show differences between brains of people with and without autism attribute the differences to negative outcomes. For example, Spencer & colleagues (2011) showed differences in the neural response to facial expression of emotion between unaffected siblings of individuals with autism and neurotypical controls with no family history of autism. They used fMRI to examine response to happy versus neutral faces. They found significant reduction within brain areas implicated in empathy and face processing in the sibling group as opposed to the control group. Though the groups did not have differences in their response time or accuracy behaviorally (i.e., not on the neuroscience task), the authors interpreted these differences in the sibling group as negative since there is a familial link to autism.

5. Mottron (2011) called on researchers to stop thinking about brain structure differences as "deficiencies" and instead recognize that many people with autism have abilities and qualities that are not just different but superior to people without autism. Thus, autism can be an advantage in some areas.

6. Mottron (2011) discusses the way in which Dawson is fact-oriented (a bottom-up thinker) while he, Mottron, is a top-down thinker. The way Dawson thinks and processes information is, of course, unique to her. However, many people with autism are detail oriented in some fashion. For example, Temple Grandin, who has autism and is an advocate for people with autism, explains that "All minds of the autism spectrum are detail-oriented, but how they specialize varies. By questioning many people both on and off the spectrum, I have learned that there are three different types of specialized thinking: 1) Visual thinking—thinking in pictures, like mine; 2) Music and Math thinking; 3) Verbal logic thinking." (Grandin, undated, p. 1). As Mottron (2011) explains, for a big-picture thinker like himself, this type of thinking is tremendously help-ful: "Because data and facts are paramount to autistic people, they tend not to get bogged down by the career politics that can sidetrack even the best scientists" (p. 35).

7. Studying and mapping the brain has become increasingly popular. For a straightforward and clear explanation of white matter and cortex, see Koch's (2012) website http://mybrainnotes.com/brain-cortex-neurons.html.

8. For more about white matter, see Fields (2008), who explains that white matter coordinates how well the brain regions work together.

9. Zimmer (2011) shows how researchers use other systems (for example, com-puter chips) to better understand the brain. He discusses how understanding the neural networks can help us understand the function of the brain better. This image is from Gigandet et al (2008).

10. According to Genesee (2000), "Learning by the brain is about making con-nections within the brain and between the brain and the outside world." Bernard (n.d.) writes: "This means that when people repeatedly practice an activity or access a memory, their neural networks—groups of neurons that fire together, creating electrochemical pathways—shape themselves accord-ing to that activity or memory. When people stop practicing new things, the brain will eventually eliminate, or 'prune,' the connecting cells that formed the pathways. Like in a system of freeways connecting various cities, the more cars going to certain destination, the wider the road that carries them needs to be. The fewer cars traveling that way, however, the fewer lanes are needed."

11. See Hebb (1949).

12. For a complete explanation of the three networks and how they are spatially distinguishable, see Rose & Meyer (1998, 2002).

13. Hall (1998) explains that neurons can be classified based on their function. Sensory neurons carry messages from sensory receptors to the spinal cord and the brain. Motor neurons control the movement of muscles, and inter-neurons form connections with other neurons.

14. Discussing the relationship between thought and speech, Vygotsky (1962) explains that there are several requirements for helping others understand when we are attempting to convey information, including understanding what we're going to use to communicate, how we're going to communicate it, and why we're trying to communicate.

15. Bloom's Taxonomy is a classification of learning objectives for education first proposed in 1956 by a committee of educators led by Benjamin Bloom. His first handbook dealt with the cognitive domain, while subsequent handbooks addressed the affective and psychomotor domains. See also Morshead (1965) and Simpson (1972).

16. Clayton Christensen's *The Innovator's Dilemma* (2003) describes disruptive innovation—a framework that describes how a product or service first begins at the bottom of a market and moves "up market," becoming a key product or service and displacing its competitors. More recently, Christensen has used the framework of disruptive innovation to provide solutions around issues in education: *Disrupting Class* (2008) and *The Innovator's Prescription* (2009).

17. Fair & colleagues (2009) explain that specific discrete areas of the brain (cerebral cortex) perform specific types of processing. These specific areas are organized into networks that interact to support cognitive functions.

18. Warren McCulloch (1945) was perhaps one of the first people who explained heterarchy in the brain. He explained that the brain was ordered, but it was not ordered hierarchically. This finding has been used both to help us better understand the brain as well as networks in computer design.

19. There are many examples of brain-environment interactions. For more information on how experience (environment) may impact the development of neural networks, see Posner & Rothbart (2005), available at www.sciencedirect.com/science/article/pii/S1364661305000264.

20. Cohen, Garcia, Apfel, & Master (2006) conducted two randomized field experiments to test an intervention designed to improve minority student performance. Since the risk of confirming a negative stereotype of one's group can negatively impact academic performance in minority students, they tested if this threat could be reduced by having students in the study reaffirm their self-adequacy. They used an in-class writing assignment and found that it improved African American students' grades (reducing the racial achievement gap by 40%—see page 1308 for an explanation of how the performance gap was reduced).

    Three years later, Cohen & colleagues (2009) conducted a follow-up study. They showed that after two years, the grade point average of African Americans was, on average, raised by 0.24 grade points. The lowest-achieving students showed grade improvements of 0.41 points. Importantly, affective improvements were also seen.

21. Steele & Aronson (1995) describe a study whereby African American and European American college students were asked to take the verbal portion of the Graduate Record Examination (GRE) and were told that the test accurately measured intellectual performance. In a subsequent experiment they did not lead participants to believe that the test accurately measured intellectual performance. They explained that by changing the instructions African-American students became less concerned about confirming negative stereotypes about their group.

    Stereotype threat has been written about extensively since then. For example, studies have been done that show stereotype threat can impact women when engaged in math tasks and entrepreneurship situations (e.g., Gupta & Bhawe, 2007; Inzlict & Ben-Seev, 2000), men when engaged in social sensitivity tests (Koenig & Egly, 2005). More recently, researchers have begun looking at the neural basis of stereotype threat (e.g., Wraga, Helt, Jacobs, & Sullivan, 2006) and continue to think about how to reduce stereotype threat so that learning can happen for all students (Boucher, Rydell, Van Loo, & Rydell, 2012).

22. See the *Journal of Social Cognitive and Affective Neuroscience* and the journal *Emotion*. Both address not just on emotion itself but the link to social phenomena and emotional functioning overall.

23. Daley (2010).

24. Rosen & Donley (2006) describe a number of lesion studies, particularly studies of primates as well as studies of humans as related to fear response.

25. Murphy & Zajonc (1993) affirmed a previous finding that positive and negative affective responses "can be evoked with minimal stimulus input and virtually no cognitive processing" (p. 723). They further found that when affective network response is elicited outside of conscious awareness, brain response is diffuse and a specific location cannot be specified.

26. Storbeck & Clore (2007) argue that "affect is not independent from cognition, that affect is not primary to cognition, nor is affect automatically elicited." They provide multiple examples of the affect-cognition connection including that the inability to use affective feedback following brain damage impacts judgment and decision making.

    Another powerful example provided by these authors is a description of the connections between the amygdala and the visual cortex. They explain, "One of the primary pathways of the visual cortex is to the amygdala, and the role of the amygdala is in part to determine the urgency of the stimulus, which eventuates in the marking of apparently important experiences hormonally and in terms of experienced arousal" (p. 1226).

The authors cite multiple other researchers who discuss the affect-cognition link. For example, to learn about facial recognition and affect see Allison, Puce, & McCarthy (2000), Kanwisher, McDermott, & Chun (1997), and Narumoto & colleagues (2001).

27. Multiple studies show how sound habituation occurs. Researchers have investigated habituation in animals as well as humans. Many studies have been carried out with infants, including that of Zelazo, Brody, & Chaika (1984) who showed habituation to sound in very young (77.5 hours old) infants.

28. Jamieson, Mendes, Blackstock, & Schmader (2009). In addition to the immediate differences in scores, somewhat unexpectedly—with no further intervention—this group of students also out-performed the comparison group on the math GRE more than a month later. Additionally, the effect held only on the math section of the GRE for both the practice and actual tests; researchers continue to examine why the verbal section was less affected but suggest that this has to do with the different kinds of cognitive skills needed for math compared to the specific kinds of skills examined on the verbal section of this test.

29. See Rosalie Fink (1995, 1998).

30. For this and other visual phenomena and optical illusions, see Michael Bach's website, www.michaelbach.de/ot/.

31. For more information, see Mountcastle (1998) and Gazzaniga (1995). Roland & Zilles (1998) provide evidence for the multiple areas in the brain that are responsible for visual processing, explaining that if two brain tasks make use of one or several identical or largely overlapping fields, "they cannot be performed simultaneously without errors or increases in latency" (p. 87). Evidence for this kind of interference in the visual cortical areas suggests that there are multiple parts of the brain contribute to visual processing. Grill-Spector (2003) explains that multiple object-selective regions in the brain respond when individuals view objects but not when they view pictures of non-objects (e.g., textures, noise, or highly scrambled objects). Objects, houses, and scenes activate ventral and dorsal regions, faces and animals activate mainly lateral and ventral regions.

32. See Bandura (1977). In addition, Ford's (1992) principle of equifinality echoes Bandura, claiming that motivating humans is best done through demonstrating that there are a "variety of pathways to a goal in complexly organized systems" (p. 257). When many students can't accomplish a task, all students lose an important opportunity to build self-efficacy because there are not enough viable models to provide a reasonable basis for believing that a given task can be accomplished.

33. One of the first scientific experiments on word recognition was conducted by James McKeen Cattell in 1886. Subjects were briefly exposed to words or letters and asked to report what they saw. They did better reporting words than even single letters! Cattell concluded: "We do not therefore perceive separately the letters of which a word is composed, but [rather we perceive] the word as a whole" (Cattell as cited in Snow & Juel, 2005, p. 503).

    Adams (1994) discusses the simultaneous top-down and bottom-up processes that occur during reading in addition to the specifics of the word superiority effect.

34. Witelson, Kigar, & Harvey (1999) explained that Einstein's brain was the same size and weight as most brains, and it had approximately the same number of neurons in the frontal or temporal lobes. But the region related to visual-spatial cognition, mathematical thought, and motor imagery were different. His inferior parietal lobes were wider than normal by about 15 percent on both sides. His supramarginal gyrus, found within the inferior parietal lobe, was not found to be divided by a sulcus, which may have allowed for more efficient connectivity of axons.

35. To learn more about the interactions between perception and affect, see Bhalla, & Proffitt's (1999) article, "Visual-motor recalibration in geographical slant perception" in the *Journal of Experimental Psychology: Human Perception and Performance* and Riener, Stefanucci, Proffitt, & Clore's (2011) work on the effect of mood on the "perception of geographical slant."

36. See Michel and colleagues 1972 paper "Cognitive and attentional mechanisms in delay of gratification," from the *Journal of Personality and Social Psychology, 21*(2), 204-218.

37. For more on the motor homunculus, see Schwerin's article at http://brain-connection.positscience.com/the-anatomy-of-movement/

38. Elbert and colleagues (1995) explain that expert violinists have between two and three times the area of cortex devoted to their left fingers than non-violinists. They also have a larger link between two sides of their brain dealing with motor coordination than people who are not violinists (Schlaug & colleagues, 1995).

39. Weiss & Jeannerod (1998) explain that motor coordination is realized by the nervous system at multiple levels. They explore how they have looked at individuals with motor impairments to see the role of different motor areas in coordination. They explain that, for example, the coordination between limbs requires a higher-order coordinating mechanism that organizes lower-level movements.

40. For a thorough review of executive function networks, see Carpenter, Just, & Reichle (2000). These authors explain that "neuroimaging studies suggest

that some constituent functions, such as maintaining information in active form and manipulating it, are not discretely localized in prefrontal regions." (p. 195). Some executive functioning processes, including goal management, have effects in several cortical regions, including posterior regions. Thus, the cortical organization of working memory and executive functions is dynamic and distributed.

41.   Burbaud & colleagues (2000) used functional magnetic resonance imaging (fMRI) to investigate the impact of cognitive strategies on cortical activation during mental calculation. They found that though a common corpus of brain areas was activated during this mental calculation in their 29 participants, differences appeared between participants based on their use of cognitive strategies. For example, individuals using verbal strategy showed activation in their left dorsolateral frontal cortex, but those using visual strategy showed a bilateral activation in the prefrontal cortex and activation in the left inferior parietal cortex.

42.   See Vince Tinto's work on persistence in higher education (1993, 1997, 1998).

43.   Ibid.

CHAPTER 4

1.   To see more about the diverse uses of the GPS see http://www.gps.gov.

2.   See Chapter 2 of this book, as well as Ertmer & Newby (1996) who explain how learners' knowledge of cognitive, motivational, and environmental strategies can help them gain control of their own learning processes. Further, Sternberg (2003) argues that expert learners—people who are flexible thinkers and who can use their knowledge in multiple and novel ways—need to be creative, analytical, and practical. In teaching students to think in these ways we prepare them to be flexible thinkers and for a variety of roles.

3.   The quotation is from Robinson (2009), p. 238. See also his TED Talks (www.ted.com/speakers/sir_ken_robinson.html) which address why education systems need to nurture creativity and why we need to shift to personalized learning environments where children can be creative.

4.   The idea of individualized instruction is pervasive throughout education. As use of instructional technology has increased, numerous theories around how technology can improve teachers' ability to individualize education have emerged. Allan Collins (1991), for example, argues that individualization will cause a shift in education to more constructivists approaches. More recently, educators in higher education have become increasingly interested in the possibility of using technology to make courses in colleges and universities more personalized (e.g., Inan, Flores, & Grant, 2010).

5. See Rappolt-Schlichtmann, Daley, & Rose's *A Research Reader in Universal Design for Learning* (Cambridge, MA: Harvard Education Press, 2012).

6. Andrews & colleagues (2000) wrote about a growing divide within the field of special education. One component of this divide was noted to be the different conceptualizations of disability that exist in the special education world. They explain that while some, described as Incrementalists, assume that a deficit exists within the individual, others, called Reconceptualists, understand that disability is a social construction. Though Reconceptualists understand the physiological aspects of disabilities, they feel that one becomes disabled only by the context in which one functions. Baglieri & colleagues (2011) explain that there are multiple examples that show us how disability is contextual. From thinking about how, in a class graded on a curve, a significant proportion of the students in that class will receive poor grades despite how much they do or do not learn to considering how a disability label might change depending on the state or even the district in which a child labeled with a disability attends school.

7. A good example of this is the case of reading difficulties, specifically dyslexia. Researchers understand that there is variability within the group of individuals diagnosed with dyslexia. Thus, several subtypes have been recognized. However, not all researchers agree on the subtype descriptions. For example, some consider that there are three different subtypes: orthographic (Roberts & Mather, 1997), surface (Caplan, 1987), and phonological (Snowling, 1981). Others argue that subtypes include dysphonetic and dyseidetic, while still others include phonological processing deficits, naming speed deficits, and double deficits (Wolf, 1999; Wolf et al., 2002). Thus, though some of these subtypes overlap, and though variability is understood, the purpose of labeling this variability is to more closely identify a type (or subtype) of disability and therefore the way to "treat" these individuals.

    Another example consists of those that want to teach to different "learning styles." In this theory it is argued that there are four primary learning styles: visual, auditory, read-write, and kinesthetic. People who give credence to this theory believe it is necessary to identify a person's learning style and to teach to each students' individual style (e.g., Dunn & Dunn, 1978; Sprenger, 2003).

8. In addition to the example of teaching to learning styles, we can think about specific programs that exist in many schools for "gifted and talented" students. For example, in New York City, students are tested as early as pre-kindergarten for entry into specific programs for students who score at the 90th percentile or above on two tests that are said to measure intellectual capability and school readiness. Within these programs, students are grouped together and receive specific instruction targeted to their learning needs.

There are many ways that teachers individualize instruction. For students on individualized educational programs (IEPs), which are designed for individuals with disabilities, instruction is particularly targeted to each student. Each IEP is designed for one student and the learning needs of that individual student are considered as the document is developed (Office of Special Education and Rehabilitative Services, U.S. Department of Education, 2000). However, IEP goals have a remedial focus and they do not address students' ability to progress in the general curriculum or ultimately to function once they leave school. Teachers who individualize in general education classrooms may use differentiated instruction (DI). These teachers do not make individual lesson plans for each student, but they do think deeply about individual student's learning needs, how the student learns best, and what the students' interests are. Within individualized instruction content, process, products, and the learning environment may be differentiated. There are many ways that differentiation can take place. For example, students may have the option to use materials at various levels, they may use individual rubrics as they work through a task, and task lists that contain in-common work for the whole class and work that addresses individual needs of students may be utilized. All of these elements require teachers to plan for specific students in their classrooms.

9. For more on T. V. Raman, see Helft (2009).

10. Ontario (2005).

11. See "New Law Will Expand TV Captions for the Deaf" in the New York Times, (October 16, 1990). Online at www.nytimes.com/1990/10/16/us/new-law-will-expand-tv-captions-for-the-deaf.html

12. One of the most common causes of such performance variation is believed to be attributable to distraction theory. Distraction theory suggests that experiencing stress, pressure, anxiety, or worries diverts an individual's attention from the task at hand and prevents the focus necessary to perform at a high level. See Beilock & Carr (2001).

13. For more information on the three networks, see Rose & Meyer (2002). See also Roland & Zilles (1998) for more information on the recognition network. Gopher (1996) discusses skill instruction builds the strategic network. Burbaud & colleagues (2000) provide insights about individual differences in neural activation patterns depending on the cognitive strategy used during problem solving. See Ledoux (1989) to learn about the connections between emotion and cognition in the brain. Ledoux explains that though emotion and cognition are mediated by separate systems of the brain, these systems interact in such a way that affect can influence cognition and cognition can influence affect.

14. The UDL Guidelines are an articulation of the UDL framework. The UDL Guidelines, Version 2.0 (CAST, 2011) are available at www.udlcenter.org/aboutudl/udlguidelines. The Guidelines are useful for educators who plans lessons or units or who develop curricula. They are particularly useful for educators attempting to identify the barriers in existing curricula.

15. The use of "desirable difficulties" can be attributed to Bjork (1994). He explains: "Conditions of practice that appear optimal during instruction can fail to support long-term retention and transfer of knowledge and, remarkably, conditions that introduce difficulties for the learner—and appear to slow the rate of the learning—can enhance long-term retention and transfer."

16. Over the past several years success in algebra has been consistently linked to success in postsecondary education and the workforce. For example, The National Mathematics Advisor Panel explains that "A strong grounding in high school mathematics through Algebra II or higher correlates powerfully with access to college, graduation from college, and earnings in the top quartile of income from employment" (2008, p. xii).

17. Algebra 1 courses have been described as "an unmitigated disaster for most students" by the National Research Council (1998) and more recently as a class that makes can make students math-aversive (Russell M. Gersten as cited in Cavanagh, 2008). Algebra textbooks reflect the problems inherent in learning algebra (Schonfield, 1992). Many traditional textbooks have a strong focus on equations and procedures for solving them and providing only a few real-world examples and a project at the end of the chapter. Support for students who are struggling is frequently in the form of additional practice problems and general advice to teachers. Little attention is given to fostering the type of reasoning that is needed for success in algebra.

18. Zarch and Kadivar (2006) found that math ability impacted math performance directly, but it also impacted performance via math self-efficacy judgments. Self efficacy judgments are impacted, in part, by students' past performance.

19. Wu & colleagues (2012) write: "Previous studies have shown that individuals with math anxiety inevitably experience more difficulty with greater performance pressure and more complicated calculations (Ashcraft & Moore, 2009). The end result is a feedback loop in which adults with math anxiety often perform poorly on standardized math tests (Hembree, 1990; Ashcraft & Krause, 2007), avoid arithmetic classes (Hembree, 1990; Ashcraft & Moore, 2009), and foster negative beliefs regarding their own math abilities (Lent et al., 1991; Ashcraft & Kirk, 2001), and in turn experience greater math anxiety and avoidance. Indeed, math anxiety has also long been cited as one of the main causes of low female enrollment in math and science courses (Ernest, 1976; Tobias & Weissbrod, 1980; Meece et al., 1982; Hembree, 1990).

20. There is a long line of research around the negative aspects of math and science textbooks. For example, Suydam (1987) explained that math teachers who help their students to become good problem solvers tend to use resources other than textbooks to generate problems. They also ask questions that are outside of the students' textbooks. Nickson (1992) explained that students tend not to connect the type of learning in textbooks with the math they encounter in real life. They begin to think of problem-solving in math in terms of right or wrong. See also Flanders (1987). There are also specific issues with the use of textbooks for females and students of color. For example, Potter and Rosser (1992) found that there were aspects of science textbooks that might deter girls from engaging with some science texts.

21. To learn more about perfect pitch, see Deutsch (2006).

22. The term "print disability" is given different definitions in different contexts. Often these definitions reference the Chafee Amendment under copyright law. The U.S. Department of Education's Office for Civil Rights (OCR, 2011) has described print disabilities as disabilities that "make it difficult for students to get information from printed sources."

23. To see details on the checkpoints that are a part of this guideline, see www. udlcenter.org/aboutudl/udlguidelines.

24. Strategic functions such as the monitoring of goals, being flexible with strategies, and switching approaches when one method is not working during problem solving are known, by some, as executive functions. Specifically, executive functions include processes such as working memory, attention, planning, problem solving, inhibition, mental flexibility, initiation, and monitoring of actions (Chan, Shum, Toulopoulou, & Chen, 2008). Executive functions develop at different rates. For example, during adolescence, inhibitory control, planning, and goal-directed behavior improve, as does attentional control and working memory (Andersonz et al., 2001; Luna et al. 2004).

25. Problem-solving novices tend to use a "working backward" strategy as they attempt to determine how to get to their end goal of solving the problem. Thus, their approaches are often more piecemeal as they work by trial and error (Larkin, Heller, & Greeno, 1980).

26. See Bandura (1977), Lave & Wenger (1991), Vygotsky (1978), and Wenger (1998).

27. See Ford (1992) and Bandura (1977).

28. Alloway (2006) explains that "within an average class of 30 children, we would expect to see working memory capacity differences corresponding to 5 years of normal development between the three highest and three lowest scoring individuals" (p. 135).

29. For more information on the use of speech recognition technologies in schools, see Follansbee & McCloskey-Dale (2000) and Loy (2012).

30. See www.corestandards.org/resources/frequently-asked-questions

31. For more on the Common Core Standards, and myths around them, see www.corestandards.org/about-the-standards/myths-vs-facts.

CHAPTER 5

1. For more on scaffolding and teaching, see Wood, Bruner, & Ross (1976).

2. In 2008, CAST published version 1.0 of the UDL Guidelines in response to calls from the field for concrete advice on how to apply the three UDL principles to curriculum design. Revised with input from educators, Version 2.0 was released in 2011 by the National Center on Universal Design for Learning (www.udlcenter.org). Derived from research in education and in the cognitive and affective neurosciences, the nine UDL Guidelines point the way to specific kinds of flexibility needed in learning experiences to meet systematic variability within and between learners.

3. Iyengar & Lepper (1999).

4. Mack & Rock (1998).

5. Simons & Chabris (1999.)

6. Seegmiller, Watson, & Stayer (2011).

7. See Malinowski (2011) at www.kunstderfuge.com/theory/malinowski.htm.

8. See Holmes (2012).

9. Ibid.

10. Rhawn Joseph's (2009) web site (http://brainmind.com/FrontalLobes.html) provides a thorough exploration of the frontal lobes. Please see his web site for a great explanation of lateralization of the frontal lobes and information about the primary and secondary motor cortices as well as the prefrontal cortex. See also Swenson (2006) for a more technical explanation of the same regions (www.dartmouth.edu/~rswenson/NeuroSci/chapter_11.html).

11. For a biography of Hawking, see www.hawking.org.uk.

12. To learn more about UDL in Maryland and in other states, go to http://www.udlcenter.org/advocacy/state.

13. Learn about the UDL@UVM Project at www.uvm.edu/~cdci/universaldesign/.

CHAPTER 6

1. For a summary of Copernicus' life from the *Stanford Encyclopedia of Philosophy*, see http://plato.stanford.edu/entries/copernicus.

2. Rose & Meyer (2002). Online at www.cast.org/teachingeverystudent/

3. See Rose & Gravel (2012).

4. DuFour, R., DuFour, R., & Eaker, R. (2008).

5. See www.udlcenter.org/aboutudl/udlcurriculum/ for further information on learning expectations.

6. See Rose & Meyer (2002). Also, see www.udlcenter.org/aboutudl/ udlguidelines/principle3/.

7. Ertmer & Newby (1996). Also, for more on the UDL perspective on expert learners www.udlcenter.org/aboutudl/expertlearners/.

8. Rose & Meyer, 2002, chapter 5.

9. Ibid.

10. For a more thorough understanding of how individuals process and react to emotional stress, see Lazarus & Folkman, 1984 (and Blascovich et al., 2003, for additional information). The foundational work from Lazarus & Folkman (1984) explores the ideas around cognitive appraisal and how individuals cope with their psychological valuations.

11. Salvia, Ysseldyke, & Bolt (2011).

12. See Phelps (2005).

13. See Supovitz (2010).

14. For more insight about the UDL perspective on assessment, see the Mislevy interview in Gordon, Gravel, & Schifter (2009), which can be found at www. udlcenter.org/resource_library/articles/mislevy.

15. See Nicol & Macfarlane-Dick (2006) for more information on formative assessment and self-regulated learning.

16. See National Center on Student Progress Monitoring at www.student-progress.org/default.asp.

17. See Nicol & Macfarlane-Dick (2006), p. 207, for more information on formative assessment and self-regulated learning.

18. Strategic Reader was created as part of the research project Monitoring Student Progress Towards Standards in Reading: A Universally Designed CBM System. For more information, see Cohen, Hall, Vue, & Ganley (2011).

19. For more on customized assessment see Walkington, Petrosino, & Sherman (2012).

20. See UDL Guidelines: Principle II. Provide Multiple Means of Action and Expression at www.udlcenter.org/aboutudl/udlguidelines/principle2.

21. See Walkington, Petrosino, & Sherman (2012) for more information on context personalization in Algebra.

22. Russell & Airasian (2011).

23. See the Mislevy interview in Gordon, Gravel, & Schifter (2009)z, which can be found at www.udlcenter.org/resource_library/articles/mislevy.

24. For more information on progress monitoring, see the National Center on Student Progress Monitoring: http://www.studentprogress.org/progresmon.asp

25. Cohen, Hall, Vue, & Ganley (2011).

26. See Rose & Meyer (2002), p. 109. Online at www.cast.org/teachingeverystudent/ideas/tes/chapter6_2.cfm.

27. See, for example, the video on "Cooperative Arithmetic" at www.edutopia.org/math-social-activity-cooperative-learning-video, which shows how a teacher and students collaborate, with students sharing ideas and providing constructive feedback.

28. See UDL Guidelines, 8.3: www.udlcenter.org/implementation/examples/examples8_3/.

29. To illustrate learner differences in group settings, one CAST instructional designer shares a story of her child whose English Language Arts class was based only on whole-class discussion. The student did not participate, even knowing that she would be penalized significantly (an entire letter grade) for a lack of participation. She felt negatively about her ability to write or to communicate her ideas. In her words, "I hate writing." Yet the following year, when the class discussed reading and writing through a monitored class blog and in class, her teacher noted that this student had "become a class leader" and that "other students valued her thoughtful comments and insights." This also had a significant impact on this student's affective engagement toward learning. She came to see herself as capable and a valuable contributor as well as thinker. That year, she won top honors in a statewide writing contest.

30. See, for example, www.edutopia.org/student-reflection-blogs-journals-technology.

CHAPTER 7

1. For example, see Ericsson, Kramp, & Tesch-Romer (1993).

2. See Lave & Wenger's book on situated learning for more information.

3. From Wenger (1998), p. 3.

4. Ibid., p. 4.

5. Ibid, p. 4.

6. Ibid.

7. See Brown (1999); Wenger, McDermot, & Snyder (2002); Polyani (1966); Somech & Bogler (1999); and Wenger, (1998).

8. Seely, Brown, & Duguid (2000).

9. Writing about students, Wenger (1998) offers a similar reflection on what things might be like if we emphasize learning from practice rather than simply testing students on how much content they can recall: "What does look promising are inventive ways of engaging students in meaningful practices, of providing access to resources that enhance their participation, of opening their horizons so they can put themselves on learning trajectories they can identify with, and of involving them in actions, discussions, and reflections that make a difference to the communities that they value" (p. 10).

AFTERWORD

1. See two articles in the June 29, 2013 edition of the *Economist*: "E-ducation: A long-overdue technological revolution is at last under way," from which the quotations are taken (www.economist.com/news/leaders/21580142-long-overdue-technological-revolution-last-under-way-e-ducation), and "Catching on at Last: New technology is poised to disrupt America's schools, and then the world's" (www.economist.com/news/briefing/21580136-new-technology-poised-disrupt-americas-schools-and-then-worlds-catching-last).

References

___. (2004; updated 2011). Achievement Gap. *Education Week*. Retrieved from
    http://www.edweek.org/ew/issues/achievement-gap/

___. (2011). Autistic people superior in multiple areas: Scientists must stop
    emphasizing autistics' shortcomings, expert urges. *Science Daily*.
    Retrieved from http://www.sciencedaily.com/releases/2011/11/
    111102161045.htm

___. (2013). Catching on at Last: New technology is poised to disrupt America's
    schools, and then the world's. *The Economist* (June 28, 2013). Retrieved
    from www.economist.com/news/briefing/21580136-new-technology-
    poised-disrupt-americas-schools-and-then-worlds-catching-last

___. (2013). E-ducation: A long-overdue technological revolution is at last under
    way. *The Economist* (June 28, 2013). Retrieved from www.economist.
    com/news/leaders/21580142-long-overdue-technological-revolution-
    last-under-way-e-ducation

___. (2012). Frequently Asked Questions. Common Core State Standards
    Initiative. Retrieved from http://www.corestandards.org/resources/
    frequently-asked-questions

___. (1990). New law will expand TV captions for the Deaf. *New York Times*.
    Retrieved from http://www.nytimes.com/1990/10/16/us/new-law-will-
    expand-tv-captions-for-the-deaf.html

___. The Brain from Top to Bottom Web Site. McGill University. Retrieved from
    http://thebrain.mcgill.ca/index.php

Adams, M. J. (1994). *Beginning to Read: Thinking and Learning about Print*.
    Cambridge, MA: MIT Press.

Adams, W. L. (2009). The Rubik's Cube: A puzzling success. *Time*. Retrieved from
    http://www.time.com/time/magazine/article/0,9171,1874509,00.html

Adelson, E. H. (1995). Checker-shadow Illusion. Retrieved from http://www
    .michaelbach.de/ot/lum_adelsonCheckShadow/index.html

Adelson, E. H. (1993). The Corrugated Plaid in Lightness Perception and Lightness Illusions. In M. Gazzaniga (Ed.) *The New Cognitive Neurosciences* (2nd Ed.) (pp. 339-351). Cambridge, MA: MIT Press.

Adelson, E. H. (1995). Why does the illusion work? Retrieved from http://web.mit.edu/persci/people/adelson/checkershadow_description.html

Allison, T., Puce, A., McCarthy, G. (2000). Social perception from visual cues: Role of the STS region. *Trends in Cognitive Sciences, 4*(7), 267–278.

Alloway, T. P. (2006). How does working memory work in the classroom? *Educational Research and Reviews, 1(4), 134–139.*

Anderson, V. A., Anderson, P., Northan, E., Jacobs, R., & Catroppa, C. (2001). Development of executive functions through late childhood and adolescence in an Australian sample. *Developmental Neuropsychology, 20,* 385–406.

Andrews, J. E., Carnine, D. W., Couthinho, M. J., Edgar, E. B., Forness, S. R., Fuchs, L., Wong, J. (2000). Bridging the special education divide. *Remedial and Special Education, 21,* 258-260, 267.

Annenberg Foundation (2011). Annenberg learner course: Neuroscience and the classroom. Retrieved from http://www.annenbergfoundation.org/news/annenberg-learner-course-neuroscience-and-classroom.

Ashcraft, M. H. & Kirk, E. P. (2001). The relationships among working memory, math anxiety, and performance. *Journal of Experimental Psychology,* 130(2), 224–237.

Ashcraft, M. H. & Krause, J. A. (2007). Working memory, math performance, and math anxiety. *Psychonomic Bulletin & Review,* 14(2), 243–248.

Ashcraft, M. H. & Moore, A. M. (2009). Mathematics anxiety and the affective drop in performance. *Journal of Psychoeducational Assessment,* 27(3) 197–205b.

Bach, M. (2002). Adelson's "Corrugated Plaid." Retrieved from http://www.time.com/time/arts/article/0,8599,1669535,00.html

Bach, M. (1997). 104 Visual Phenomena & Optical Illusions (Website). Retrieved from http://www.michaelbach.de/ot/

Baglieri, S., Valle, J. W., Connor, D. J., & Gallagher, D. J. (2011). Disability studies in education: The need for a plurality of perspectives on disability. *Remedial and Special Education, 32, 267–278.*

Bandura, A. (1977). *Social Learning Theory.* Englewood Cliffs, N.J.: Prentice-Hall.

Bandura, A. & Wood, R. (1989). Effect of perceived controllability and performance standards on self-regulation of complex decision-making. *Journal of Personality and Social Psychology, 56,* 805–814.

Barney, M. (1998). Leaping over walls: With technology integration, the sky's the limit. *Edutopia*. Retrieved from http://www.edutopia.org/leaping-over-walls

Beliner, D. (2001). Learning about learning from expert teachers. *International Journal of Educational Research, 35*(5), 463–483.

Bernard, S. (2010). Neuroplasticity: Learning physically changes the brain. *Edutopia*. Retrieved from http://www.edutopia.org/neuroscience-brain-based-learning-neuroplasticity

Bernard, J.-L. & Wade-Woolley, L., Co-Chairs. (2005). Education for All: Report of the Expert Panel on Literacy and Numeracy Instruction for Students with Special Education Needs, Kindergarten to Grade 6. Ontario, Canada: Ministry of Education. Retrieved from http://www.edu.gov.on.ca/eng/document/reports/speced/panel/speced.pdf

Bhalla, M. & Proffitt, D. R. (1999). Visual-motor recalibration in geographical slant perception. *Journal of Experimental Psychology: Human Perception and Performance, 25*(4), 1076-1096. doi: 10.1037/0096-1523.25.4.1076.

Bishop, P. C. & Strong, K. E. (2010). Why teach the future? *Journal of Futures Studies, 14*(4), 99-106.

Björk, R. A. (1994). Memory and metamemory considerations in the training of human beings. In J. Metcalfe & A. Shimamura (Eds.), *Metacognition: Knowing About Knowing* (pp. 185-205). Cambridge, MA: MIT Press.

Blascovich, J., Mendes, W. B., Tomaka, J., Salomon, K., & Seery, M. (2003). The robust nature of the biopsychosocial model challenge and threat: A reply to Wright and Kirby. *Personality and Social Psychology Review, 7*(3), 234-43.

Bloom, B. S. (1974). An introduction to mastery learning theory. In Block, J. H. (Ed.) *Schools, Society, and Mastery Learning* (pp. 3-14). New York, NY: Holt, Rinehart, & Winston.

Bloom, B. S., Engelhart, M. D., Furst, E. J., Hill, W. H., & Krathwohl, D. R. (1956). *Taxonomy of Educational Objectives: The Classification of Educational Goals; Handbook I: Cognitive Domain*. New York, NY: Longmans, Green.

Bloom, B. S. & Sosniak, L. A. (1985). *Developing Talent in Young People*. New York, NY: Ballantine Books.

Boss, S. (2009). High tech reflection strategies make learning stick. *Edutopia*. Retrieved from http://www.edutopia.org/student-reflection-blogs-journals-technology

Boucher, K. L., Rydell, R., Van Loo, K., & Rydell, M. (2012). Reducing stereotype threat in order to facilitate learning. *European Journal of Social Psychology, 42*(2),174-179.

Brain Connection (n.d.). The anatomy of movement. Retrieved from http://
brainconnection.positscience.com/topics/?main=anat/motor-anat

Bransford, J. D., Brown, A. L., & Cocking, R. R. (2000). *How People Learn: Brain,
Mind, Experience, and School.* Washington, DC: National Academy
Press.

Burbaud, P., Camus, O., Guehl, D., Bioulac, B., Caillé, J. M., & Allard, M. (2000).
Influence of cognitive strategies on the pattern of cortical activation
during mental subtraction: A functional imaging study in human subjects.
Neuroscience Letters, 287(1), 76–80.

Burke, J. (1978). Connections. New York: Time Warner/Macmillan.

Caplan, D. (1987). Disturbances of the sound system. In D. Caplan (Ed.).
Neurolinguistics and Linguistic Aphasiology: An Introduction (pp. 201-
232). New York, NY: Cambridge University Press.

Carpenter, P. A., Just, M. A., & Reichle, E. D. (2000). Working memory and
executive function: Evidence from neuroimaging. *Current Opinion in
Neurobiology,* 10, 195–199.

CAST, Inc. (2012). Learning Tools. Retrieved from http://www.cast.org/
learningtools/

CAST, Inc. (2012). Staff Biography: Todd Rose. Retrieved from http://www.cast.
org/about/staff/trose.html

CAST, Inc. (2012). UDL Book Builder. Retrieved from http://bookbuilder.cast.org/
library.php

CAST, Inc. (2008). UDL Editions. Retrieved from http://udleditions.cast.org/

CAST, Inc. (2012). UDL Exchange. Retrieved from http://udlexchange.cast.org/
home

CAST, Inc. (2011). UDL Guidelines 2.0. Retrieved from http://www.udlcenter.org/
aboutudl/udlguidelines

CAST, Inc. (2012). UDL Guidelines 2.0: Checkpoint 8: Foster collaboration
and communication. Retrieved from http://www.udlcenter.org/
implementation/examples/examples8_3

CAST, Inc. (2012). UDL Guidelines 2.0: Principle II. Provide Multiple Means
of Action and Expression. Retrieved from http://www.udlcenter.org/
aboutudl/udlguidelines/principle2

CAST, Inc. (2012). UDL Guidelines 2.0: Principle III. Provide Multiple Means
of Engagement. Retrieved from http://www.udlcenter.org/aboutudl/
udlguidelines/principle3

CAST, Inc. (2012). UDL Studio. Retrieved from http://udlstudio.cast.org/

CCSSO (2008). Attributes of Effective Formative Assessment. Formative
Assessment for Students and Teachers (FAST) Collaborative (p. 3).

Retrieved from http://www.ccsso.org/documents/2008/attributes_of_
effective_2008.pdf

Chan, R. C. K., Shum, D., Toulopoulou, T., & Chen, E. Y. H. (2008). Assessment of
executive functions: Review of instruments and identification of critical
issues. *Archives of Clinical Neuropsychology, 23*(2), 201–216.

Chase, W. G. & Simon, H. A. (1973). Perception in chess. *Cognitive Psychology, 4,*
55–81.

Chase, W G. & Simon, H. A. (1973). The mind's eye in chess. In W. G. Chase (Ed.).
Visual Information Processing (pp. 215-281). San Diego, CA: Academic
Press.

Chi, M. (2006). Two approaches to the study of experts' characteristics. In K. A.
Ericsson, N. Charness, P. Feltovich, & R. Hoffman (Eds.), *The Cambridge
Handbook of Expertise and Expert Performance* (pp. 21-30). New York,
NY: Cambridge University Press.

Chi, M. T. H., Glaser, R., & Farr, M. J. (1988). *The Nature of Expertise.* Hillsdale,
NJ: Erlbaum.

Christensen, C. M. (2001). Assessing your organization's innovation capabilities.
Leader to Leader, 21, 27–37. Retrieved from http://www.utdallas.edu/
~chasteen/Christensen%20-%202nd%20article.htm

Christensen, C. M. (2008). *Disrupting Class: How Disruptive Innovation Will
Change the Way the World Learns.* New York, NY: McGraw-Hill.

Christensen, C. M. (2011). *The Innovator's Dilemma: When New Technologies
Cause Great Firms to Fail.* Cambridge, MA: Harvard Business Review
Press.

Christensen, C. M. (2008). The Innovator's Prescription: A Disruptive Solution
for Health Care. New York, NY: McGraw-Hill.

Cohen, G.L., Garcia, J., Apfel, N., & Master, A. (2006). Reducing the racial
achievement gap: A social-psychological intervention. *Science, 313*(5791),
1307-1310.

Cohen, G. L., Garcia, J., Purdie-Vaughns, V., Apfel, N., & Brzustoski, P. (2009).
Recursive processes in self-affirmation: Intervening to close the minority
achievement gap. *Science, 324*(5925), 400–403.

Cohen, N., Hall, T., Vue, G., & Ganley, P. (2011). The strategic reader: Using
curriculum-based measurement and universal design for learning to
support reading instruction in a digital environment. In P. E. Noyce & D.
T. Hickey (Eds.), *New Frontiers in Formative Assessment* (pp. 129-140).
Cambridge, MA: Harvard Education Press.

Coles, G. (2000). *Misreading Reading: The Bad Science that Hurts Children.*
Portsmouth, NH: Heinemann.

Collins, A. (1991). The role of computer technology in restructuring school. *Phi Delta Kappan, 73*(1), 28–36.

Common Core State Standards Initiative (2011). Myths vs. Facts. Retrieved from http://www.corestandards.org/about-the-standards/myths-vs-facts

Common Core State Standards Initiative (2012). Preparing America's Students For College And Career. Retrieved from http://www.corestandards.org/

Computer Hope (2012). Computer history—1980-1990. Retrieved from http://www.computerhope.com/history/198090.htm

Coyne, P., Pisha, B., Dalton, B., Zeph, L. A., & Cook Smith, N. (2012). Literacy by design: A universal design for learning approach for students with significant intellectual disabilities. *Remedial and Special Education, 33,* 162–172. Retrieved from http://www.cast.org/library/bycast/Literacy_by_design_coynepishadaltonzephcook.pdf

Daley, S. G. (2010). *Emotional responses during reading tasks: What shapes them and how they relate to reading comprehension.* Dissertation Abstract International. Retrieved from Dissertations and Theses database.

Damasio, A. R. (1994). *Descartes' Error: Emotion, Reason, and the Human Brain.* New York, NY: Harper Collins.

Damasio, A. (2003). *Looking for Spinoza: Joy, Sorrow, and the Feeling Brain.* New York, NY: Harcourt.

Davidson, R. J. & Lutz, A. (2008). Buddha's brain: Neuroplasticity and meditation. *IEEE Signal Processing Magazine, 25*(1), 176–174.

Dennett, D. C. (1995). Review of Damasio, *Descartes' Error. Times Literary Supplement,* 4821 (August 25, 1995), pp. 3–4.

de Posada, J. (2009). Don't eat the marshmallow! [Video.] Retrieved from http://www.ted.com/talks/lang/en/joachim_de_posada_says_don_t_eat_the_marshmallow_yet.html

Deutsch, D. (2006). The enigma of absolute pitch. *Acoustics Today, 2,* 11–18.

Dewey, J. (2002). *Child and the Curriculum.* Chicago, IL: University of Chicago Press.

DuFour, R., DuFour, R., & Eaker, R. (2008). *Revisiting Professional Learning Communities at Work: New Insights for Improving Schools.* Bloomington, IN: Solution Tree.

Duncan, A. (2011). Winning the Future with Education: Responsibility, Reform, and Results. Testimony given to Congress, Washington, DC. Retrieved from http://www.ed.gov/news/speeches/winning-future-education-responsibility-reform-and-results

Dweck, C. S. (2000). *Self-Theories: Their Role in Motivation, Personality, and Development.* Philadelphia, PA: Psychology Press.

Dweck, C. S. & Leggett, E. L. (1988). A social-cognitive approach to motivation and personality. *Psychological Review, 95*(2), 256–273.

Dunn, R. & Dunn, K. (1978). *Teaching Students Through Their Individual Learning Styles: A Practical Approach.* Reston, VA: Reston Publishing Company.

Education for All Handicapped Children Act. (1975). Pub. L. 94-142, 20 U.S.C. § 1401.

Education Week. (2012). A nation at risk: 25 years later. *Education Week.* Retrieved from http://www.edweek.org/ew/collections/nation-at-risk-25-years/

Elbert, T. H., Pantev, C., Wienbruch, C., Rochstroh, B., & Taub, E. (1995). Increased cortical representation of the fingers of the left hand in string players. *Science, 270,* 305–307.

Elmore, R. F. (1996). Getting to scale with good educational practice. *Harvard Education Review, 66*(1). Retrieved from http://ed-share.educ.msu.edu/scan/TE/danagnos/te9206B.PDF

Ericsson, K. A., Charness, N., Feltovich, P. J., & Hoffman, R. R. (2006). *The Cambridge Handbook of Expertise and Expert Performance.* New York, NY: Cambridge University Press.

Ericsson, K. A., Krampe, R. T., & Tesch-Römer, C. (1993). The role of deliberate practice in the acquisition of expert performance. *Psychology Review, 100*(3), 363–406.

Ericsson, K. A. & Smith, J. (1991). Prospects and limits of the empirical study of expertise: An introduction. In K. A. Ericsson & J. Smith (Eds.), *Toward a General Theory of Expertise: Prospects and Limits* (pp. 1-39). Cambridge, England: Cambridge University Press.

Ernest, J. (1976). Mathematics and sex. The *American Mathematical Monthly, 83*(8), 595–614.

Ertmer, P. A. & Newby, T. J. (1996). The expert learner: Strategic, self-regulated, and reflective. *Instructional Science, 24*(1), 1–24.

Fair, D. A., Cohen, A. L., Power, J. D., Dosenbach, N. U. F., Church, J. A., Miezin, F. M., & Petersen, S. E. (2009). Functional brain networks develop from a "local to distributed" organization. *PLoS Computational Biology, 5*(5).

Feldon, D. F. (2007). Cognitive load and classroom teaching: The double-edged sword of automaticity. *Educational Psychologist, 42,* 123–137.

Ferlazzo, L. (2012). Classroom Q&A with Larry Ferlazzoc. Education Week Teacher. Retrieved from http://blogs.edweek.org/teachers/classroom_qa_with_larry_ferlazzo/2012/01/matt_townsley_asked_carol_boston.html

Fields, R. D. (2008). White matter matters. *Scientific American, 298,* 54–61. doi:10.1038/scientificamerican0308-54. Retrieved from http://www.nature.com/scientificamerican/journal/v298/n3/full/scientificamerican0308-54.html

Fink, R. P. (1995/1996). Successful dyslexics: A constructivist study of passionate interest reading. *Journal of Adolescent and Adult Literacy, 39*(4), 268–280.

Fink, R. P. (1998). Literacy development in successful men and women with dyslexia. *Annals of Dyslexia, 48,* 311 346.

Fischer, G. (2011, October). Social Creativity: Exploiting the Power of Cultures of Participation. *Proceedings of SKG2011: 7th International Conference on Semantics, Knowledge and Grids* (Beijing, China), pp. 1–8. Retrieved from http://l3d.cs.colorado.edu/~gerhard/papers/2011/SKG-China.pdf

Fischer, K. W. & Rose, L. T. (2001). Webs of skill: How students learn. *Understanding Learning Differences, 59*(3).

Fischer, K. W. & Tangney, J. P. (1995). Self-conscious emotions and the affect revolution: Framework and overview. In J. P. Tangney & K. W. Fischer (Eds.), *Self-Conscious Emotions: The Psychology of Shame, Guilt, Embarrassment, and Pride* (pp. 3-24). New York, NY: Guilford.

Fisher, L. M. (1999). An interview with John Seely Brown. *Strategy & Business Magazine, 17,* 86–95.

Flanders, J. (1987). How much of the content in mathematics textbooks is new? *Arithmetic Teacher, 35,* 18–23.

Follansbee, B. & McClosky-Dale, S. R. (2000). Proceedings from the Center On Disabilities Technology and Persons with Disabilities Conference 2000: *Speech recognition in schools: An update from the field.* Northridge, CA: California State University. Retrieved from http://www.csun.edu/cod/conf/2000/proceedings/0219Follansbee.htm

Ford, M. (1992). Summary of Motivational Systems Theory. In *Motivating Humans* (pp. 244-257). Newbury Park, CA: Sage Publications.

Frijda, N. H. (1986). *The Emotions.* London, England: Cambridge University Press.

Fullan, M. (2007). *The New Meaning of Educational Change.* New York, NY: Teacher's College Press.

Fullan, M. (2002) Principals as leaders in a culture of change. *Educational Leadership,* Special Issue. Alexandria, VA: ASCD. Retrieved from http://www.michaelfullan.com/media/13396053050.pdf

Galton, F., Sir (1869/1979). *Hereditary Genius: An Inquiry into its Laws and Consequences.* London, England: Julian Friedman Publishers.

Garfinkel, N. (2011). A braille Rubik's Cube! Finally? Sure, finally! Retrieved from http://www.bestweekever.tv/2010-03-18/a-braille-rubiks-cube-finally-sure-finally/

Gazzaniga, M. S. (1995). *The Cognitive Neurosciences*. Cambridge, MA: MIT Press.

Genesee, F. (2000). Brain Research: Implications for Second Language Learning. Center for Applied Linguistics. *ERIC Digest*. Retrieved from http://www.cal.org/resources/digest/0012brain.html

Gigandet, X., Hagmann, P., Kurant, M., Cammoun, L., Meuli, R., & Thiran, J.-P. (2008). Diffusion MRI tractography in the brain white matter. In Estimating the Confidence Level of White Matter Connections Obtained with MRI Tractography. *PLoS ONE Journal*. Retrieved from http://www.plosone.org/

Gobet, F. & Charness, N. (2006). Expertise in chess. In K. A. Ericsson, N. Charness, P. Feltovich, & R. Hoffman (Eds.), *Cambridge Handbook of Expertise and Expert Performance* (pp. 523-538). Cambridge, England: Cambridge University Press.

Gopher, D. (1996). Attention control: Explorations of the work of an executive controller. *Cognitive Brain Research, 5*, 23–38.

Gordon, D. T. (2003). *A Nation Reformed? American Education 20 Years After A Nation at Risk*. Cambridge, MA: Harvard Education Press.

Gordon, D. T., Gravel, J. W., & Schifter, L. A. (2009). Perspectives on UDL and assessment: An interview with Robert Mislevy. In D. T. Gordon, J. W. Gravel, & L. A. Schifter (Eds.), *A Policy Reader in Universal Design for Learning (pp.* 209-218). Cambridge, MA: Harvard Education Press.

Greenhow, C., Robelia, B., & Hughes, J. E. (2009). Learning, teaching, and scholarship in a digital age: Web 2.0 and classroom research: What path should we take now? *Educational Researcher, 38*(4), 246–259.

Gregson, J. (2001). System, environmental, and policy changes: Using the social-ecological model as a framework for evaluating nutrition education and social marketing programs with low-income audiences. *Journal of Nutrition Education, 33*(1), 4–15.

Grill-Spector, K. (2003). The neural basis of object perception. *Current Opinion in Neurobiology, 13*, 1–8.

Gupta, V. K., & Bhawe, N. M. (2007). The influence of personality and stereotype threat on women's entrepreneurial intentions. *Journal of Leadership & Organizational Studies, 13*(4), 73–85.

Hall, R. (1998). The neuron. Retrieved from http://web.mst.edu/~rhall/neuroscience/01_fundamentals/neuron.pdf

Hargreaves, A., Lieberman, A., Fullan, M., & Hopkins, D. (2010). Second International Handbook of Educational Change. [Volume 2.] Dordrecht, Germany: Springer.

Hargreaves, A. (2011). Personal web site. Retrieved from http://www.andyhargreaves.com/

Hawking, S. (1994). *Black Holes and Baby Universes and Other Essays.* New York, NY: Bantam Books.

Hawking, S. (1998). *A Brief History of Time.* New York, NY: Bantam Books.

Hawking, S. (2001). *The Universe in a Nutshell.* New York, NY: Bantam Books.

Hawking, S. (2012). *Stephen Hawking.* Retrieved from http://www.hawking.org.uk/

Hayes, J. R. (1981). *The Complete Problem Solver.* Philadelphia, PA: Franklin Institute Press.

Helft, M. (2009). For the blind, technology does what a guide dog can't. *The New York Times.* Retrieved from http://www.nytimes.com/2009/01/04/business/04blind.html?em=&pagewanted=all.

Hembree, R. (1990). The nature, effects, and relief of mathematics anxiety. *Journal for Research in Mathematics Education, 21*(1), 33–46.

Henry, S. (2009). The (only) three ways to improve performance in schools. Harvard Graduate School of Education Web Site. Retrieved from http://www.uknow.gse.harvard.edu/leadership/leadership001a.html

Higher Education Opportunity Act (2008). Pub L. 110-315, 20 U.S.C. §

Holmes, K. (2012). Animating Björk's Biophilia: Q&A With Stephen Malinowski. The Creator's Project. Retrieved from http://thecreatorsproject.com/blog/animating-bjorks-ibiophiliai-qa-with-stephen-malinowski

Hord, S. M. (1997). Professional learning communities: What are they and why are they important? *Issues About Change, 6(1), 1–7.*

Huet, N. & Mariné, C. (2009). Expertise and self-regulation processes in a professional task. *Applied Cognitive Psychology, 23,* 1027-1041.

Individuals With Disabilities Education Act (2004). Pub L. 94-142, 20 U.S.C. § 1400.

Inan, F. A., Flores, R., & Grant, M. M. (2010). Perspectives on the design and evaluation of adaptive web-based learning environments. *Contemporary Educational Technology, 1*(2), 148–159.

Inzlicht, M. & Ben-Zeev, T. (2000). A threatening intellectual environment: Why females are susceptible to experiencing problem-solving deficits in the presence of males. *Psychological Science, 11*(5), 365–371.

Isaacson, N. & Bamburg, J. (1992). Can schools become learning organizations? *Educational Leadership, 50(3), 42–44.*

Iyengar, S. S. & Lepper, M. R. (1999). Rethinking the value of choice: A cultural perspective on intrinsic motivation. *Journal of Personality and Social Psychology, 76*(3), 349–366.

Jamieson, J. P., Mendes, W. B., Blackstock, E., & Schmader, T. (2009). Turning the knots in your stomach into bows: Reappraising arousal improves performance on the GRE. *Journal of Experimental Social Psychology, 46*, 208–212.

Johanning, D. I. (2004). Supporting the development of algebraic thinking in middle school: A closer look at students' informal strategies. *Journal of Mathematical Behavior, 23*, 371–388.

Joseph, R. (Ed.) (2000). *Neuropsychiatry, Neuropsychology, Clinical Neuroscience.* (3rd Ed.) New York, NY: Academic Press.

Kahn, J. (1993). The music animation machine. Retrieved from http://www.musanim.com/mam/kahnarticle.html

Kanwisher, N., McDermott, J., & Chun, M. (1997). The fusiform face area: A module in human extrastriate cortex specialized for the perception of faces. Journal of Neuroscience, 17, 4302-4311.

Kepler (2011). Venezuela's historical homunculus. Retrieved from http://venezuela-europa.blogspot.com/2011/04/venezuelas-historical-humunculus.html

Kids marshmallow experiment (2009). [Video.] Retrieved from http://www.youtube.com/watch?v=6EjJsPylEOY

King, D. (2011). Neurons and Support Cells. Retreived from http://www.siumed.edu/~dking2/ssb/neuron.htm#myelin

Klein, D. (2005). The state of state math standards (p. 15). Washington, DC: Thomas B. Fordham Foundation.

Koch, S. N. (2012). Brain Structure and Neurons. MyBrainNotes.com. Retrieved from http://mybrainnotes.com/brain-cortex-neurons.html

Koenig, A. M. & Eagly, A. H. (2005). Stereotype threat in men on a test of social sensitivity. *Sex Roles, 52*(7-8), 489–496.

Kohn, A. (1994). The risk of rewards. *ERIC Digest.* Retrieved from http://www.alfiekohn.org/teaching/ror.htm

Kovelman, I., Baker, S. A., & Petitto, L. A. (2008). Bilingual and monolingual brains compared: A functional magnetic resonance imaging investigation of syntactic processing and a possible "neural signature" of bilingualism. *Journal of Cognitive Neuroscience, 20*(1), 153–169.

Larkin, J. H., Heller, J. I., & Greeno, J. G. (1980). Instructional implications of research on problem solving. In W. J. McKeachie (Ed.) *Cognition,*

College Teaching, and Student Learning (pp. 51-66). San Francisco, CA: Jossey-Bass.

Lave, J. & Wenger, E. (1991). *Situated Learning: Legitimate Peripheral Participation (Learning in Doing: Social, Cognitive and Computational Perspectives)*. Cambridge, England: Cambridge University Press.

Lazarus, R. S. & Folkman, S. (1984). *Psychological Stress and the Coping Process*. New York, NY: Springer.

Leadershop (2011). *Out of our minds: Learning to be creative*. [Review.] Retrieved from http://www.leadershipnow.com/leadershop/1841121258.html

LeDoux, J. E. (1989). Cognitive-emotional interactions in the brain. *Cognition and Emotion, 3,* 267–289.

LeDoux, J. E. (1994). Emotion, memory, and the brain. *Scientific American, 270*(6), 50–57.

Lehrer, J. (2009). DON'T!: The secret of self-control. *The New Yorker.* Retrieved from http://www.newyorker.com/reporting/2009/05/18/090518fa_fact_lehrer

Lent, R. W., Lopez, F. G., & Bieschke, K. J. (1991). Mathematics self-efficacy: Sources and relation to science-based career choice. *Journal of Counseling Psychology, 38,* 424–430.

Linn, M. C. & Björk, R. A. (2006). The science of learning and the learning of science: Introducing desirable difficulties. *Observer, 19*(3). Retrieved from http://www.psychologicalscience.org/index.php/uncategorized/the-science-of-learning-and-the-learning-of-science.html

Loy, B. (2012). Options to Consider: Speech Recognition. Retrieved from http://askjan.org/media/speechrec.html

Lublin, Nancy. (2009). How to write a mission statement that isn't dumb. Fast Company. Retrieved from http://www.fastcompany.com/1400930/how-write-mission-statement-isnt-dumb

Luna, B., Garver, K. E., Urban, T. A., Lazar, N. A., & Sweeney, J. A. (2004). Maturation of cognitive processes from late childhood to adulthood. *Child Development, 75,* 1357-1372.

Lutz, A., Greischar, L.L., Rawlings, N.B., Ricard, M., & Davidson, R. J. (2004). Long-term meditators self-induce high-amplitude gamma synchrony during mental practice. *Proceedings of the National Academy of Sciences of the United States of America (PNAS) 101*(46), 16369-73.

Mack, A. & Rock, I. (1998). Inattentional blindness: An overview. *Psyche, 5*(3).

Maddox, W. T. & Ashby, F. G. (2004). Dissociating explicit and procedural learning-based systems of perceptual category learning. *Behavioral Processes, 66,* 309–332.

Malinowski, S. (2011). Music animation machine. Retrieved from http://www.musanim.com/

Malinowski, S. (2011). Music animation machine theory. Retrieved from http://www.kunstderfuge.com/theory/malinowski.htm

Matthews, M. S. & Farmer, J. L. (2008). Factors affecting the Algebra I achievement of academically talented learners. *Journal of Advanced Academics, 19*(3), 472–501.

McClure, C. T. (2009). Algebraic thinking: What it is and why it matters. *District Administration, 45,* 4.

McCullouch, W. (1945). A heterarchy of values determined by the topology of nervous nets. *Bulletin of Mathematical Biophysics, 7,* 89–93.

McKeithen, K. B., Reitman, J. S., Rueter, H. H., & Hirtle, S. C. (1981). Knowledge organization and skill differences in computer programmers. *Cognitive Psychology, 13,* 307–325.

Meadows, D. H. (2008). *Thinking in Systems.* White River Junction, VT: Chelsea Green Publishing Company.

Medina, J. (2008). *Brain Rules.* Seattle, WA: Pear Press. http://www.brainrules.net/

Meece, J. L., Parsons, J., Kaczala, C. M., Goff, S. B., & Futterman, R. (1982). Sex differences in math achievement: Towards a model of academic choice. *Psychological Bulletin, 91,* 324–348.

Mischel, W., Ebbesen, E. B., & Zeiss, A. R. (1972) Cognitive and attentional mechanisms in delay of gratification. *Journal of Personality and Social Psychology, 21,* 204–218.

Minow, M. (1990). *Making all the difference: Inclusion, exclusion, and American law.* Ithaca, NY: Cornell University Press.

Morrow, D. G., Leirer, V. O., & Altieri, P. A. (1992). Aging, expertise, and narrative processing. *Psychology and Aging, 7,* 376–388.

Morshead, R. W. (1965). Taxonomy of educational objectives handbook II: Affective domain. *Studies in Philosophy and Education, 4*(1), 164–170.

Mountcastle, V. B. (1998). *Perceptual Neuroscience: The Cerebral Cortex.* Cambridge, MA: Harvard Press.

Mottron, L. (2011). Changing perceptions: The power of autism. *Nature, 479*(7371), 33–35.

Murphy, S. T. & Zajonc, R. B. (1993). Affect, cognition, and awareness: Affective priming with optimal and suboptimal stimulus exposures. *Journal of Personality and Social Psychology, 64*(5), 723–739.

Murray, P. (1989). Poetic genius and its classical origin. In Murray, R. (Ed.) *Genius: The History of an Idea* (pp. 9-31). Oxford, England: Basil Blackwell.

Nadler, J. (2007). Squaring up to the Rubik's cube. *Time Magazine*. Retrieved from http://www.time.com/time/arts/article/0,8599,1669535,00.html

National Center on Student Progress Monitoring Web Site. Retrieved from http://www.studentprogress.org/default.asp

National Center on UDL (2013). What is meant by the term curriculum? Retrieved from http://www.udlcenter.org/aboutudl/udlcurriculum

National Center on UDL (2013). UDL and Expert Learners. Retrieved from http://www.udlcenter.org/aboutudl/expertlearners

National Coordination Office for Space-Based Positioning, Navigation, and Timing and the Civil GPS Service Interface Committee. (2012). GPS.GOV: Official U. S. Government information about the Global Positioning System (GPS) and related topics. Retrieved from http://www.gps.gov/

National Education Technology Plan (2010). U. S. Department of Education (pp. 14-18). Retrieved from http://www.ed.gov/technology/netp-2010

National Federation of the Blind (2011). http://www.nfb.org/nfb/Braille_coin.asp

National Institute of Child Health and Human Development. (2000). *Report of the National Reading Panel. Teaching children to read: An evidence-based assessment of the scientific research literature on reading and its implications for reading instruction* (NIH Publication No. 00-4769). Washington, DC: U. S. Government Printing Office.

National Mathematics Advisory Panel. (2008). *Foundations for Success: The Final Report of the National Mathematics Advisory Panel.* Washington, DC: U. S. Department of Education. Retrieved from http://www2.ed.gov/about/bdscomm/list/mathpanel/report/final-report.pdf

National UDL Task Force (2012). UDL in Your State. Retrieved from http://www.udlcenter.org/advocacy/state

Narumoto, J., Okada, T., Sadato, N., Fukui, K., & Yonekura, Y. (2001). Attention to emotion modulates *f*MRI activity in human right superior temporal sulcus. Kyoto, Japan: Kyoto Prefectural University of Medicine.

Nickson, M. (1992). The culture of the mathematics classroom: An unknown quantity? In D. Grouws (Ed.). *Handbook of Research on Mathematics Teaching and Learning.* New York, NY: MacMillan.

Nicol, D. J., & Macfarlane-Dick, D. (2006). Formative assessment and self-regulated learning: A model and seven principles of good feedback practice. *Studies in Higher Education*, 31(2), 199–218.

O'Connor, J. J., & Robertson, E. F. (2002). Nicholas Copernicus. Retrieved from http://www-groups.dcs.st-and.ac.uk/history/Biographies/Copernicus.html

OECD/CERI (2008). Learning in the 21st Century: Research, Innovation, and Policy. International Conference, Paris, France.

Office of Special Education and Rehabilitative Services, U. S. Department of Education (2012). A Guide to the Individualized Education Program. Retrieved from http://ed.gov/parents/needs/speced/iepguide/iepguide.pdf

Office for Civil Rights, U. S. Department of Education (2011). Frequently Asked Questions About the June 29, 2010 Dear Colleague Letter. Retrieved from http://www2.ed.gov/about/offices/list/ocr/docs/dcl-ebook-faq-201105.pdf

Ontario Ministry of Education (2005). Education for All: *The Report of the Expert Panel on Literacy and Numeracy Instruction for Students With Special Education Needs, Kindergarten to Grade 6.* Retrieved from http://www.edu.gov.on.ca/eng/document/reports/speced/panel/speced.pdf

Partnership for 21st Century Skills (n.d). 21st Century Learning Environments. Retrieved from http://www.p21.org/storage/documents/le_white_paper-1.pdf

Phelps, R. P. (2005). *Defending Standardized Testing.* New York, NY: Psychology Press.

Polanyi, M. (2009). *The Tacit Dimension.* Chicago, IL: University of Chicago Press.

Posner, M. I., & Rothbart, M. K. (2005). Influencing brain networks: Implications for education. *TRENDS in Cognitive Sciences, 9*(3), 99-103.

Potter, E. F., & Rosser, S. V. (1992). Factors in life science textbooks that may deter girls' interest in science. *Journal of Research in Science Teaching, 29*(7), 669–686.

Price, D. (2005) Learning Communities and Student Success in Post-Secondary Education. A Background Paper. New York, NY: MDRC. Retrieved from http://www.mdrc.org/publications/418/full.pdf

PBIS.org (2013). Frequently Asked Questions. Retrieved from http://www.pbis.org/pbis_faq.aspx

PBIS.org (2013). What is School-Wide Positive Behavioral Interventions & Supports? Retrieved from http://www.pbis.org/school/what_is_swpbs.aspx

Rakes, C. R., Valentine, J. C., McGatha, M. B., & Ronau, R. N. (2010). Methods of instructional improvement in algebra: A systematic review and meta-analysis. *Review of Educational Research, 80*(3), 372–400.

Raman, T. V. (2007). Solving a braille Rubik's cube. Retrieved from http://video.google.com/videoplay?docid=-4180435763269825467

Rappolt-Schlichtmann, G. S., Daley, S., & Rose, L. T. (2012). *A Research Reader in Universal Design for Learning*. Cambridge, MA: Harvard Education Press.

Raven, J., Raven, J. C., & Court, J. H. (1998). *Raven manual: Section 1, general overview, 1998 edition*. Oxford, England: Oxford Psychologists Press Ltd.

Recht, D. R., & Leslie, L. (1988). Effect of prior knowledge on good and poor readers' memory of text. *Journal of Educational Psychology, 80*, 16–20.

Rehabilitation Act of (1973). Pub L. 93-112, title V, Sec. 504, 29 U.S.C. § 794.

Richman, H. B., Gobet, F., Staszewski, J. J., & Simon, H. A. (1996). Perceptual and memory processes in the acquisition of expert performance: The EPAM model. In K.A. Ericsson (Ed.) *The Road to Excellence: The Acquisition of Expert Performance in the Arts and Sciences, Sports, and Games* (pp. 167-187). Mahwah, NJ: Erlbaum.

Roberts, R., & Mather, N. (1997). Orthographic dyslexia: The neglected subtype. *Learning Disabilities Research & Practice, 12*(4), 236–250.

Robinson, K. (2001/2011). *Out of Our Minds: Learning to be Creative*. Chichester, England: Capstone.

Robinson, K. (2006). Ken Robinson says schools kill creativity. [Video.] TED Ideas worth spreading. Retrieved from http://www.ted.com/talks/ken_robinson_says_schools_kill_creativity.htm

Robinson, K. (2010). Sir Ken Robinson: Bring on the learning revolution! [Video.] TED Ideas worth spreading. Retrieved from http://www.ted.com/talks/lang/en/sir_ken_robinson_bring_on_the_revolution.html

Robinson, K. (2010). Ken Robinson: Changing education paradigms. [Video.] TED Ideas worth spreading. Retrieved from http://www.ted.com/talks/lang/en/ken_robinson_changing_education_paradigms.html

Robinson, K., & Aronica, L. (2009). *The Element: How Finding Your Passion Changes Everything*. London, England: Viking Penguin.

Roland, P. E., & Zilles, K. (1998). Structural divisions and functional fields in the human cerebral cortex. *Brain Research Reviews, 26*, 87-105.

Rose, D., & Gravel, J. (2012). Curricular Opportunities in the Digital Age. Boston, MA: Jobs for the Future. Retrieved from http://www.studentsatthecenter.org/papers/curricular-opportunities-digital-age

Rose, D., & Meyer, A. (1998). Learning to Read in the Computer Age. Cambridge, MA: Harvard Education Press. Retrieved from http://www.cast.org/library/books/ltr/chapter1.html

Rose, D. H., Meyer, A., Strangman, N., & Rappolt, G. (2002). *Teaching Every Student in the Digital Age*. Alexandria, VA: Association for Supervision and Curriculum Development. Retrieved from http://www.cast.org/teachingeverystudent/

Rose, L. T., Daley, S. G., & Rose, D. H. (2011). Let the questions be your guide: MBE as interdisciplinary science. *Mind, Brain, and Education, 5*(4): 153–162.

Rose, D. H., & Rose, T. (2011). Learner Variability and UDL. [Presentation.] Retrieved from http://community.udlcenter.org/forum/topics/learner-variability-and-udl

Rosen, J. B., & Donley, M. P. (2006). Animal studies of amygdala function in fear and uncertainty: Relevance to human research. *Biological Psychology, 73*, 49–60. Retrieved from http://people.usd.edu/~cliff/Courses/Advanced%20Seminars%20in%20Neuroendocrinology/fear/Rosen06.pdf

Rubik's Official Web Site (2011). https://www.rubiks.com/index.php

Russell, M. K., & Airasian, P. (2011). *Classroom Assessment: Concepts and Applications.* (7th Ed.) New York, NY: McGraw-Hill.

Ryan, R., & Deci, E. (1991). Motivation and education: The self-determination perspective. *Educational Psychologist, 26*(3&4), 325–346. Retrieved from http://selfdeterminationtheory.org/SDT/documents/1991_DeciVallerandPelletierRyan_EP.pdf

Ryan, R., & Deci, E. (2000). Self-determination theory and the facilitation of intrinsic motivation, social development, and well-being. *American Psychologist, 55*(1), 68–78.

Salvia, J., Ysseldyke, E., & Bolt, S. (2011). *Assessment: In Special and Inclusive Education.* (12th Ed.) Belmont, CA: Wadsworth Cengage Learning.

Samanez-Larkin, G. R. & D'Esposito, M. (2008). Group comparisons: Imaging the aging brain. *Social & Affective Neuroscience, 3*(3), 290–297.

Samson, F., Mottron, L., Souliéres, I., & Zeffiro, T. A. (2011). Enhanced visual functioning in autism: An ALE meta-analysis. *Human Brain Mapping.* Retrieved from http://www.ncbi.nlm.nih.gov/pubmed/21465627

Savage, K. L. (1993). Literacy through competency-based educational approaches. In Crandall, J. & Peyton, J. K. (Eds.), *Approaches to Adult ESL Literacy Instruction* (pp. 15-33). Washington, DC: Center for Applied Linguistics.

Schlaug, G., Jäncke, L., Huang, Y., Staiger, J. F., & Steinmetz, H. (1995). Increased corpus callosum size in musicians. *Neuropsychologia, 33*, 1047-1055.

Schnall, S., Harber, K. D., Stefanucci, J. K., & Proffitt, D. R. (2008). Social support and the perception of geographical slant. *Journal of Experimental Social Psychology, 44*(5): 1246-1255. doi: 10.1016/j.jesp.2008.04.011.

Schoenfeld, A. H. (1992). Learning to think mathematically: Problem solving, metacognition, and sense making in mathematics. In Grouws, D. (Ed.) *Handbook of Research on Mathematics Teaching and Learning* (pp. 334-370). New York, NY: MacMillan.

Schunk, D. H., & Zimmerman, B. J. (1997). Social origins of self-regulatory competence. *Educational Psychologist, 32*, 195–208.

Seegmiller, J. K., Watson, J. M., & Strayer, D. L. (2011). Individual differences in susceptibility to inattentional blindness. *Journal of Experimental Psychology, Learning, Memory, and Cognition, 37*(3), 785-91.

Seely Brown, J., & Duguid, P. (2000). Structure and Spontaneity: Knowledge and Organization. In I. Nonaka & D. Teece (Eds.), *Managing Industrial Knowledge* (pp. 44-67). Thousand Oaks, CA: SAGE Publications.

SERC. (2012). Teaching Methods. In Pedagogy in Action SERC Portal. Northfield, MN: Carleton College. Retrieved from http://serc.carleton.edu/sp/library/pedagogies.html

Simons, D., & Chabris, C. (1999.) The Invisible *Gorilla: How Our Intuitions Deceive Us*. New York, NY: Random House.

Simpson, E. (1972). *The Classification of Educational Objectives in the Psychomotor Domain: The Psychomotor Domain*. [Vol. 3.] Washington, DC: Gryphon House.

Sloboda, J. (1976). Visual perception of musical notation: Registering pitch symbols in memory. *Quarterly Journal of Experimental Psychology, 28*, 1–16.

Smith, T. A. (1996). Anatomy of a Fugue. Retrieved from http://www2.nau.edu/tas3/fugueanatomy.html

Snow, C. E., & Juel, C. (2005). Teaching children to read: What do we know about how to do it? In M. J. Snowling & C. Hulme (Eds.), *The Science of Reading: A Handbook* (pp. 501-520). Malden, MA: Blackwell Publishing.

Snowling, M. J. (1981). Phonemic deficits in developmental dyslexia. *Psychological Research, 43*, 219–234.

Somech, A., & Bogler, R. (1999) Tacit knowledge in academia: Its effects on student learning and achievement. *The Journal of Psychology, 133*(6), 605–616.

Souliéres, I., Dawson, M., Samson, F. Barbeau, E. B., Sahyoun, C. P., Strangman, G. E., … Mottron, L. (2009). Enhanced visual processing contributes to matrix reasoning in autism. *Human Brain Mapping, 30*, 4082-4107.

Spencer, M. D., Holt, R. J., Chura, L. R., Suckling, J., Calder, A. J., Bullmore, E. T., & Barron-Cohen, S. (2011). A novel functional brain imaging endophenotype of autism: The neural response to facial expression of emotion. *Translational Psychiatry, 1*(19), e16.

Spilich, G. J., Vesonder, G. T, Chiesi, H. L., & Voss, J. F. (1979). Text processing of domain-related information for individuals with high- and low-domain knowledge. *Journal of Verbal Learning and Verbal Behavior, 18*, 275–290.

Sprenger, M. (2003). *Differentiation Through Learning Styles and Memory*. Thousand Oaks, CA: Corwin Press.

Steele, C. M., & Aronson, J. (1995). Stereotype threat and the intellectual test performance of African Americans. *Journal of Personality and Social Psychology, 69*(5), 797–811.

Sternberg, R. J. (2003). What is an "expert student?" *Educational Researcher, 32*(8), 5–9.

Sternberg, R. J., & Horvath, J. A. (1995). A prototype view of expert teaching. *Educational Researcher, 24*(6), 9–17.

Storbeck, J., & Clore, G. L. (2007). Emotional controls on cognitive processes. *Cognition and Emotion, 21*, 1212-1237.

Stout, B. L., & Smith, J. B. (1986). Competency-based education: A review of the field and a look to the future. *Journal of Vocational Home Economics Education, 4*(2), 109–134.

Supovitz, J. (2010). Is High-Stakes Testing Working? @Penn GSE Research. Philadelphia, PA: University of Pennsylvania Graduate School of Ecuation.

Suydam, M. (1987). Indications from research on problem solving. In Curcio, F. (Ed.) *Teaching and Learning: A Problem-Solving Focus*. Reston, VA: NCTM.

The National Commission on Excellence in Education (1983). *A nation at risk: The imperative for educational reform: A report to the nation and the secretary of education*. United States Department of Education. Retrieved from http://datacenter.spps.org/uploads/SOTW_A_Nation_at_Risk_1983.pdf

The Obsolete Technology Web Site. (2012). Apple Macintosh. Retrieved from http://oldcomputers.net/macintosh.html

Tinto, V. (1997). Classrooms as communities: Exploring the educational character of student persistence. *The Journal of Higher Education, 68*(6), 599–623.

Tinto, V. (1998). Colleges as communities: Taking research on student persistence seriously. *The Review of Higher Education, 21*(2), 167–177.

Tinto, V. (1993). *Leaving College: Rethinking the Causes and Cures of Student Attrition*. [2nd Ed.] Chicago, IL: University of Chicago Press.

Tobias, S., & Weissbrod, C. (1980). Anxiety and mathematics: An update. *Harvard Educational Review, 50*(1), 63–70.

UDL Connect (2013). Universal Design for Learning: Theory and Practice Discussions. Retrieved from http://community.udlcenter.org/group/universal-design-for-learning-theory-and-practice/forum

U. S. Department of Education (2011). Advisory Commission on Accessible Instructional Materials in Postsecondary Education for Students with Disabilities. Retrieved from http://www2.ed.gov/about/bdscomm/list/aim/index.html

U. S. Department of Education (2012). Summary of considerations to strengthen state requests for ESEA flexibility. Retrieved from http://www.ed.gov/sites/default/files/considerations-strengthen.pdf

U. S. Department of Education (2012). *Elementary and secondary education: ESEA reauthorization: A blueprint for reform.* Retrieved from http://www2.ed.gov/policy/elsec/leg/blueprint/index.html

University of Vermont (2012). UDL@UVM. Retrieved from http://www.uvm.edu/~cdci/universaldesign/

Vogel, E. K., Woodman, G. F., & Luck, S. J. (2001). Storage of features, conjunctions, and objects in visual working memory. *Journal of Experimental Psychology: Human Perception and Performance, 27,* 92-114.

Vygotsky, L. S. (1978). *Mind and Society: The Development of Higher Mental Processes.* Cambridge, MA: Harvard University Press.

Vygotsky, L. (1962). *Thought and Language.* Cambridge, MA: MIT Press. Retrieved from http://www.marxists.org/archive/vygotsky/works/words/index.htm

Walkington, C., Petrosino, A., & Sherman, M. (2012). Supporting algebraic reasoning through personalized story scenarios: How situational understanding mediates performance and strategies. *Mathematical Thinking and Learning, 15*(2), 89-120.

Weddel, K. S. (2006). Competency-Based Education and Content Standards. Retrieved from http://www.cde.state.co.us/cdeadult/download/pdf/CompetencyBasedEducation.pdf

Weiss, P., & Jeannerod, M. (1998). Getting a grasp on coordination. *News in Physiological Sciences, 13,* 70–75.

Wenger, E. (1998). *Communities of Practice: Learning, Meaning, and Identity.* New York, NY: Cambridge University Press.

Wenger, E., McDermott, R., & Snyder, W. C. (2002). *Cultivating Communities of Practice: A Guide to Managing Knowledge.* Cambridge, MA: Harvard Business School Press.

Wentzel, K. R., & Wigfield, A. (2009). *Handbook of Motivation at School.* New York, NY: Taylor Francis.

Witelson, S., Kigar, D., & Harvey, T. (1999). The exceptional brain of Albert Einstein. *The Lancet, 353*(9170), 2149-2153.

Wolf, M., O'Rourke, A. G., Gidney, C., Lovett, M. W., Cirino, P., & Morris, R. (2002). The second deficit: An investigation of the independence of phonological and naming-speed deficits in developmental dyslexia. *Reading and Writing: An Interdisciplinary Journal, 15*, 43–72.

Wolf, M. (1999). What time may tell: Towards a new conceptualization of developmental dyslexia. The Norman Geschwind Memorial Lecture. *Annals of Dyslexia, 43*, 1–28.

Wood, D., Bruner, J. S., & Ross, G. (1976). The role of tutoring in problem solving. *The Journal of Child Psychology and Psychiatry, 17*(2), 89-100.

World Cube Association. (2012). http://www.worldcubeassociation.org/

Wraga, M., Helt, M., Jacobs, E., & Sullivan, K. (2006). Neural basis of stereotype-induced shifts in women's mental rotation performance. *Social Cognitive and Affective Neuroscience, 2*(1), 12–19.

Wu, S. S., Barth, M., Amin, H., Malcarne, V., & Menon, V. (2012). Math anxiety in second and third graders and its relation to mathematics achievement. *Frontiers in Psychology, 3*, 162.

Yanko Design. (2012). Color Rubik's cube for the blind. Retrieved from http://www.yankodesign.com/2010/03/17/color-rubik-cube-for-the-blind/

Zambo, D., & Brem, S. K. (2004). Emotion and cognition in students who struggle to read: New insights and ideas. *Reading Psychology, 25*, 189–204.

Zarch, M. K., & Kadivar, P. (2006). The role of mathematics self-efficacy and mathematics ability in the structural model of mathematics performance. Proceedings of the 9th WSEAS International Conference on Applied Mathematics (pp. 242-249). Istanbul, Turkey: WSEAS.

Zeki, S. (1999). *Inner Vision: An Exploration of Art and the Brain*. Oxford, England: Oxford University Press.

Zelazo, P. R., Brody, L. R., & Chaika, H. (1984). Neonatal habituation and dishabituation of head turning to rattle sounds. *Infant Behavior and Development, 7*, 311–321.

Zemdegs, F. (2011). Interview with Feliks Zemdegs. [Video.] Retrieved from http://youtu.be/mgbNYznXxEE

Zemdegs, F. (2011). Rubik's Cube World Record: 5.66 Seconds. [Video.] Retrieved from http://www.youtube.com/watch?v=3v_Km6cv6DU

Zimmerman, B. J., & Campillo, M. (2003). Motivating self-regulated problem solvers. In J. E. Davidson & R. Sternberg (Eds.), *The Nature of Problem Solving* (pp. 233- 262). New York, NY: Cambridge University Press.

Zimmerman, B. J., & Kitsantas, A. (2002). Acquiring writing revision and self-regulatory skill through observation and emulation. *Journal of Educational Psychology, 94*, 660–668.

Zimmerman, B. J., & Kitsantas, A. (2005). The hidden dimension of personal competence: Self-regulated learning and practice. In A. J. Elliot, & C. S. Dweck (Eds.), *Handbook of Competence and Motivation* (pp. 509-526). New York, NY: Guilford.

Zimmer, C. (2011). 100 trillion connections. *Scientific American, 304*, 58–63.

Acknowledgments

The authors gratefully acknowledge essential contributions from our CAST research colleagues, including Director of Research Gabrielle Rappolt-Schlichtmann and Research Scientists Samantha Daley, Tracey E. Hall, Sam Johnston, and Todd Rose. Each of them shared lessons from their inspiring work to expand our understanding of the research underpinnings of UDL and their implications for practice. Their scholarship and leadership ensures a vibrant future for the UDL field.

We also wish to thank Linda Butler for her extraordinary project management, multimedia editing, and online production which transformed a mere book into a universally designed online resource with media-rich print and e-book editions. Since CAST's founding in 1984, Linda has made numerous contributions to the work described in this book.

Kristin Robinson led the instructional design for the online version and provided expertise in developing scaffolds and learning supports.

Significant contributions to media production were made by Brielle Domings, Graham Gardner, Mary O'Malley, and Alan Leney, as well as design expertise provided by Lisa Spitz and Kim Ducharme.

Rachel Currie-Rubin, Rick Birnbaum, Scott Lapinski, Billie Fitzpatrick, and Valerie Hendricks made substantial editorial contributions in researching, fact-checking, and editing.

CAST's technology team led by Boris Goldowsky and including Lynn McCormack and Matthew Brambilla provided us with an online platform and expert technical development throughout the project.

We also extend a special thanks to all the teachers, students, parents, experts, and CAST staff who took part in the media creation process.

We are tremendously grateful to Anne Schneider and the LD ACCESS Foundation, as well as an anonymous donor, for contributing the funds that made this work possible. Thanks also to CAST's president, Ada Sullivan, for her patient support and good advice along the way.

About the Authors

Anne Meyer is Co-Founder (with David Rose) of CAST, a nonprofit education research and development organization, and its Chief of Education Design. Building on a career-long interest in the intersection of curriculum design and educational psychology, particularly affect and motivation in learning, Dr. Meyer is a primary author of the principles of universal design for learning (UDL). Meyer has led the development of CAST's award-winning multimedia technology based on UDL. She is the author or editor of five previous books, including the seminal *Teaching Every Student in the Digital Age: Universal Design for Learning* (with David H. Rose, ASCD, 2002). With her colleagues at CAST, she was awarded the Computerworld/Smithsonian Innovation Award in 1992.

David H. Rose is Co-Founder (with Anne Meyer) of CAST and its Chief Education Officer. He is primary author of the principles of the educational reform framework called universal design for learning (UDL), which now influences educational policy and practice throughout the United States and beyond. For more than 30 years, he has taught at Harvard's Graduate School of Education. He was one of the authors of the U.S. Department of Education's National Educational Technology Plan (2010). He is the author or editor of five previous books, including *Universally Designed Classroom: Accessible Curriculum & Digital Technologies* (with Chuck Hitchcock and Anne Meyer, Harvard Education Press, 2005). He is the winner of numerous awards, and George Lucas's *Edutopia* magazine has named him one of education's "Daring Dozen" of innovators.

David Gordon directs CAST's publishing and communications programs. He is the editor of several books about education, including *The Digital Classroom* and *A Nation Reformed? American Education 20 Years after 'A Nation at Risk'* (Harvard Education Press). Prior to joining CAST, Gordon was editor of the *Harvard Education Letter*, where he won a National Press Club Award for distinguished reporting and analysis of national teaching certification programs. He has also been a senior editor of the Harvard Education Press and an associate editor of *Newsweek*.

Index

Note: Italicized page numbers indicate figures; underlined page numbers indicate Web links.

Copernicus, Nicolaus, *127–128*
CCSSO (Council of Chief State School Officers), 15
Cube designs, 28. *See also* Rubik's Cube
"Cubers," 23–26
Cultivating Communities of Practice, <u>40</u>
curriculum. *See also* UDL curriculum
    assessment, 14–15
    goals, 14–15
    instructional components, 14–15
    interaction of learners with, 4
    materials, 14–15
    methods, 14–15
curriculum practices, integrating UDL into, 159
curve-ball example, *87*

D

Daley, Samantha
    affect, <u>64</u>
    affective states of learners, <u>102</u>
    designing for "average learner," <u>4</u>
    emotion and learning, <u>91</u>
    progress monitoring, <u>103</u>
Damasio, Antonio, 12
Datz, Konstantin, 28
Davidson, Richard, 12–13
Dawson, Michelle, 50
Descartes' Error, 12
digital books, creation of, 3
digital materials, flexibility of, <u>3</u>
digital media, malleability of, 18
"digital river," <u>19–20</u>
disabilities
    intellectual, 7
    of schools, 5
    shift from, <u>9</u>
    shift from medical model, 5
    in UDL curriculum, <u>129</u>
"disability" vs. variability, <u>81</u>
disengagement, 166. *See also* Engagement
    Principle
distributed intelligence, metaphor for, <u>44</u>
distributed specialization, 67–68
diverse presentations, 104
Domings, Yvonne, <u>17</u>
Duncan, Arnie
    accountability systems, 14–15
    "Tight on goals, loose on means," 15

Dweck, Carol, 30–<u>31</u>
dyslexia, 6–7
dyslexic astrophysicists, <u>71</u>

E

Edgren, Kate, <u>141</u>
education
    dynamic-systems perspective, 42
    goal of, <u>8</u>, <u>84</u>
    raising expectations about, 19
    standardization, 6
    uniformity, 6
educational environment
    affordances of, 38
    community, 38
educators. *See also* teachers
    Mundorf, Jon, 39
    Posey, Allison, 39
    Reid, Alexis, 38–<u>39</u>
efficacy expectations, development of, 13
emotion
    and cognition, 12–13
    tie to learning, <u>91</u>
emotional profiles, differences in, <u>4</u>
emotional strategies, <u>64</u>
emotional supports, <u>64</u>
EnACT (Ensuring Access through Collaboration
    and Technology Project), 171
engagement
    enhancing, <u>98</u>
    increasing, <u>124</u>
    with learning, 11
    social and academic, 80
    in UDL Guidelines, 14
engagement and attention, reframing, 113–115
Engagement Principle. *See also* disengagement;
   "why" of learning
    explained, 89
    iSolveIt project, 92–98
    learning contexts, 91
    learning environment, 91
    overview, 90–98
    recruiting interest, *91, 114*
    self-regulation, *91, 111, 114*
    sustaining effort, *91, 111, 114*
    sustaining persistence, *91, 111, 114*
    variability, 91–92

Hillaire, Garron, 94
"how" of learning, 90. *See also* strategic networks

I

Ignitemedia.com film, 74
"inattention blindness," *113*
inkblot, 63
instructional adjustments, making, 163–168
instructional methods. *See* methods
interactions, parts of, 3
interactive media, 18
interactivity, examples of, 18
Internet, impact of, 18–19
iSolveIt project
    iPad apps, 94
    MathScaled puzzle, 94–95
    MathSquared puzzle, 93–94
    overview, 92–95
    recruiting interest, 95–96
    self-regulation, 97–98
    sustaining effort, 96–97
    sustaining persistence, 96–97

J

Johnson, Mindy, 94, 164–165
Johnston, Sam, 12, 38, 44

K

K-12 environments
    applied systems thinking, 42
    Common Core State Standards, 107

L

language arts, bridging with other content, 126
Laswell, Rhonda
    alternate pathways, 110
    brain science, 123
    variability, 112
    varying routes to learning, 148
Lave, Jean, 157
learner capacities, 85
learners. *See also* expert learners
    categorizing, 85
    interaction with curricula, 4
    "in the margins," 2

positive sense of self, 57–58
    proactivity of, 154
    purposeful & motivated, *32*
    resourceful & knowledgeable, *32*
    strategic & goal-oriented, *32*
    strengths of, 90
    variability of, 9
    weaknesses of, 90
learning
    basic components of, 55
    contextual nature of, 30
    developing love of, 8
    in dynamic interaction, 11
    engagement, 55
    engagement with, 11
    evaluating, 6
    "how" of, 90
    impact of biology on, 10
    meaning of, 53
    and mindset, 31
    practice-based, 158
    prerequisites, 55
    recognition, 55
    self-efficacy of, 12
    social nature of, 30
    strategies, 55
    traditional approach toward, 4
    understanding, 6
    "what" of, 90
    "why" of, 90
learning brain, 56. *See also* brain
learning context, significance of, 10–11
learning environments
    interactions of students with, 11
    students' appraisals of, 98
    UDL Editions, 153
learning experiences, designing with flexibility,
    115–118
learning expertise
    designing for variability, 26–29
    developing, 23
    requirements, 25
    selecting strategy, *27*
learning progress, blocks to, 5
learning sciences. *See also* sciences
    context dependency, *87*
    variability, 85, *87*

student progress
    indicating, _140_
    monitoring, 146, 148
students
    abilities of, 10
    boredom, _11_
    diversity of, 84
    engagement, _11_
    as experts, _149_
    interaction with learning environments, 11
    learning from, 39
    with special needs, 86
success
    occurrence of, 4
    pathways to, _12_
summative assessment
    development of, 141
    explained, 136–137
    vs. formative assessment, 15–16
summative tests, 136–137
syllabus, design of, 173
"systems change," 41
systems thinking, applied, 42

T

Tavares, Lindsay
    lesson goals, _136_
    planning assessments, _146_
    planning UDL curriculum, _130_
    UDL Guidelines, _110_
teachers. See also educators
    as expert learners, 37–38
    learning from students, 39
    role in classrooms, _56_
teaching
    evaluating effectiveness of, _139_
    pervasiveness of, 36–37
    unseen aspects of, 38
Teaching Every Student in the Digital Age, 5, 19, 128, 147
teaching methods. See methods
teaching practice, shifting, _125_
theory and practice
    changes in, 8–16
    cognition and emotion, 12–13
    individual differences, 9–10
    individual interactions, 10–12

    individual-context interactions, 10–12
    updated goals, 8
    variability, 9–10
"Tight on goals, loose on means," 15
Tinto, Vincent, 80
"Toccata and Fugue in D Minor," _116_–_117_
traditional education, barriers in, 4

U

UDL (Universal Design Learning)
    adoption by states, _17_
    affective networks, 90
    coining, _5_
    in context of lesson goal, 98
    "design" aspect, 89
    fixing curriculum, 6
    founding of, 3
    framework, _87_
    growing acceptance of, 17
    and Internet, 18–19
    "learning" aspect, 89
    National Center, _18_
    as pedagogy, 19
    policy developments, _18_
    practice of, 109
    recognition networks, 90
    strategic networks, 90
    systematic application of, 6
    translational framework, 88
    "universal" aspect, 89
UDL assessments. See assessments
UDL Book Builder, 18, _153_–_154_
UDL changes
    media, 19–20
    societal and context, 16–19
    theory and practice, 8–16
UDL Connect, _88_, _147_
UDL culture, building, 168–169
UDL curriculum. See also curriculum
    assessment, 136–146
    assessment of, 137
    defined, 128–129
    design practices, 160–163
    digital learning tools, 130
    goals, _131_–_136_
    interrelationships, _129_
    location of disability, _129_